Serial Television

Serial Television
Big Drama on the Small Screen

Glen Creeber

 Publishing

For Catrin

First published in 2004 by the
British Film Institute
21 Stephen Street, London W1T 1LN

The British Film Institute is the UK national agency with
responsibility for encouraging the arts of film and television
and conserving them in the national interest.

Cover image: *The Sopranos* (HBO, 1999–)
Cover design: Ketchup
Set by Fakenham Photosetting Ltd, Fakenham, Norfolk
Printed in the UK by Cromwell Press, Trowbridge, Wiltshire

British Library Cataloguing-in-Publication Data
A catalogue record for this book is available from the British Library

ISBN 1–84457–021–5 (pbk)
ISBN 1–84457–020–7 (hbk)

CONTENTS

ACKNOWLEDGMENTS

Firstly, I would like to thank Professor John Tulloch who helped to appoint me as a Research Fellow at Cardiff University in 1999. This book would simply not have been written without that initial help and I thank him and the Department of Journalism, Media and Cultural Studies for three precious years of research. While writing the book I have attended many conferences and would like to thank all those people whose help and hospitality was so important to me. In particular, I am indebted to Val Jacobs, Jason Jacobs, Graeme Turner and John Hartley in Brisbane, Nuntiya Doungphummes and St John's University in Bangkok and all of the 'Pilots' team in Barcelona. Gratitude must also go to Andrew Lockett whose support while he was at the BFI made the act of writing and publishing this book a great deal more pleasant and painless than it probably should have been. Finally, thanks to everyone in the Department of Film, Theatre and Television at Aberystwyth, University of Wales – particularly those who still believe in the power and significance of the text.

Some of the material in this book is revised from earlier articles written and published in various places. I would therefore like to thank all those concerned for allowing me to republish material in this form. Parts of the Introduction and Chapter One first appeared as 'Taking Our Personal Lives Seriously: Intimacy, Continuity and Memory in the Television Serial', *Media, Culture & Society*, vol. 23, no. 4, 2001 and '*Heimat*' in Creeber, *Fifty Key Television Programmes*, 2004. Parts of Chapter Two first appeared as 'Surveying *The Kingdom*: Explorations of Medicine, Memory and Modernity in Lars von Trier's *The Kingdom*', *European Journal of Cultural Studies*, vol. 5, no. 4, 2002 and '"Reality or Nothing?": Dennis Potter's *Cold Lazarus*', in Wayne, *Dissident Voices: The Politics of Television and Social Change*, 1998. Parts of Chapter Three first appeared as 'Cigarettes and Alcohol: Investigating Gender, Genre and Gratification in *Prime Suspect*', in *Television & New Media*, vol. 2, no. 2, 2001, '*Prime Suspect*' in Creeber, *Fifty Key Television Programmes*, 'Old Sleuth or New Man?: Investigations into Rape, Murder and Masculinity in *Cracker* (1993–1996)', *Continuum: Journal of Media and Cultural Studies*, vol. 16, no. 2, 2002 and '"TV Ruined the Movies": Television, Tarantino and the Intimate World of *The Sopranos*' in Lavery, *This Thing of Ours: Investigating The Sopranos*, 2002. Parts of Chapter Four first appeared as '*Queer as Folk*' in Creeber, *Fifty Key Television Programmes*. Finally, parts of the Conclusion first appeared as '"Hideously White" British Television: Glocalisation and National Identity' in *Television and New Media*, vol. 5, no. 1, 2004.

INTRODUCTION
From Small to Big Drama[1]

Since their origins in commercial radio in the 1930s, many serials have been dismissed as 'soap opera'. Yet their persistence and popularity is significant, in a period in which, in so much traditionally serious drama and fiction, there has been a widespread withdrawal from general social experience.

Raymond Williams (1974: 58)

During his celebrated last interview in 1994 the British television dramatist Dennis Potter attacked the sort of 'formula-ridden' television that he felt was increasingly characterising the medium. 'Where is the single play?' he asked, and 'the series, you can punch the buttons in the predictability … You can call the shot numbers in advance' (Potter, 1994: 16).[2] In a similar vein, the television writer John Wilsher gave a talk to the Australian Screenwriters' Conference which was later published in 1997 under the title, 'TV Series Drama: A Contradiction in Terms?' Like Potter, Wilsher argued that the single play had been resigned to television history because in the current economic climate the industry was looking for 'long-form drama' that (acting as 'star vehicles') could be guaranteed to bring back an audience week after week. According to Wilsher, such thinking inevitably produces the sort of 'assembly line' aesthetics which now sadly dominate television drama and which inevitably prioritises the personal over the political, the sexual over the social and the conventional over the experimental. As Wilsher puts it (1997: 11):

Whether you watch a series about medics, cops, firefighters, lawyers, customs officers, oil-rig workers, life boat crew or soldiers, what you end up seeing is not them doing the job that gives the show its basic premise. You see them falling in and out of love, committing adultery, having babies, getting on well or badly with teenage kids. Personal life is privileged at the expense of questions of power, politics, economics, social structure, religion, science, or ethics (other than sexual). Plays give way to series; now series are mutating into soaps, in content if not in form.

This consistent lament for the single play and polemical attack on long-form drama is a recurring theme for many British television critics, practitioners and observers of the industry. It seems particularly true of a certain generation who were brought up on a diet of theatrical 'one-offs' provided in Britain by the likes of *Armchair Theatre* (ITV, 1956–74), *The Wednesday Play* (BBC, 1964–70) and *Play for Today* (BBC, 1970–84). In particular, single plays like *Up the Junction* (BBC, 1965) and *Cathy Come Home* (BBC, 1966) were regarded as politically progressive, seemingly alerting the whole nation to important social concerns such as abortion and homelessness (see Creeber, 2001e).[3] So while the single play is seen as somehow epitomising quality television's 'golden age', long-form drama is generally associated with the commercially standardised and aesthetically conservative. Such an assumption runs through Carl Gardner's and John Wyver's article, 'The Single Play: from Reithian Reverence to Censorship and Cost-Accounting', published in *Screen* in 1983. According to Gardner and Wyver, the regrettable demise of the single play was the result of a restrictive ideological and economic condition which valued profit more than it did artistic freedom and expression (1983: 118):

> Series … are obviously easier to schedule, filling the same neatly-timed hole for a
> comfortable number of weeks. They are designed from the start to fit in with fixed points in
> the schedule (like the 9 o'clock 'watershed' and *News at Ten*) and, because the audience is
> led back to them week after week, they build and attain far better ratings than single dramas,
> even when these are forced into anthology slots. And exactly because they are expected,
> indeed conceived to collect these high ratings, there is always the pressure on them to opt for
> the safe, the predictably popular, the tried-and-tested.

But why has it simply been assumed by so many critics that the slow death of the single play also equals the destruction of television drama itself? Could its demise in the late 1970s not have actually signalled the very 'coming of age' of television drama which was finally breaking away from the aesthetic constraints of its past? For the single play arrived out of a set of historical circumstances that were actually more *theatrical* than they were inherently *televisual*. Whether the aesthetics of early TV drama were simply mimicking the theatre as critics have argued (a claim recently contested by Jason Jacobs [2000]), surely there can be no doubt that the early predominance of the single play was itself a theatrical inheritance which would, by definition, run its course. In many ways, the single television 'play' does still exist, but due to the developments in technology it is now almost indistinguishable (in form, content and initial distribution) from the cinema. Where once the titles of *Armchair Theatre* and *The Wednesday Play* deliberately celebrated TV's allegiance to the stage, titles like *Channel Four Films* or the BBC's *Screen Two* foreground their aspirational cross-over onto the big screen. Seen in this light, the demise of the single play is the inevitable result of a form that could never play to the strengths and inherent possibilities of the medium, but could only ape the conventions and narrative structure of its nearest rivals.

FROM SINGLE PLAY TO 'FLEXI-NARRATIVE'

In contrast to the single play the drama series and serial has flourished on the small screen, reflecting and celebrating the inherent dynamics of the medium for which it has proved to be so uniquely suited. Such has been its success that even natural history television (*Big Cat Weekly* [BBC, 2004]) and television advertising (as in the *Nescafé* series) has successfully mimicked the form. Indeed, the cinema itself has increasingly copied the style and structure of serialisation with films like *Star Wars* (Lucas, 1997–), *The Lord of the Rings* (Jackson, 2000–3), *Harry Potter* (Columbus, 2000–) and *Kill Bill* (Tarantino, 2003–4) actually emulating and adopting the continuous dynamics of small screen drama, frequently complete with cliffhangers at the end of each feature-length segment.

The Singing Detective: psychological depth in serial form

Yet, serialisation is still more commonly associated with television drama (a form originally inherited, as was soap opera, from radio). Indeed, rather than being characterised by the notion of a singular text, the unparalleled success of continuous drama on the small screen appears to particularly lie in its ability to reflect and exploit what Raymond Williams once defined as the 'flow' of the televisual image (1974: 86–96). Like soap opera, serialised drama recurs regularly throughout the schedule, weaving in and out of the domestic space and deliberately tapping into and playing with an audience's sense of time in a way never imagined before by the cinema, theatre or single play.[4] Simply in terms of hours alone the series and serial can produce a breadth of vision, a narrative scope and can capture an audience's involvement in a way equalled by few contemporary media. One need look no further than Potter's own award-winning serials like *Pennies from Heaven* (BBC, 1976) and *The Singing Detective* (BBC, 1986) or Wilsher's controversial and highly acclaimed police series, *Between the Lines* (BBC, 1992–4) to realise that 'long-form drama' need not be any less provocative, complex and aesthetically challenging than any other televisual form.

As these celebrated examples suggest, it is important not to simply deride the impact of serialisation on all television drama. In particular, the conventions borrowed from continuous genres like soap opera often allow a narrative complexity to be introduced to television fiction in a way that was perhaps impossible to conceive in terms of the single play. According to Jane Root, 'Soap opera characters live in a complicated world. For them, as for us, nothing will ever be completely resolved or totally worked out. In single plays a wedding can tie everything into a happy ending. Soap operas, however, treat marriage as the opportunity for a whole series of other stories about marital relationships, infidelity and children' (1986: 45). As this suggests, part of the appeal of serialisation lies in its ability to construct 'open' rather than 'closed' narrative forms. While the single play tends to have a clearly defined narrative trajectory, like soap opera the continuous nature of serial drama means that resolution is frequently delayed, conclusion is evaded and the neat tying up of all major storylines generally avoided. As Robert C. Allen puts it (1995: 7–8):

> Soap operas operate according to very different narrative and dramatic principles than more closed narrative forms: they are predicated upon the impossibility of their never ending . . . Put in semiotic terminology, US daytime soap operas trade an investment in syntagmatic determinacy (the eventual direction of the overall plotline) for one in paradigmatic complexity (how particular events effect the complex network of character relationships).

It is this 'paradigmatic complexity' that has inspired so much serial drama, helping it to expand and redefine the narrative horizons of television fiction as a whole. Indeed, Robin Nelson argues that series drama has gradually learnt to employ a complex form of 'flexi-narrative' which harnesses the narrative complexity of soap opera for other forms of television genre. By weaving together a number of interrelating, continuous, connecting and disconnecting storylines, Nelson suggests that a police series like *Hill Street Blues* (NBC, 1981–7) produced a heightened form of realism that enabled it to explore and examine social and human issues in a more 'authentic' manner (see Nelson, 2004: 100–4).

Hill Street Blues: going even further than soaps

In particular, the way some storylines were developed and resolved while others were often left partly developed, undeveloped and frequently unresolved gave a greater sense of realism to the crime genre that, by definition, often prided itself on reaching a conclusive narrative conclusion. By increasing its narrative complexity in this manner, Nelson argues that the 'flexi-narrative' form better responds to and reveals the complexity, ambiguity and lack of closure that typifies the contemporary world. Implicitly opposed to single (or closed) narrative consistency, this 'flexi-narrative' structure tends to celebrate narrative indeterminacy, character density and thematic ambiguity. As Nelson puts it (1997: 38):

> *Hill Street* [*Blues*] ... extended the function of a richer texture achieved by a juxtaposition of a number of narratives variable in tone, with a range of diverse characters. Going even further than soaps, many of the narrative strands were left open to be taken up in later episodes whilst others simply trailed off unresolved. Thus *Hill Street* achieved its dense textures and sense of a lack of resolution to difficult problems for an audience who sensed the complexity of things in the historical world.

Seen in this light, it is perhaps no surprise that the big screen adaptation of a television serial like *The Singing Detective* failed to receive the critical applause of the original. Not only did Dennis Potter's own screenplay seemingly 'sanitise' certain aspects of the narrative for a mainstream cinema audience, but the sheer longevity of the psychoanalytical process (an integral element of the narrative as a whole) had to be compressed into the format and limitations of a single text (see *The Singing Detective* [Gordon, 2003]). In contrast, the television serial (with its long-form, episodic nature) arguably possessed a greater potential to represent the prolonged and enduring process of psychoanalysis; complete with its developments, regressions and frequent psychological blockages. It could even be argued that long-form drama is intrinsically better suited to explore and dramatise the complexity of character psychology as a whole, at least compared with the contemporary feature film that seemingly needs to pack psychological change and development into an ever decreasing number of scenes and minutes. Notice, for example, how the complex, difficult and sometimes less than productive therapy sessions so crucial to a television serial like *The Sopranos* (HBO, 1999–) were simply turned into quick-fire comedic encounters in a film like *Analyze This* (Ramis, 1999).

No wonder, then, that big screen directors like Steven Spielberg (*Band of Brothers* [HBO, 2000]), David Lynch (*Twin Peaks* [ABC, 1990–1]), Oliver Stone (*Wild Palms* [Fox, 1993]) and Lars von Trier (*The Kingdom* [Danish TV, 1994]) have inevitably been seduced by the serial form; realising that the sheer breadth of the television serial frequently allows them room and possibilities that cinema or theatre simply cannot. As Robert J. Thompson has put it (1996: 32):

> The series is, indeed, broadcasting's unique aesthetic contribution to Western art. Unlike any other medium but old-time radio and the comic strip, television presents stories that can go on forever. In soap operas and long-running series, we can see characters age and develop both physically and narratively in a way that even Wagner's longest operas or Dickens's most extended novels didn't allow. Even serialized comics and movies, which may be released over long periods of time, lack the regularity of the television series.

This might explain why classic novels often find their 'natural' home in the television serial. Six, seven or even eleven (see *Brideshead Revisited* [ITV, 1981]) separate episodes allow greater room for the adaptation of a complex and dense novel. Indeed, it is well known that nineteenth-century writers like Charles Dickens originally wrote their novels in serialised form, publishing them in monthly or weekly magazine instalments that echo television and radio serialisation today (see Coolidge, 1967). According to the British screenwriter Michael Eaton, it is not the dynamics of the big screen that so perfectly captures the magnitude and complexity of Dickens' original text, but the sheer scope and breadth of television. For Eaton, 'it's the TV serial – its lack of fixed length allowing room for multinarrative strands and subplot digression – which has proved a more appropriate medium. This was the form through which my generation was introduced to Dickens … to the multifarious characters, active plots and rich thematic concerns … (Eaton, 1999: 29).[5]

It is no surprise that grand historical epics are now commonly regarded as prime material for serialised television drama. From the 1970s onwards miniseries like *I, Claudius* (BBC, 1976), *Roots* (ABC, 1977), *Holocaust* (NBC, 1978), *The Winds of War*

(ABC, 1983), *Das Boot* (Bavaria Atelier, 1984), *Heimat* (WDR, 1984), *North and South* (ABC, 1985) and *War and Remembrance* (ABC, 1989–90) quickly demonstrated the genre's potential to take on large and difficult narratives that covered huge areas of both space and time. It is hard to imagine, for example, that a single play could ever attempt to do justice to *Roots* (Alex Haley's epic generational story about his family history from slavery to emancipation) in any narrative form other than the TV miniseries. More recent examples like *Our Friends in the North* (BBC, 1996) and *Band of Brothers* certainly suggest that in terms of history the broad sweep of the television serial offers a narrative poten-tial that the feature film and the single play can never quite achieve (see Chapter One).

In particular, many critics have recognised the power of the television serial to give voice to an increasing number of perspectives and points of view. Although the Russian theorist Mikhail Bakhtin applied his notion of 'heteroglossia' to explain the multilayered intertextual possibilities of the novel, such a theory could equally be applied to serial television (see Newcomb, 1984). According to John Caughie, it is this kind of narrative complexity that produces serial television's unique relationship with its audience. It cre-ates a form of viewing practice that inherently exploits its extended and interrupted construction of time (2000: 205):

> The particular patterns of regularity which scheduling offers, and the domestic accessibility
> of broadcasting provide the conditions in which serial narrative becomes the staple diet of
> broadcasting fiction. Well trained by soap operas, crime series, and other forms of serial or
> series narrative to sustain plots and characters over time, the audience develops an aptitude
> for interrupted and interruptable narrative. More than that, lacking the concentrated forms of
> identification which the articulation of point of view invites in the cinema, television drama
> substitutes familiarity, repetition, and extension of time. If the space of the look is
> foundational for our engagement in cinematic forms of narrative, the extension of interrupted
> time gives us forms of engagement, involvement, and subjectivity specific to television.

Seen in this light, serialised television drama need be no less 'progressive' or inherently 'radical' than the single play. In fact, its tendency towards narrative complexity, particu-larly its ability to produce a 'flexi-narrative' structure that mixes a number of narrative levels together (frequently without offering any neat resolutions), is arguably better able to reflect and respond to the increasing uncertainties and social ambiguities of the con-temporary world. Of course, the single play should still have its place in the television schedules, but the development and evolution of serialised drama appear to suggest that rather than simply emulate other forms of dramatic media, television fiction has gradu-ally learnt to utilise and exploit the episodic and continuous flow of television itself.

THE SERIAL, MINISERIES AND 'MEGAMOVIE'

Revealingly, those critics who continue to mourn for the single play tend to group all long-form television drama together. Yet, long-form drama can refer to an infinite num-ber of programmes and genres. Put in crude terms, these are the basic structures of television drama that have traditionally existed:

- **Single play**: 'One-off' drama (sometimes referred to as the 'tele-film') that begins and ends within a single episode. Early examples of single play series included *Goodyear TV Playhouse* (NBC, 1951–60), *Armchair Theatre* and *The Wednesday Play*.
- **'Made-for-TV movie'**: Structurally the same as the single play, but were generally regarded as more 'filmic' than 'theatrical'. They sometimes (although not always) acted as a 'pilot' for a series. Examples include *ABC Movie of the Week* (ABC, 1970–1) and *ABC Monday Night Movie* (ABC, 1975–6). Originating in America the term has generally lost its currency.
- **Soap opera**: A continuous, never-ending drama series usually set around the domestic and intimate lives of a small community that explicitly resists narrative closure. Examples include *Coronation Street* (Granada, 1960–), *Dallas* (CBS, 1978–91) and *Neighbours* (Grundy, 1985–).
- **Series**: Continuous stories (usually involving the same characters and settings) which consist of self-contained episodes possessing their own individual conclusion. As such, the episodes in a traditional drama series can be broadcast in any order without losing narrative coherence. Examples include *The Avengers* (ITV, 1961–9), *Charlie's Angels* (ABC, 1976–81) and *Star Trek* (NBC, 1966–9).
- **Anthology series**: A number of single stories that are connected by a related theme, setting or set of characters. Examples include *The Twilight Zone* (CBS, 1959–64), *Boys from the Blackstuff* (BBC, 1982) and *Clocking Off* (BBC, 2000–3).
- **Serial**: A continuous story set over a number of episodes that usually comes to a conclusion in the final instalment (even if a sequel follows). Examples include *The Singing Detective*, *Prime Suspect* (Granada, 1991–) and *Brideshead Revisited*.
- **Miniseries**: Structurally the same as the serial but usually associated with epic dramas (sometimes run over consecutive evenings). Examples include *Rich Man, Poor Man* (NBC, 1976), *Roots* and *Holocaust*. Originating in America the term has gradually lost its currency.

As this very basic account suggests, there are obvious differences between various types of long-form drama. In particular, there is a distinct contrast between the narrative form and structure of the series and the serial (sometimes referred to as a miniseries, see above). While the traditional *series* is usually never-ending and involves self-contained episodes that can frequently be broadcast in any order, a *serial* follows an unfolding and episodic narrative structure that moves progressively towards a conclusion. So while, as John Ellis puts it, 'the series implies the form of the dilemma rather than that of resolution and closure' (Ellis, 1982: 154), the drama serial often produces a distinct and discernible narrative arc.[6] As Sarah Kozloff explains (1992: 90–1):

> *Series* refers to those shows whose characteristics and setting are recycled, but the story concludes in each individual episode. By contrast, in a *serial* the story and discourse do not come to a conclusion during an episode, and the threads are picked up again after an hiatus. A series is thus similar to an anthology of short stories, while a serial is like a

serialised Victorian novel. Serials can be further divided into those that do eventually end (despite the misnomer, miniseries belong in this category) and those, such as soap opera, that may be cancelled but never reach a conclusion, a new equilibrium.

As this suggests, the series and the serial can be seen as offering distinctly separate structural forms. Although both the series and serial are episodic, the series tends to offer an infinite number of self-contained episodes while the serial produces what Jane Feuer has referred to as 'arc shows' (1995: 112), i.e. dramas that follow a distinct narrative trajectory over a number of limited episodes. As such, the serial employs a number of generic forms, including elements borrowed from the traditional single drama. As Patricia Holland puts it, serials are dramas 'in which the plot develops over several episodes, sometimes three or four, sometimes as many as ten or twelve', yet '... in many ways are an expansion on the creative coherence of the single play' (1997: 114).

However, unlike the single play the episodic nature of the serial form means that it also shares important characteristics with the series. This means that the serial can frequently break free of the narrative limitations of single drama and exploit some of the most seductive elements of serialisation. In particular, the viewer is often able to get to know the characters and the story in a serial almost as well as they might do in a series or soap opera. Writing about soap as early as 1974, Horace Newcomb argued that the genre's two most important elements were 'intimacy' and 'continuity' (253). According to Newcomb, the serial nature of the genre allows a far greater 'audience involvement, a sense of becoming a part of the lives and actions of the characters they see' (ibid.). So, while adopting the narrative arc of the single play, the serial also employs the episodic nature of television so that levels of intimacy and continuity can be developed and maintained. It is perhaps this combination of a 'flexi-narrative' form within a single narrative arc that makes the serial so unique a space for contemporary television drama. With its combination of a continuous narrative structure contained within a clearly defined narrative arc, it allows television to exploit its tendency towards 'intimacy' and 'continuity' yet without dispensing with the power and possibilities offered by its gradual movement and progression towards narrative closure and conclusion.

The serial's re-branding as the '*miniseries*' in America during the 1970s and 1980s highlighted the difference between the serial and series. Influenced by the success on public television of British serials like *The Forsyte Saga* (BBC, 1967), *Elizabeth R* (BBC, 1971) and *The Six Wives of Henry VIII* (BBC, 1970), American television began to conceive the serial in a particular light, viewing it as the perfect vehicle for the dramatisation of popular novels. In particular, the miniseries became associated with 'event' television. Sometimes broadcast over consecutive evenings, miniseries like *Rich Man, Poor Man* (ABC's hugely successful adaptation of Irwin Shaw's best-selling novel) and historical epics like *Roots* and *Holocaust* made the miniseries a particularly attractive and lucrative re-invention of the traditional serial (see Chapter One). However, the truth was that the structure and form of the miniseries was actually no different than the traditional serial – they simply consisted of a number of *limited* episodes that led progressively towards a conclusion.

An explicit example of the serial and miniseries today would be *24* (Fox, 2001), a television drama whose very title advertised its limited trajectory. Famously mimicking 'real time', *24* became well known for running for exactly twenty-four hours. Consisting of only twenty-four episodes of an hour long (including commercial breaks when it was shown in the US) the intention was that *24* provided the viewer with one single day in the life of Jack Bauer (Kiefer Sutherland). In this way, it explicitly set out in advance its precisely defined beginning (zero hour) and conclusion (the climatic twenty-fourth episode) (see Brookes, 2004: 1–5). Consequently, its gradual movement towards narrative closure distinguished it from the never-ending storylines of the series (or soap opera) by constructing a well-defined narrative arc that eventually promised some form of resolution and conclusion at its end (even if a sequel was already in the pipeline). According to the *New York Times* television critic Vincent Canby, such a form allows many of the most sophisticated characteristics of film and television to combine, resulting in a new type of contemporary storytelling. As Canby puts it (2000: 59):

> *The Singing Detective* and *The Sopranos* are something more than mini-series. Packed with characters and events of Dickensian dimension and color, their time and place observed with satiric exactitude, each has the kind of cohesive dramatic arc that defines a work complete unto itself. No matter what they are labelled or what they become, they are not open-ended series, or even miniseries.
> They are megamovies.

Such has been the seductive power of the television serial (or 'megamovie') that in more recent years the distinguishing characteristics between the serial and the series are gradually beginning to merge. In particular, self-contained episodes that can be broadcast in *any* order and still make sense are now increasingly rare in the series as the narrative progression and sequential development of the serial form is increasingly incorporated into other television genres. The phenomenal success of the American soap opera *Dallas* around the world seems to have had an enormous effect on other forms of drama. As Robert J. Thompson has put it, *Dallas* 'gave memory to an entire medium. Soon dramatic shows – even those that weren't exactly soaps – began employing ongoing storylines' (1996: 34).

Although it set an important precedent, these developments were taking place long before *Dallas*. MTM Enterprises (an independent production company formed in 1970 after the success of *The Mary Tyler Moore Show* [CBS, 1970–7]) promoted cumulative narratives in a number of series during the 1970s and 1980s (see Feuer, Kerr and Vahimagi, 1984). Producing shows like *Lou Grant* (CBS, 1977–82), *Hill Street Blues* and *St Elsewhere* (NBC, 1982–8), MTM's dramas tended to incorporate elements of the serial form into the traditional series, with their storylines developing and continuing week after week. The company even appeared to inspire narrative continuity among sitcoms like *Cheers* (NBC, 1982–93) where the courtship between central characters Sam (Ted Danson) and Diane (Shelley Long) stretched sequentially from episode to episode.[7] Whatever its origins, this genre breakdown between the serial and series form is now part of the contemporary television landscape. As Graeme Turner explains (2001: 6):

Television genres and programming formats are notoriously hybridised and becoming more so. John Ellis, in the first edition of *Visible Fictions* (1982), confidently outlined the difference between the series and the serial. One of the key differences, it seemed then, was the series' use of self-contained episodes with relatively autonomous plotlines as against the serial's use of continuing storylines with characters who learned from episode to episode. Today, there are elements of the serial in many of what the industry would regard as series: US sitcoms such as *Friends*, hospital dramas such as *ER*, and cop shows such as *NYPD Blue*. In the UK, the self-contained, narratively low-key, realist format of the police series *The Bill* has given way to the continuing storylines and the focus on characters' private lives that is typical of soap opera.

Such an account of small screen hybridisation would seem to support Wilsher's worse fears that all television drama is now mutating into soap opera. The need for a successful serial to be continued and recycled (*The Bill* [ITV, 1984–] actually started life as a single play)[8] and the need to allow audiences to come in at any moment of the story certainly means that frequently a well-defined narrative arc is less pronounced than it may have once been. You can certainly see this in the way that *The Sopranos* went from having a strongly defined narrative development in the first series to adopting a more self-contained, episodic narrative structure in subsequent series. Indeed, episodes in series two of *The Sopranos* could almost stand alone as single plays in their own right while many of the narrative developments that take place within an episode are often completely forgotten in subsequent episodes. As its creator David Chase has explained, he had a 'personal goal' of making episodes that 'could have been made as a stand-alone feature film', i.e. entirely 'self contained' (2001: 8).

The traditional differences between the serial and the series now need to be redefined, taking into account the merging of the two separate forms. In brief, the changes can be defined in this way:

- **Series**: While the series is still continuous and never-ending, storylines now often develop from one episode to another (even introducing cliffhangers). This produces a cumulative narrative of sorts that does not exactly prevent viewers watching episodes in any order but which can be (and often are) watched in sequence. Examples include *Friends* (NBC, 1994–2004), *NYPD Blue* (ABC, 1993–) and *The Bill*.
- **Serial**: While the serial (and miniseries) still generally moves towards a narrative conclusion over a number of limited episodes, continuity between separate episodes is not as foregrounded as it may have once been, allowing greater entry points for viewers who have not followed the entire story. Final resolutions are also discouraged, leaving the opportunity for another series an option. Examples include *The Sopranos*, *The West Wing* (NBC, 1999–) and *Six Feet Under* (HBO, 2001–).

This increasing hybridity of television drama (particularly the apparent merging between the serial, series and soap opera) means that the unique style and structure of the television serial is probably not always as pronounced as it once was. However, it also means that the serial form is increasingly flexible, that it can adopt various genre styles and structures within its loosely defined narrative structure. While it is true that series are now emulating serials and that serials are now emulating series, it is also equally true that narrative fluidity between types of drama are more flexible than ever before. While it may be a shame that some of the more traditional structures of television drama are changing, these changes may offer new and surprisingly novel ways of reflecting and dramatising the contemporary world.

FROM SOAP TO SURREALISM

The result of this breakdown between the traditional series and serial may mean that for many viewers a great deal of television drama now has a 'soap-like' quality to it. Many may view contemporary serials (and miniseries) like *Six Feet Under*, *The Sopranos*, *Queer as Folk* (Channel Four, 1999–2000), *The West Wing*, *Nip/Tuck* (NBC, 2003–) and *Shameless* (Channel Four, 2004) as essentially continuous and developing narratives – dramas that they can dip in and out of at ease without having to watch every episode religiously and in close detail in order to follow the story. Yet, while their connection to continuous drama is there for anyone to see, there is still a discernible difference between these serial dramas and soap opera. Unlike most soap operas these serials:

- Are usually broadcast post-watershed (meaning that their content and characterisation can be decidedly more adult and intense in tone).
- Combine a mixture of 'flexi-narrative' techniques within a loosely defined narrative arc (meaning that elements of narrative progression towards conclusion can and still take place but within a complex exchange of narrative and character complexity). *What becomes payoff of each episode)*
- Sometimes reveal a tendency towards more 'experimental' techniques (meaning that definitions of social reality can be and are increasingly called into question. This clearly includes the subversion and re-invention of genre [see Chapter Three]).
- Offer examples of a new relationship between politics and the self (meaning that political issues are now increasingly centred convincingly around the domain of personal and private interaction).

It is this last point that perhaps reveals one of the most important changes that has taken place in television drama over the last twenty years or so. This reconception of the relationship between 'politics' and the 'self' means that the 'soap opera' techniques (generally derided by so-called 'serious' television writers, directors and producers of the 1960s and 1970s) have now become the very means by which 'radical' and 'progressive' drama is frequently conceived and constructed for a contemporary audience. This can partly be explained in the very changes and evolution of 'realism' itself. According to Andrew Higson, the history of British realism can be understood as 'the history of the changing conceptualisation of the relation between the public and the private, between the political and the personal ...' (1986: 83). While in early forms of the genre this relationship tended to be centred on the 'social' and 'political' space, in more recent years the shift has been towards matters of a more 'personal' and 'private' realm.

Put crudely, traditional forms of British social realism (of the 'documentary'-influenced *Cathy Come Home* and *Up the Junction* type) tended to suggest that the problems in a character's life could be remedied by structural changes in society. In contrast, newer forms of realism have tended to reflect a less optimistic belief in the power of political and social change as a whole, forcing a shift towards narratives of a more 'psychological' rather than overtly 'political' nature. As Julia Hallam and Margaret Marshment put it (2000: 216):

> Contemporary social realism comes in a range of stylistic variations, incorporating hybridised elements garnered from traditions of European art cinema to advertising, remaining committed to a humanist politics of individual self-worth but offering little by way of political solutions to environmental and social factors. There are clear correspondences here with Italian neo-realism, which, as recent reassessments have pointed out, tends to focus on the psychological depiction of characters governed by the chaotic forces of everyday life, rather than proffering political solutions to their problems.

Not surprisingly, then, the employment of 'soap opera' techniques has become a convenient means by which contemporary social realism attempts to re-articulate and re-examine the 'psychological' depiction of character. In this context, the 'soap opera-isation' of long-form television drama should not be conceived purely as a move away from the 'social' and the 'political' towards the 'personal' and the 'trivial', but as a gradual progression towards newer forms of representation which offer an arguably more contemporary articulation of present social experience. This also means a widening of 'social realism' as a term and an aesthetic choice to include sections of society other than the working class (where it was usually located during the so-called 'golden age' of the single play [see Jordan, 1981]).

It is important to recognise the 'political' nature of the personal lives so frequently dramatised by these newer forms of 'realism'. Serialised drama like *thirtysomething* (ABC, 1987–91), *Northern Exposure* (CBS, 1990–5), *This Life* (BBC, 1996–7), *Queer as Folk* and *Sex and the City* (HBO, 1998–2004) may appear to devalue the political landscape of its characters' lives in favour of their personal and private existence. However, the personal nature of the 'politics' under discussion is arguably still explored in such shows, their narratives constantly questioning and examining 'political' issues of self-identity in a way rarely examined before. In fact, the 'soap opera' conventions that typify such narratives may actually offer a more complex means by which the intricacies and personal ambiguity of contemporary life (particularly surrounding issues of identity, gender and sexuality) can be dramatised for a more self-knowing and self-reflexive audience (see Chapter Five).

It could also be argued that part of the success of historical serials like *Roots*, *Holocaust* and *Our Friends in the North* was the way in which they were similarly able to balance

Our Friends in the North: balancing the 'political' with the 'personal'

and address the 'personal' and the 'political' within one complex narrative trajectory. In particular, their reliance on 'soap opera' conventions (the historical narrative often centred around one single family or family tree) meant that they could explicitly dramatise and explore the *personal* nature of history – to analyse the minutiae of the past so that history itself increasingly became a self-reflexive, interpretative and subjective experience. While a serial like *Our Friends in the North* may have primarily revolved around a 'soap'-like fascination with the personal lives of its four central characters, this did not necessarily mean that the social, political and historical framework of the narrative itself was diminished. In fact, it could be argued that the political nature of the characters' personal lives was explored all the more convincingly and the 'politics of the everyday' more wholly imagined because of its fusion of 'soap-like' characteristics within a serialised and episodic form.

Similarly, television drama has seen a shift away from the depiction of external social/political realities to a more self-reflexive, multidimensional and subjective form. Dramas like *Edge of Darkness* (BBC, 1985), *Moonlighting* (NBC, 1985–9), *The Singing Detective, Twin Peaks, Cop Rock* (ABC, 1990), *Wild Palms, GBH* (Channel Four, 1991), *The X-Files* (Fox, 1993–2002), *Buffy the Vampire Slayer* (WB, 1977–2001), *Six Feet Under* and *The Kingdom* certainly appear to dispense with more traditional notions of 'naturalism'; their heightening levels of fantasy constructing a narrative universe in which social reality itself is continually set against subjective, individual and multiple perspectives (see Chapter Two). In other words, the external reality once offered by earlier forms of 'social realism' seems to be increasingly supplanted by a form that can (perhaps playfully) be referred to as 'social surrealism' – one that (in their flexi-narrative structure and their serialised hybridity) appears to more accurately reflect the social inconsistencies and moral uncertainties of a 'postmodern' world. As Lez Cooke puts it (2003: 178):

> For these dramas a faster tempo and such stylistic innovations as hand-held camerawork, elliptical editing, unusual shot transitions, montages, fantasy sequences and surreal inserts contrive to introduce something new into British television drama, a new form for a new postmodern audience, an audience that has not been reared on studio naturalism and which is impatient with the slow narrative development and 'realist' *mise en scène* traditionally associated with British television drama.

Recent television drama has learnt a great deal from the power and possibility of soap opera. Given a more complex narrative structure in which to create, it has both exploited and subverted the means by which the genre has generally been conceived and understood. It frequently employs complex forms of 'flexi-narrative', introducing intricate and sophisticated layers of plot and subplot narrative levels which gradually enhance character and narrative density beyond the scope of the single 'closed' narrative. On the other hand, it also seems to be able to play around with and sometimes even subvert the realist aesthetics upon which soap opera has generally been formed, often using its 'post-watershed' and 'quality' distinction as a means by which newer forms of televisual narrative can be conceived, imagined and re-imagined for a contemporary audience.

There is still arguably room within the serial form (even taking into account the increasing merging of the series and serial format) to allow other narrative styles, structures and generic possibilities to take place. The progression from single play to 'megamovie' has not been without its problems or loses, but surely the time is now ripe to celebrate the generic hybridity of television drama in the contemporary age, and to take stock of its enormous achievements and remarkable possibilities. This is the primary purpose of this book and the reason why, as a viewer, I still find myself enchanted and amazed by the potential and actualities of fiction on the small screen. The sheer breadth, narrative complexity and adult-orientated agenda of long-form television drama as a whole (and the television serial in particular) continues to give it a crucial and relevant place in the televisual depiction of contemporary life. Rather than continue to mourn for the demise of the single play, I suggest we celebrate the ability of television drama to continue to do what it does best, i.e. to take on large, personal and multi-dimensional narrative structures that reflect and respond to the contemporary world in a way that the cinema, theatre and the single play can rarely hope to emulate.

TEXTS AND CONTEXTS

In this book I will attempt to offer an insight into the political, aesthetic and generic possibilities of contemporary television drama. In particular, I will set out to explain how the television serial may actually better reflect, engage with and respond to the subtle nuances, political preoccupations and social realities of the contemporary age. Of course, such an undertaking is incredibly ambitious, particularly if it aims to do justice to all the important dramas, genres and issues that have spanned our screens in the last thirty years or so. However, this is not the purpose of this book. Instead, I will simply offer twelve case studies around which certain issues and debates can be contextualised, explored and addressed. Of course, this will mean that not all issues, programmes, genres and debates can be represented in full. There is, for example, no section on 'costume drama' (i.e. serials adapted from classic novels). While this may seem to be a tragic omission to many, I simply had to be selective in what I chose to look at, supplying 'snapshots' of the contemporary scene rather than a comprehensive and complete picture.[9]

Looking mainly at limited serials (i.e. dramas that still generally have a clearly defined beginning, middle and end) I will attempt to offer nothing more than examples of and insights into the debates, genres and programmes that make up the complex and prolific field that is contemporary television drama. If it is a complete picture you want (if that were even possible) then you will be disappointed, but I hope to suggest some of the most important and revealing fields of enquiry that this area has to offer. It will not satisfy every reader, but I hope that whatever your personal interests it will have something to say about an important and ever-growing form of contemporary fiction.

With this approach in mind, the first chapter (dealing primarily with *Roots*, *Holocaust* and *Heimat*) will examine the means by which the miniseries can dramatise the private and political issues of an historical landscape frequently more skilfully and revealingly than other media representation. In particular, it will explore how the 'personalised' preoccupation of soap opera can actually help to re-examine historical matter, casting a critical and often self-reflexive eye on official and objective notions and conceptions of 'historical fact'. The second chapter (dealing primarily with *Twin Peaks*, *The Kingdom* and *Cold Lazarus* [Channel Four/BBC, 1996]) will then explore the issue of aesthetic experimentation, suggesting ways in which contemporary television drama can still manage to be both innovative and challenging within the apparent limitations and restrictions of the 'new broadcasting age'; asking questions concerning the role of fantasy and subjectivity within both a 'modernist' and 'postmodern' political landscape.

Chapter Three (dealing primarily with *Prime Suspect, Cracker* [Granada, 1993–6] and *The Sopranos*) will address similar issues but particularly within the context of genre and consider the means by which the reconstruction of genre can frequently aid and promote new dramatic forms. Contradicting the apparently conservative and restricting limitations of genre as a televisual form, it will argue that genre itself can ironically become the means by which traditional forms of representation can be subverted and re-invented for a contemporary world. Finally, the last chapter (dealing primarily with *This Life*, *Queer as Folk* and *Sex and the City*) will look at the means by which the serial and series form both exploits and subverts the traditional conventions of soap opera, suggesting ways through which the 'politics' of everyday life can be successfully examined and exhumed for a contemporary audience. Isolating characteristics of the 'soap drama' it will attempt to re-examine the politics of identity and community (looking particularly at issues of gender and sexuality) within the generic conventions of both drama and comedy.

For some readers my method of analysis may seem a little 'old-fashioned'. I employ no primary ethnographic research, no detailed statistical charts and little 'scientific' evidence to support many of my claims. Instead my method of approach revolves mainly around close textual and contextual analysis, offering detailed readings of certain programmes, debates and issues that are open to conjecture and discussion. While some critics may dismiss such 'readings' as entirely subjective, what I would argue is that they are not meant to be understood as concrete factual suppositions. I do not pretend for one moment that I have discovered the final 'meaning' or 'truth' behind the programmes and debates I address. Instead, what this book aims to do is simply add to an ongoing *dialogue* around television drama, one that puts certain arguments and hypotheses up for debate and discussion without ever attempting to insist that any one of these readings is more valid or justifiable than any other that may (or may not) be in circulation. While I worry about the dominance of audience research in film and television in recent years, I do welcome the insight that such approaches have given to the discipline, i.e. that as many readings of a piece of film and television exist as there are members of the audience. As Hodge and Tripp point out (1986: 7):

> A television show is not a single stimulus; it is a vast meaning-potential complex, an interrelated set of verbal and visual meanings. But this potential is only abstract until there is someone to realise it. Interpretation is an intensely active process. Meaning is always constructed, or reconstructed, by the interaction of a set of signs with an overall code.

While I have the means and power of publication at my grasp, this book does not intend to somehow set these readings in stone or play down the 'vast meaning-potential complex' that television undoubtedly produces. Like any other member of the audience I have my own personal concerns, debates and issues that I will inevitably bring to my discussion. Textual analysis is not meant to be a science, indeed it could be argued that to apply even a 'semi-scientific' approach to drama of this sort (one that attempts to find the 'real' meaning behind a piece of fiction) defeats the very object of the drama itself. By definition drama is most commonly open-ended, multidimensional and ripe for interpretation. Hopefully this account of contemporary television attempts to accept and embrace these tendencies; to do otherwise would perhaps do an injustice to the power and potential of the very drama under discussion. Put simply, it is not my intention here to reduce episodic television drama to a manageable and sustainable size but to hopefully reveal its sheer breadth, structural complexity and narrative possibilities. In doing so, I hope to suggest some reasons why we should stop mourning for the so-called 'golden age' of the single play and start appreciating and understanding the staggering strength and diversity of serial television; a form that continues to provide a space for big drama on the small screen.

NOTES

1. Part of this introduction first appeared in a slightly different form in Creeber (2001a).
2. In 2003 there was a Royal Television Society panel discussion on the disappearance of the single play. Research presented there highlighted just how steep the decline in one-off single drama actually was. According to Richard Langridge, 'In 1983 there were 215 original single

dramas filling 330 hours of television, which averaged 6.4% original dramas a week. Now there are 63 original dramas a year, which averages 0.6% of programmes a week' (cited by Radio, 2003: 31).

3. *Cathy Come Home*'s depiction of modern homelessness is generally credited for helping to create *Shelter*, a charity designed to help the homeless in Britain.

4. As Christine Geraghty explains, 'The characters in a serial, when abandoned at the end of an episode, pursue an 'unrecorded existence' until the next one begins. In other words, we are aware that day-to-day life has continued in our absence … ' (Geraghty, 1981: 10).

5. Eaton is currently adapting *The Pickwick Papers* for television.

6. In successful cases a serial can be re-commissioned, such as *Prime Suspect 2, 3, 4* and so on. However, usually each serial should be able to stand up as an independent and self-sustaining narrative in its own right. Although a sitcom series like *Seinfeld* (NBC, 1990–8) or *M*A*S*H* (CBS, 1972–83) is initially designed to run indefinitely, it may manufacture a conclusion and resolution when the time finally comes. Exceptions such as these are important reminders of the fact that all such definitions can never be rigidly applied (see Kozloff, 1992: 92).

7. *Cheers* wasn't actually made by MTV, but its creative team included figures like James Burrows, Les Charles and Glen Charles who were all originally employed by the company.

8. *The Bill* actually began as a one-off play called *Woodentop* in Thames TV's *Storyboard* series in 1983.

9. In fact, there are now plenty of books devoted to 'costume drama', not least Giddings and Sheen (2000).

1 ADAPTING THE PAST

Empirical and Emotional Realism in the Historical Miniseries[1]

INTRODUCTION

> By creating their show for NBC, the authors have forced themselves to be equally responsive
> to the demands of both primetime show biz and historical accuracy. They prove that such a
> marriage of commerce and art can bear remarkable fruit.
>
> Frank Rich on *Holocaust* (cited in Doneson, 2002: 148–9)

Taking into account the sheer breadth of the television miniseries (allowing room for
multinarrative strands and subplot digression), as well as its ability to produce a clearly
defined beginning, middle and end (creating a usually well-defined narrative arc), it is
not surprising that the form eventually found itself uniquely suited to dramatising
increasingly large and complex narrative trajectories. *Rich Man, Poor Man* (PSB, 1976),
a hugely successful twelve-hour weekly adaptation of the Irwin Shaw novel, is often
stated as starting off the trend for the miniseries in the United States, its story's own
relatively large passage of time perhaps suggesting possibilities and inspirations for serials that encompassed large historical landscapes.[2] Often based on bulky, popular novels
of the time, television (with its unparalleled temporal breadth) seemed to be the natural
home for the adaptation of such epic fiction. According to John Thornton Caldwell, the
miniseries itself soon became huge television 'events' around which the schedules could
be arranged even if the individual programme itself failed to do well in the ratings. As
Caldwell puts it (1994: 162):

> Given the financial risks of high-production value programming, event status shows function,
> for cable and broadcasters alike, somewhat like retailing loss leaders. Even if showcased
> spectacles – miniseries, MOWs, primetime soaps, and international sports – lose money
> because production costs outweigh spot sales, they typically provide marquee points of entry
> that entice viewers to sample more commonplace products in the programmer's store.
> Sometimes the value implicit in such shows is more widespread. Miniseries can, for example,
> create network identities as high-profile banner carriers intended to rally the troops.

Perhaps the evolution of this style of epic drama may have been partly inspired by the
huge success of films like David Lean's *Doctor Zhivago* (1965) and Francis Ford
Coppola's *The Godfather Part I* (1972) and *Part II* (1974). Both adapted from best-selling
novels, they produced long, complex and historically situated narratives that were both

temporally expansive and narratively multilayered. Tellingly, Coppola's two epic movies would eventually be re-edited for television a year after the success of *Rich Man, Poor Man* so that the story could finally take place in chronological order. Calling itself *Mario Puzo's The Godfather: The Complete Novel for Television* (NBC, 1977), it spread itself over four consecutive evenings starting on 12 November and running to over seven hours long. In comparison to *The Godfather Part I & II*'s relatively disappointing ratings when shown separately on American television, this new format apparently resulted in an average hundred million viewers (see Cowie, 1997: 103); a huge ratings success that only confirmed the television miniseries as both an artistic and economic success.[3]

After the popularity of *Rich Man, Poor Man*, *Roots* (ABC, 1977), apparently seen by 130 million viewers during its initial US broadcast, certainly appeared to trigger a wave of historically based serials. *Roots*, *Holocaust* (NBC, 1978), *The Winds of War* (ABC, 1983), *North and South* (ABC, 1985), and *War and Remembrance* (ABC, 1989–90) clearly helped to define a whole subgenre of new historical television drama. Focused around a particular time or story in history, these dramas came with an unusual degree of cultural capital. Sometimes (rather misleadingly) billed as 'docudramas', their attempt to represent real and important historical issues and events led them to be taken seriously both by audiences and critics alike; while also appealing to those viewers who just fancied a damn good yarn spun over a number of nightly episodes. Dramas about the recent past were also popular, with miniseries like *Helter Skelter* (CBS, 1976) (the story of Charles Manson) and *Rumor of War* (CBS, 1980) (about the Vietnam conflict) dramatising recent historical events.

As discussed in the Introduction, perhaps the rise of the American miniseries can partly be attributed to the success of British (particularly historical) serials on American public television channels during the 1970s. *The Six Wives of Henry VIII* (BBC, 1970), *Edward and Mrs Simpson* (ITV, 1978) and *Testament of Youth* (BBC, 1979) were all hugely popular historical serials, while the Roman epic *I, Claudius* (BBC, 1976) serialised Robert Graves' (apparently 'unfilmable') 1934 novel in twelve award-winning episodes that found international acclaim. The British series *Upstairs Downstairs* (ITV, 1971–5) even went on to win an Emmy® in the US, showing the marketability of British historical drama that presented a particular (what some have called 'idealised') version of Britain's past. Yet despite its limitations the genre became an increasingly popular form during the late 1970s and 1980s, winning large audiences at home, selling internationally and often attracting important co-production money from abroad, especially from America (see Bennett *et al.*, 1981: 285).

One now famous exception to this type of 'heritage' drama was Ken Loach and Jim Allen's controversial serial *Days of Hope* (BBC, 1975), which took as its central story the rise of the British working-class movement. Consisting of four episodes, it focused its narrative on an English working-class family during the period from 1916 (the year in which conscription was introduced) to 1926 (the year of Britain's General Strike). Interestingly, it became the talking point for television and film academics at the time about the use of 'classical realism' in film and television generally. In particular, the argument (now most frequently referred to as the '*Days of Hope* Debate') took place in the pages

Rich Man, Poor Man: one of the first television miniseries

of the film journal *Screen* and discussed how history could and should be best represented on screen. While Colin McCabe (1981) argued that a 'classic realist text' (of which, he suggested, *Days of Hope* was an example) could never offer a 'progressive' view of history, Colin McArthur (1981) argued that the apparent 'realism' of the drama did little to diminish its radical agenda.

Such a debate neatly articulates some of the central arguments that almost inevitably

Days of Hope: creating debate about TV realism

take place around the issue of representing history as screen fiction. According to McCabe, in attempting to pass itself of as accurately representing 'the real', a classic real-ist text privileges itself as offering an unproblematic version of both history and truth. As such, he argued that *Days of Hope* 'falls within a bourgeois conception of history in which the past is understood as having a fixed and immutable existence rather than being the site of constant struggle in the present' (1981: 312). In contrast, Colin McArthur stated that despite *Days of Hope*'s apparent adherence to a realist mode, it still managed to remain 'progressive' by offering a view of history that explicitly challenged the 'domi-nant ideology' of the time. Added to this, its progressive content was reflected in a form that involved 'the shedding of certain classical (primarily Hollywoodian) mechanisms and strategies, most notably the star and the dramaturgical device (most evident in the melodrama) of the climax' (1981: 309).

When discussing the following historical miniseries then, it is important to remember the issues that surround such a debate. Unlike other examples discussed in this book, all the dramas below attempt to represent *real* historical times and events. How 'accu-rately' these events are represented will therefore prove to be an important (although not always the only) element by which their eventual 'success' will be judged. However, the question of whether historical fiction should or should not represent history as a piece of 'realism' (and what sort of *'realisms'* are actually employed) will remain a pertinent point around which issues of historical accuracy and interpretation will be discussed. None of the three case studies below explicitly uses 'non-naturalistic' devices in which to portray their historical narratives, but nor do they simply attempt to render the real as a simple piece of unproblematic verisimilitude. Indeed, I will argue that all three dramas are extremely conscious and sometimes even self-conscious about the way in which they are representing history, offering a version of the past that is implicitly aimed at and constructed for a contemporary, frequently nationally based, mass audience.

In many ways, a subject as rich, dense and as complex as the historical miniseries deserves a number of books to itself.[4] However, all I hope to do in this small chapter is to simply point out ways in which the miniseries can offer insights and representations of history that few other media could hope to emulate. Rather than long-form drama destroying the political and critical potential of television drama, I will argue that the very 'soap-like' dynamics that such a form inevitably employs, actually makes it an unusually versatile vehicle for exploring and investigating the philosophical nature of history and indeed its relevance and significance for a contemporary audience.

Roots (ABC, 1977)

> Here's a twelve-hour story where the whites are villains and the blacks are the heroes in a country that is 85 per cent white. It doesn't sound like a good idea at first blush.
>
> Fred Silverman (cited in Stark, 1997: 200)

Roots is now regarded as 'a milestone in television history' (Smith, 1995: 101–2). Based on Alex Haley's hugely popular novel of the same name and primarily directed by Marvin Chomsky (although David Greene of *Rich Man, Poor Man* fame directed the all-important first episode and the first hour of the second), it traced the semi-factual story of Haley's ancestors back to Africa, beginning with the journey of Kunta Kinte (LeVar Burton/John Amos) into slavery in the United States.[5] *Roots* was twelve hours long and run over eight successive nights by ABC (beginning on 23 January, 1977); the final episode was watched by a total of eighty million viewers. Later it would go on to win nine Emmys®, the George Foster Peabody Award, six Television Critics Circle Awards and a Golden Globe for Best Drama Series.[6] Perhaps testament to its enduring popularity was the recent issue of *Roots: the 25th Anniversary Edition* (2002) on a Warner Bros DVD, which includes a feature-length audio commentary and its own documentary simply entitled, *Remembering Roots*.

Roots came out of a certain moment in American cultural history. In particular, the US bicentennial celebrations occurred only six months before its first broadcast, encouraging an interest in American genealogy and the nation's search for its own complex heritage. This was also compounded by the Civil Rights movement in the 1960s that had produced a greater pride among black Americans who were now demanding to determine not only their future but also discover and re-represent the details of their past. Although it may not have been as historically 'accurate' as some critics would have liked (in fact, Haley's own book later received much criticism for the liberties it apparently took with the details of his own family tree), the enormity of it as a 'television event' was unmistakable. For a rare moment in American television history, a national audience was actively made to identify with black characters and black history, an event that arguably forced viewers to re-evaluate the issue of racial discrimination from within both a contemporary and historical context.

Legend has it that the idea to schedule *Roots* over a number of successive evenings was partly an attempt to get it over with quickly if it proved to be a unanimous flop (see Fishbein, 1983: 279–80). Many within ABC were nervous about the sensitivity of its subject matter. However, as Wolper reveals, it was the serial nature of the drama that played a large role in its remarkable success. Although audiences were attracted to the historical context of the story as a whole, its serialised narrative structure meant that it kept them as hooked as any soap opera or drama series. According to Wolper, 'People would get up in the morning, would go to work and talk about what they saw last night, and if you didn't watch *Roots* you were out of the conversation. So when you went home the second night you said, I'd better watch *Roots* otherwise I've nobody to talk to tomorrow morning' (cited by Wheen, 1985: 152).

However, many critics felt that *Roots* had made too many concessions in a bid for mainstream success, simply watering down and sanitising its difficult subject matter in a desperate bid to appeal to as wide a demographic as possible. Most recently, Lauren R. Tucker and Hemant Shah have argued in their 'production of culture' analysis of the drama that the network executives transformed the original novel into a 'dominant white' interpretation (1992: 335):

> In the case of TV *Roots*, the white producers and network executives made several structural changes during the production process that altered the original characterizations, content, and theme of Haley's story in such a way as to promote an entirely different social meaning and ideology. By placing the black experience in the context of the classic immigrant story, the creators ignore the distinctiveness of Kunta Kinte's struggle – and the struggle of all black Americans – against the institution of slavery and oppression in favor of an emphasis on the idea of universal assimilation implicit in the immigrant myth.

Indeed, even the most casual viewer could probably spot the way that *Roots* seemed to be deliberately orientating itself towards a white audience. Although its opening takes place in an African village in Gambia in 1750, the tribe itself is actually portrayed speaking rather 'middle-brow' English. The decision not to use subtitles in the first episode can also be seen as simply pandering to an American audience's apparent refusal to accept anything too 'strange' or 'difficult'.[7] Such apparent compromises to its audience may also be suggested in the employment of well-known black faces such as Maya Angelou and even O. J. Simpson (a couple of decades before his infamous murder trial and still at the height of his national fame as a sporting hero), an attempt to limit the alienation of the white audiences watching. This could also apply to the other popular TV stars that the drama employed like Edward Asner, Ralph Waite (previously the father in *The Waltons* [CBS, 1972–81]) and Cicely Tyson, familiar faces that all American audiences (both white and black) would have possibly felt comfortable with.

As Tucker and Shah point out, the African 'Mandingo' village portrayed in the opening episode of *Roots* is an Americanised version of what such a community may have been like. Filmed in Savannah, Georgia, its picture of a surprisingly tolerant and liberal society appears to construct a veritable Eden. In fact, Kunta Kinte's father and mother are overwhelmingly portrayed as an almost perfect 'Western' family unit, strict but inherently kind-hearted with only two children. When one of the goats Kunta Kinte is meant to be guarding is killed by a leopard, his father shows concern only for his son's safety (quickly correcting himself when he briefly and initially loses his temper). And while there is brief mention of male circumcision, there is certainly no reference to its female equivalent; or, for that matter, any strange rituals, slaughtering of animals or unsettling practices that an American television audience may have taken exception to. The values here, then, are derived more from contemporary middle-class America than eighteenth-century Africa. At times its vision of Gambia certainly threatens to look more like a Disney film than an historical miniseries. Indeed, one can't help but wonder if parts of Disney's *The Lion King* (Allers, 1994) may have even been influenced by the series, so similar is some of its Africanesque iconography and visual imagery.

Similarly, one can see other attempts to include an audience that may have been alienated by the drama's uncomfortable subject matter. While the principal female characters of the African village are suitably covered up for an American family audience, the extras and black background women are all nude from the waste up; perhaps an attempt to titillate its potential audience as much as pay respect to any notion of historical accuracy. In fact, some of the opening shots of the whole series involve a bevy of bare-breasted black women washing and carrying clothes from the river. This naked titillation is possibly part of the reason why the white slave-traders' sexual interest in the black slave girls is so frequently alluded to. While offering us an important insight into the way that black slaves were perceived as white property, it also helps to keep the drama carefully spiced with a healthy balance of sex and violence.

This attempt to capture a white American audience may also suggest reasons why Ed Asner (previously of *Lou Grant* [CBS, 1977–82] fame and a well-known American liberal)[8] plays the captain of a slave ship who does not approve of the practice of slavery. Not happy with the ethical or theological implications of carrying human cargo, perhaps his personal struggle helps the white audience to alleviate their historical guilt. So while he is morally ambiguous (he ultimately does work for the slave trade and we never actually discover if he actually uses a black 'belly warmer' in his cabin or not), his ethical struggle itself is perhaps an important part of the serial's attempt to lessen the alienation of a large part of the American public.

However, the most recurring criticism of *Roots* (echoed by Tucker and Shah [1992]) is that it simply perpetuates and reinforces an idealised vision of the 'immigrant myth' and ultimately the 'American Dream'. As we later follow the lives of Kunta Kinte's daughter Kizzy (Leslie Uggams) (raped by a white plantation owner) and her son Chicken George (Ben Vereen), through to Kinte's grandson Tom Harvey's (Georg Stanford Brown) eventual emancipation in post-Civil War America, so the 'triumph of an American family' and the apparent meritocracy of the US is insidiously supported. By the end of the miniseries (which includes a personal appearance by Haley himself) the Haleys are a respectable, educated American family, their assimilation into white middle-class

American culture complete. While the struggle to get there had been brutal, horrific and notoriously unjust, by its end America appears to finally atone for its sins and accepts Kunta Kinte's ancestors into its seemingly tolerant and multicultural bosom. As Karen Ross has put it, *Roots* was (1996: 98):

> the quintessential rags-to-riches story which could hold for black communities as well as white. The awesome power of television is its ability to gloss over or ignore inconvenient truths in order to present a more hopeful scenario, where hard work can overcome every disadvantage, even endemic racism.

While this sort of criticism has much weight, it is important not to play down the day-to-day horrors that typify the story told by *Roots* as a whole. For twelve hours we witness one black generation after another being horse-whipped, mutilated, beaten, broken, treated like animals, humiliated, raped and abused by their white slave owners and fellow countrymen, yet overcoming all with a quiet dignity, an irrepressible pride and a stoic self-respect. Above all, the story of black slavery is not told from the white perspective as was so often the case (particularly in historical books and journals of the period), but from the point of view of those who were enslaved and those who suffered from it the most. This is no mean feat for an American miniseries of the 1970s when heroic black images were considerably less common than they are today. Concessions are made for a white audience, but it would have been strange if liberties had not been taken with history for the sake of getting this profoundly difficult and socially inflammable story across to a possibly less than receptive and even hostile American public.

Seen in this light, many of the possible concessions made to a white audience can be explained and even justified as an attempt to get a great deal of history (some of it very unpleasant indeed) to as large an audience as possible. Firstly, it was crucial that if viewers were to follow the story across its entire twelve hours (and thereby absorb its important historical message) it needed to immediately hook its audience directly into the narrative, to make them care about and empathise with its central black characters. Anything that may have meant that viewers (particularly white viewers) were less likely to switch off may have been justified in an attempt to bring harsher historical facts and issues to the audience later on in the series. As Wolper puts it when defending the drama's 'middle-brow' aesthetics and its need to capture an audience's attention (my emphasis, cited by Wheen, 1985: 152):

> American television is 'middle-brow', and I wanted to make a subject that was important in a middle-brow way so a large audience could appreciate it, understand it and get something out of it. I mean, people actually turned off basketball games in bars around America and put on *Roots* because they wanted to learn and they wanted to learn *on their own terms* – they wanted terrific drama, entertainment and stars.

Perhaps the sheer power of *Roots* lay in its ability to create a heady but carefully balanced mixture of titillation, melodrama, human interest and history to make it both entertaining and educational on a number of different levels. An historical miniseries like *Roots* is perhaps best understood in terms of its ability to offer viewers a form of 'the real' that may go beyond traditional notions of realism or historical accuracy alone. While historical 'facts' are inevitably crucial in its successful rendering of history, perhaps just as important is its ability to breathe life into the emotional side of the past, thereby personalising the political nature of history and imbuing these sometimes stale facts with individual power and relevance to a contemporary audience.

This might explain, for example, the programme-maker's decision to make the ship's captain so strongly anti-slavery. His dramatic purpose (particularly as he is new to transporting this human cargo) is to ask questions about thumb-screws, chains and how (and how *many*) slaves are carried on board and how it could be justified by apparently good-minded Christian people. The conversations between him and the brutal Slater (Ralph Waite), inform and remind the audience of the theological and moral questions of the time (as well the terrible realities of the slave trade as a whole). Historically, of course, his position does also remind us that many white people *were* indeed against slavery and were actively involved in trying to bring it to its end, just as we see black Africans helping the white slave traders capture other Africans. In order that the slave trade is not reduced to simply 'whites' against 'blacks', it could be argued that the drama had a moral responsibility to show the different shades of grey in between. Such a theme is arguably continued later when a poor white family becomes friends with a black slave family and are subject to racism and violence as a result of that association.

Perhaps, then, the power of *Roots* lies not in its *historical* but its *emotional* reality, a concept reminiscent of Ien Ang's ground-breaking work on the American soap opera *Dallas*. Ang found that despite the soap opera's inherently 'escapist', 'glamorous' and 'Americanised' *mise en scène*, the viewers she interviewed in Holland still found the drama provided a great deal of relevance to their lives, mainly through a technique she referred to as '*emotional realism*'. By this she meant that the narrative potency of *Dallas* did not rely so much on its social verisimilitude or empiricist reality, as much as its characters' ability to engage and involve an audience on a personal and emotional level. For Ang, *Dallas* both cultivated and exploited the 'melodramatic imagination', allowing viewers to intimately relate to and empathise with the personal problems encountered by the characters despite the trappings of sensationalism that also defined it. As Ang puts it (1985: 47):

> The realism of *Dallas* is therefore produced by the construction of a *psychological* reality, and it is not related to its (illusory) fit to an externally perceptible (social) reality. It could even be said that in *Dallas* an 'inner realism' is combined with an 'external realism'.

While *Roots* claims to be more than simply a soap opera (or indeed 'costume drama'), it perhaps nonetheless exploits the 'melodramatic imagination' in an attempt to 'adapt' or 'translate' history to its viewers. Both Kunta Kinte's African and American experiences may be a travesty of classical and empirical realism, but its 'emotional' appeal plays a major factor in its success at realising and articulating history for a contemporary audience. One of the reasons why Kunta Kinte's capture, imprisonment and eventual slavery seemed so compelling to an American audience, is possibly because the viewer's identification with its black characters takes place over such a large narrative space. Interestingly, *Roots* appears to allow itself time to first capture the emotional heart of its audiences before *gradually* and *slowly* forcing them to witness and take on board the sheer horror of its history lesson (a luxury that perhaps only the relative longevity of the miniseries can really afford). The opening episode of *Roots* may owe more to America in the 1970s than Gambia in the 1700s, but it is a device that brutally brings home the sheer unadulterated misery of being torn from everything you know of and understand as home. For an American audience to really understand that (and thereby really begin to appreciate the personal consequences of the slave trade), it could be argued that they had to eventually feel that, for a brief period of time, at least, eighteenth-century Gambia could have been their home.

In fact, by the time Kunta Kinte is captured by the white slave traders (actually two thirds of the way into the first episode), many viewers would have so closely identified with him (the start of the episode actually begins with his birth) that they will feel all the more shocked and personally traumatised by his brutal capture. The horror of such an event is arguably made more terrible because he, rather than being a native African whose culture and customs are inherently 'strange' to an American audience, is actually now readily identifiable and empathetic to the audience as a whole. In terms of American television, it is as if slave traders were to suddenly arrive in *The Waltons* and drag off John Boy in chains!

In this sense, *Roots* harnessed the continuity techniques of soap opera by having us identify with characters over a surprisingly large period of screen time. While a single play would have inevitably needed to condense its complex history into two or three hours, *Roots* had the luxury of bringing difficult historical facts gradually and carefully to a possibly less than receptive audience by mixing them together with a large number of other (perhaps more 'sensational') elements. While the audience slowly but inevitably becomes captivated and seduced by the more intrinsically 'soap-like' elements of the drama (family relations, love, marriage, the birth of children, divorce, death and so on), the history (the brutality of slavery, the social consequences of racism, the black struggle for freedom) is also conveyed. Perhaps it is only through such an epic structure (taking place over a number of days and episodes) that such issues can be convincingly interwoven, realising a narrative complexity that can effectively juggle many themes at once.

It might be interesting to compare *Roots* to a single film that deals with similar historical events. Perhaps most revealing, it can be likened to Steven Spielberg's big-screen portrayal of American slavery, *Amistad* (1997). While the expansive narrative arc of *Roots* crosses multiple generations, *Amistad* centres its storyline around *one* event (focusing on the true uprising of a slave ship and the slaves' subsequent struggle for freedom through the US courts). This remarkable story attempts to bring the atrocities of slavery to an audience without producing an overwhelmingly depressing and morally despairing narrative. However, the film's fundamental desire to celebrate the power of the human spirit in the face of all adversity risks misrepresenting history at the expense of finding and foregrounding a central moral imperative. While a similar moral framework is discernible in *Roots* as a whole (particularly in its overly upbeat ending and the potential of a slave uprising at the end of episode one, creating a convenient cliffhanger), it could be argued that its multigenerational narrative structure offers a more complex and pluralistic reading of history than could ever be matched by Spielberg's true, but *exceptional* storyline. Ironically, Spielberg's use of the true story of the *Amistad* ship threatens to make it less representative of the history of the American slave trade than Haley's own semi-fictional account. No wonder that Wolper originally urged Haley to sell the rights of the novel over to television, arguing that a movie version of his 885-page novel would simply need to cut out too much of the plot (Stark, 1997: 200).

As 'soap-like' and melodramatic as it was, *Roots*' ability to produce complex, multiple storylines over a multigenerational narrative arc meant that the intrinsic complexity of history itself was alluded to in its structure, if not always in its content. As flawed as it may be historically, the sheer breadth of its epic structure means that it produces the framework to get both the social and emotional complexity of slavery across to millions of people who may otherwise never have contemplated the subject in any historical depth. As such, *Roots* may be best seen as a case study in the power of 'emotional realism' to translate and humanise historical facts for a contemporary audience. It is clearly more successful as a piece of drama than a piece of history, but the history itself is still there and is brought home more forcibly and convincingly because of the dramatic techniques and emotional narrative dynamics that it so shrewdly and carefully employs.

Roots: offering a form of emotional realism

In particular, it created a narrative journey that an exceptionally large contemporary American audience could relate to and empathise with; something which empirical realism and historical accuracy were unlikely to achieve alone.

Holocaust (NBC/Titus, 1978)

> I wanted a real German family, the equivalent of American Jews who think of themselves first as Americans. We didn't want to do *Fiddler on the Roof* Jews, although they were prime victims of the Holocaust. We were afraid they would vitiate what we were trying to do – appeal to a broad audience.
>
> Gerald Green (cited in Doneson, 2002: 151)

The huge success of *Roots* guaranteed that it was a winning formula television executives wanted to emulate time and again. Only a year later came *Holocaust*, a four-part 'miniseries' about Hitler's extermination of the Jews. Like its predecessor, it was aired over a number of consecutive evenings (16–18 April 1978), hoping to capture the nation's imagination in a similar way to *Roots*.[9] Written by Gerald Green and also (partly) directed by Marvin Chomsky, it surpassed all expectations, winning the biggest television audience in the United States in 1978 with an estimated 120 million viewers worldwide.[10] Beginning in Germany in 1935 with the marriage of the German Gentile Inga Helms (Meryl Streep) into the Jewish Weiss family, the story allows viewers the opportunity to follow the various fortunes of two German families from the origins of Nazi Germany, through to the Holocaust and the end of hostilities in 1945.

Such was its success, the makers of *Holocaust* found that despite originally being aimed at an American audience, the miniseries also went on to become surprisingly popular and have a huge influence outside the US. Transmitted in West Germany on 22, 23, 25 and 26 January 1979 to a total of twenty million viewers, the *FAZ* cultural page argued that 'After *Holocaust* one can no longer speak of the fundamental impotence of art' (cited by Herf, 1980: 39). Indeed, each episode in Germany was followed by a television debate that brought to the fore issues and concerns that, according to many commentators, were virtually buried and 'repressed' before its broadcast. 'Having destroyed a taboo', wrote Jean-Paul Bier, the miniseries 'created a climate favourable to discussing it in the family, at school or at work' (1980: 29).[11] Although critics like Jeffrey Herf were right to point out that the pre-*Holocaust* vision of complete national 'amnesia' was not entirely accurate – 'that numerous books, articles and documentary films about the Holocaust had [already] been printed and shown in West Germany' (Herf, 1980: 32) – nothing seemed to capture the public consciousness in a way that was comparable to the American miniseries. As Heinz Hohne put it in the German magazine, *Spiegel* (1979: 22):

> An American television series, made in a trivial style, produced more for commercial than for moral reasons, more for entertainment than for enlightenment, accomplished what hundreds of books, plays, films, and television programmes, thousands of documents, and all the

concentration camp trials have failed to do in more than three decades since the end of the war: to inform Germans about crimes against Jews committed in their name so that millions were emotionally touched and moved. ... Only since, and thanks to, *Holocaust* does a large majority of the nation know what was hidden behind the seemingly innocuous bureaucratic phrase, 'the final solution'. They know it because US filmmakers had the courage to free themselves from the crippling precept that it is impossible to portray mass murder.[12]

Like *Roots*, the serial nature of *Holocaust* was clearly one of the major reasons for its success. Its appropriation of the serial form enabled it to capture an audience's attention and imagination in a way rarely possible within the smaller dynamics of the cinema or single play. While its central narrative arc allowed a clear historical thread to be continued and developed over four consecutive nights, its employment of 'soap opera' techniques (particularly the audience's intense and emotional familiarity with its characters) meant that issues of history and personal responsibility could be portrayed and explored on a number of different narrative levels.

Despite its international success, *Holocaust* was also the subject of much criticism and debate. Many commentators, for example, felt that the human drama at the centre of the narrative inevitably trivialised (and took liberties with) the history it was attempting to portray; more concerned perhaps with *entertaining* its audience than *educating* them about one of the most complex and horrifying aspects of twentieth-century history. 'It tries to show what cannot be imagined' wrote Elie Wiesel, novelist and survivor of Auschwitz, in the *New York Times*. 'It transforms an ontological event into soap-opera' (cited by Wiesel, 1978: 175 and Kaes, 1989: 28). According to the German magazine *Der Spiegel*, it presented Fascism 'in the format of a family album ... genocide shrunken to the level of *Bonanza* with music appropriate to *Love Story*' (cited by Herf, 1980: 37).

In particular, *Holocaust* was frequently criticised for simply trying to portray the 'Final Solution' on television at all. Reacting to its controversy, the screenwriter Paddy Chayefsky explained that 'Trivialization is television' (cited by Avisar, 1988: 130). Chayefsky's comments (surprising for a writer who made his name in the so-called 'golden age' of television drama)[13] echoed numerous critics who felt that television was simply not the place for a narrative dealing with such historical gravity. As Molly Haskell put it, 'the Holocaust is simply too vast, the elimination of six million people from the earth too incomprehensible, to fit into ... the reductive context of the small screen' (Haskell, 1978: 79). The sheer presence of commercial breaks during the miniseries was also seen as implicitly 'commodifying' genocide, 'much like toothpaste' (cited by Shandler, 1997: 158). Jean Baudrillard famously compared the death camps with television itself. *Holocaust*, he argued (1984: 22):

Replays the extermination – but too late for it to profoundly unsettle anything, and above all it does so via a medium which itself is cold, radiating oblivion, dissuasion and extermination in an even more systematic manner, if this is possible, than the camps themselves. TV, the veritable final solution to the historicity of every event.

In fact, the opening credits of *Holocaust* would have probably done little to reassure a cynical viewer that this was anything other than prime-time soap opera. The concentration on personality rather than historical context (each major actor is framed during the opening credits with their real name and their character's name superimposed underneath) seems to immediately prioritise the human story over its social or political implications. Added to this, the flamboyant orchestral score by Morton Gold signifies that we are in the presence of melodrama, a narrative that will have little trouble emphasising human drama over any other aspect of the story. Opening (like *The Godfather*) with a lavish wedding, viewers are rather less than subtly introduced to all the major characters during the speeches, the rather furtive look of Heinz Muller (Anthony Haygarth) immediately signalling to the audience who is to be the villain of the piece. In contrast, the warm, charming and good-looking Dr Josef Weiss (Fritz Weaver) is quickly established in the role of hero and as the symbol of a good, decent man. But like *Roots*, perhaps the most biting criticism is that this was clearly an 'Americanised' view of history. Although set in Berlin in 1935, all the actors here are American, speak in broad American accents and appear (despite efforts in costume) to display the manners, the tastes and the culture of contemporary, middle-class America.

Echoing the problems with the portrayal of Kunta Kinte's homeland in *Roots*, the filmmaker and critic Claude Lanzmann argued that the series particularly attempted to 'normalise' its Jewish characters at the expense of historical accuracy. For Lanzmann, the television miniseries simply had to do away with the 'Otherness' of its Jewish family in order that the story become acceptable for an American audience (1979/80: 138–9):

> It was necessary that the Jewish victims differ in no way from the spectators or even from their executioners: everything that could make the Jews seem different had been erased in order to make their humanity visible and perceptible. All trace of otherness has been effaced; thus the Jewish family is 'assimilated', and most of the actors are not themselves Jewish. But the opposite would have been right. The humanity of the victims ought to have been made more striking and more profound to the extent that they had at the start appeared different from us. Would television viewers of the world have identified so easily with the Jewish men and women of Poland, of the Ukraine, or of Belorussia, with their clothing, their traditions, their particularity, their strangeness?

Such a criticism seems difficult to defend, particularly if the miniseries was simply meant to be a *faithful* and *naturalistic* reconstruction of historical events. But as shown above, how 'faithful' a miniseries is to historical authenticity is not the only criteria upon which its success can or should be judged. Just as different forms of realism (including 'emotional realism') attempt to portray something of what life feels like rather than simply what it looks like, so it is important to judge an historical miniseries like *Holocaust* on more than its historical accuracy alone. What critics like Lanzmann seem to forget is that all historical dramas are 'adaptations' or 'translations' of history that have to make choices about how best to portray real historical events. While verisimilitude is clearly a crucial element of any historical 'adaptation' it is not the only factor that needs to be taken into consideration when dramatising the past.

In this sense, maybe some of the problems of adapting a literary work to film or television may also be relevant in the adaptation of history. For example, some 'fidelity critics' tend to judge the success of an adaptation simply by how 'faithful' it is to the original novel. The literary critic Brian McFarlane (1996: 164, also cited by Giddings and Sheen, 2000: 2) suggests that if these critics experience a sense of 'dissatisfaction' with an adaptation, it is usually because

> the illusion of reality created by the film does not coincide with their perception of the illusion of reality created by the novella. They write as though the latter were somehow fixed and that it is merely obtuse of the film-maker not to have noticed this and reproduced it in the new medium.

However, it has been argued that those that attempt to be explicitly faithful to a book do not always do the most justice to the original material. Sometimes, liberties have to be taken with the original source to enable the very essence of the story to be translated and transferred to another medium. Although the adaptation of history and fiction are clearly two different projects, they both nonetheless demand a similar process of selection and revision that involves being literally faithful or not to the original source.

For example, while the decision to make the Jewish characters in *Holocaust* appear essentially 'American' in appearance and behaviour may seem to be taking extreme liberties with historical truth, it proved to be a crucial means by which this particular story (for this particular national audience) attempted to translate or 'adapt' these real historical events. To heighten the 'Otherness' of the Jews in the serial would have undoubtedly offered a greater empirical realism (an empirical realism more faithfully rendered, for example, by Lanzmann's *Shoah* [1985], his own nine-and-a-half-hour documentary account of the Holocaust).[14] But in doing so, it would have risked alienating a television audience whose very act of identification may have enabled them to appreciate more fully how the Nazi Holocaust happened to people no fundamentally different to themselves. As one character puts it in Auschwitz, 'It's hard to remember we are all people. Individual humans. Names. Homes. Families.' Indeed, having explicitly identified and empathised with these characters in a manner akin to soap opera, to see many of them finally walk into gas chambers arguably produces an emotional response in its audience that few narratives could hope to emulate.

Like *Roots*, then, the very 'soapiness' of the serial form *Holocaust* employs, attempts to force an American audience to explicitly identify with its central Jewish family so that they gradually learn to see the Holocaust *through their eyes*; enabling them to understand more completely how it might have felt to be persecuted for a 'strangeness' which they themselves (like the actual Holocaust victims) could not have perceived. As Judith E. Doneson explains, it could also make a non-Jewish audience ask questions about their own potential for hatred and discrimination (2002: 151):

Green did not expect the audience to identify with the Weisses but rather to sympathize with them, to understand that they were not 'foreign' but the equivalent of middle-class American Jews whose lives were destroyed only because they were Jewish. The moral, of course, is evident: the bystander – the neighbor – is often as guilty as the perpetrator, be it Nazi Germany or contemporary America.

Making the Nazis in the story also appear similar to the intended audience arguably produces the same effect. By heightening their 'normality', i.e. '*Americanising*' them, the spectator is perhaps forced to face up to the banality of evil, the possibility that it inevitably lies within us all. The central Nazi in the narrative is Major Erik Dorf (Michael Moriarty) who is initially seen to possess no real hatred towards the Jews. Indeed, he tells his wife early on in the first episode that not only is he apolitical himself but his father was a Socialist. 'I'm no fire-eater,' he rather mildly explains when she suggests he work for the Nazis. 'I hate guns, I hate parades. I'm a baker's son who worked his way through law school.' However, through a *gradual* combination of careerism, greed and self-preservation he eventually plays a major role in the relentless and brutal extermination of millions of his own countrymen and women. Perhaps it might have been more realistic to portray Dorf as a fanatical racist and Jew-hater from the start, but an audience's intense and initial identification with him (as with Asner's character in *Roots*) is crucial if the viewer is to see how the atrocities of the Holocaust were not carried out by monsters, but by ordinary (and often mild-mannered) people like themselves. Obviously the makers of the miniseries may well have had other motives for not wanting to alienate American audiences, but the result is nonetheless the same. In attempting to dramatise the personal dimensions of the history, the audience is slowly and carefully forced to make sense of it, not as rhetoric but as discursive practice, not as knowledge but as 'private' and '*emotional*' experience.

As with *Roots*, it is also interesting to compare *Holocaust* with films that depict similar historical events. Interestingly, Steven Spielberg's cinematic representation of history appears to offer another revealing comparison. In contrast to the earlier miniseries, Spielberg's depiction of the Holocaust in the movie *Schindler's List* (1993) was almost universally acclaimed as dramatically authentic and a 'masterpiece' of the cinema (for example, see Rich, 1994: 9). Perhaps the film's auteurist credentials and black-and-white cinematography more easily satisfied critics who might have felt that colour television was not an appropriate medium for the portrayal of genocide.[15] Yet, despite their differences, it is useful to note the many similarities between the TV miniseries and Spielberg's Hollywood movie. Each takes and dramatises a central human narrative in order to suggest and reveal the *general* atrocities of Nazi Germany. In doing so, both hoped that the human dimensions of their stories could encapsulate the historical 'facts' of the Holocaust and repackage them for a mass audience (see Shandler, 1997: 158–9). Yet, the contrasting focus of each narrative reveals an important difference between the film and the television serial. Whereas the four-part miniseries fictionalises the lives of two families in the hope of representing various and different aspects of Holocaust history, *Schindler's List* (like *Amistad*) chose to centre the narrative around a single true story

Holocaust: breathing humanity into history

(in this case, that of Oskar Schindler [Liam Neeson] and the rescue of his Jewish factory employees).

It is this central difference between the two narratives that seems to have a profound effect on its audience's understanding and interpretation of history. Compared with the three hours' running time of Spielberg's movie, the TV serial's seven and a half hours of screen time provided its film-makers with a huge canvas upon which to dramatise almost every important aspect of the war. While quantity doesn't necessarily denote quality, the miniseries was never bound by the relatively limited restrictions of Hollywood, so was able to widen the storyline to encompass many different and multifarious historical events. In contrast, Spielberg's decision to centre his film around the exceptional figure of Schindler arguably limits its telling of history, hoping that the single storyline is emblematic of the much wider historical conditions in which it originally took place. Such a decision may be seen as unavoidable or even more respectful to the dead and to the survivors of the Holocaust, but it has also been criticised for offering a far too selective and biased reading of history. According to Jacob Epstein, Schindler's story is simply nothing more than an 'exotic exception' which dangerously misleads its audience by overemphasising its significance (1994: 65).[16]

Similarly, Sara R. Horowitz argues that Schindler's overwhelming and benevolent presence meant that 'the film consistently draws our attention *away* from the ongoing atrocity and genocide . . .' (my emphasis, Horowitz, 1997: 135).[17] In contrast, *Holocaust* was actually attacked for being *over* ambitious in its attempt to tell the whole story of World War II, frequently at the expense of its internal realism. As Ilan Avisar points out, 'almost everything important in the history of the Third Reich and the persecution of the Jews from 1933 to 1945 happens to the members of two families' (1988: 129). Yet, in terms of simply bringing historical 'facts' before a mass audience, *Holocaust* (like *Roots* before it) has the edge on its Hollywood rivals that can never adequately compete with its sheer length of screen time, narrative scope and the possibility of complex, multiple, historical storylines.

Seen in this light, it is perhaps possible to understand the central *raison d'être* of *Holocaust* along similar lines to that of *Roots* – as a process of historical *adaptation*. As such, both serials should be judged not purely on their 'fidelity' to an original 'source', but their ability to translate 'the essence' of complex and difficult histories for a (primarily) American mass audience. If television drama has a role in such matters at all, both serials are testament to the unsurpassed ability of television drama (particularly the historical miniseries) to create an 'emotional' sense of reality that goes far beyond the historical limitations of a 'classical' or 'empiricist' rendering of the real. As such, their purpose lies not in *recreating* the past, but in *reassembling* it in such a way that it begins to take on a shape and a structure as almost recognisable as our own. Perhaps only then, can we ever truly begin to appreciate the humanity of the past, i.e. the fact that history happens to people no fundamentally different to ourselves. Against all the odds, *Holocaust* seemed to achieve this, and for that, if nothing else, it should be praised.

Heimat (WDR/SFB, 1984)[18]

> Authors all over the world are trying to take possession of their history . . . but they often find that it is torn out of their hands. The most serious act of expropriation occurs when people are deprived of their history. With *Holocaust*, the Americans have taken away our history.
>
> Edgar Reitz, 'Let's Work on Our Memories' (1979) (cited in Elsaesser, 1996: 176)

After *Holocaust*, there seems to have been a resurgence of films dealing with World War II. In particular, German films like *Our Hitler* (Syberberg, 1977), *The Marriage of Maria Braun* (Fassbinder, 1978) and *The Tin Drum* (Schlondorff, 1979) all seemed to re-investigate Nazi Germany in quick succession after the miniseries was first broadcast.[19] It seemed that the controversy sparked by *Holocaust* had somehow found its answer in a number of other texts that specifically dealt with German history. Or perhaps it just so happened that the German nation was finally able to examine itself some forty odd years after the atrocities of the war. Whatever the reasons, it seemed that the representation of the past (and the problems involved in representing history) seemed to be a recurring theme in German literature and film during the 1980s.

Appropriately enough, one of these representations came in the form of a television drama. *Heimat*, directed and conceived by German film-maker Edgar Reitz, was subtitled 'A Chronicle in Eleven Parts', spanning sixty-three years of German history from 1919 to 1982, watched in West Germany alone by twenty-five million viewers (see Kaes, 1989: 163). According to Reitz, *Holocaust* was an *Americanised* version of the war, or as he put it, 'German History – Made in Hollywood' (ibid; 184). In contrast, the large rock that stands at the beginning of each episode of *Heimat* is inscribed with the unambiguous words, 'Made in Germany'. Reitz even wrote a 'manifesto' on the subject entitled, 'Let's Work on Our Memories', published a year after the American miniseries was originally screened in Germany (see Elsaesser, 1996: 176).

Five years in the making, both Reitz and (and his writing partner, Peter Steinbach) spent more than a year researching oral history and writing the script on location (including many of the villagers they met as extras in the film). Set in a small fictional rural community called Schabbach (located somewhere in the Hunsrück region of Germany where Reitz himself grew up), the serial spends a great deal of time portraying personal and private existence. The central figure of the narrative is Maria (Marita Breuer) born in 1900 whose life story (until her death in the 1980s) acts as the linchpin around which all the other stories from four generations of three large families revolve. Above all, then, *Heimat* is an historical 'soap opera', charting a century of German history primarily through the eyes of one small community. Despite its obviously political and historical context, a great deal of the drama simply revolves around ordinary rural people as they go about their day-to-day lives, the camera often lingering lovingly and leisurely over frequently trivial and daily routines.

Part of this obsession with everyday life is suggested by its title. *Heimat* is a German word that remained for an English-speaking audience because it was generally believed to be untranslatable. In its crudest form Heimat simply means 'home' or homeland', but the word also has other important artistic and cultural connotations. In fact, Heimat was originally a literary genre with its origins in the 1890s, a style of storytelling that tended to hark back to a pre-industrial, romantic conception of rural Germany, depicting its people as existing in perfect harmony with nature. However, by the 1920s the National Socialists had begun claiming the genre for themselves, imbuing it with racist and anti-Semitic connotations that embedded it in notions of race and nationality. Although after World War II its Nazi associations were exorcised, hugely popular Heimat films still offered German audiences a nostalgic retreat into a sentimental depiction of a rural idyll, perhaps reflecting the country's own longing to return to some mythical homeland that was now seemingly lost forever. As such, the word Heimat produces a host of complex and ambiguous connotations among the German people, a word that has been claimed and re-claimed by numerous ideologies but still manages to retain some of its simple and honest longing for home and identity. As Anton Kaes puts it, 'Like no other the word, Heimat encompasses at once kitsch sentiment, false consciousness, and genuine emotional needs' (ibid: 166).

It is in this context that this eleven-part television serial is best understood; as both a reaction against the Americanisation of German history and as an attempt to re-claim the Heimat tradition from its Nazi contamination. Like Heimat films and literature before it, the story primarily centres on a nostalgic depiction of German village life, a seemingly innocent world far away from the corrupt metropolis. This is perhaps one of the reasons for its obsession with the private and domestic as opposed to the social and political world. In fact, many of the political and social concerns of World War II are discernible only at the very margins of *Heimat*, and this (perhaps most controversially) includes the Holocaust. Although at one point we follow a village boy on his bicycle as he accidentally and briefly comes across a concentration camp, the Holocaust itself is never portrayed and neither is it discussed openly in any detail throughout the entire serial. In fact, the gradual rise of the Nazi regime comes about so slowly and gradually that it seems almost barely noticeable at times, so caught up is the story in the personal and emotional dynamics of its characters' lives.

This pushing of social and political history to one side is particularly true of the episodes that deal directly with the war years (seen almost entirely through the eyes of rural Germany). Episode seven, for example, 'Soldiers' Love', is set during 1945 but provides little information about the war or the wider consequences of Nazi rule. Instead, it revolves around the 'illicit' love affair between two characters, Otto (Jörg Hube) and Maria. At just under one hour long, twelve minutes are devoted simply to the couple as they sit talking about their feelings for each other in Maria's bedroom. This could be a love story set in almost any historical period, were it not for the noise of the distant bombers flying overhead. For a moment, Otto's awareness and discussion of the aircraft threatens to disturb this purely personal narrative, but Maria quickly transforms the noise into a domestic context, i.e. a means of getting to sleep. In this way, she takes the wider social setting of the war and intuitively brings it back into the personal and domestic space of the home (taken from its English subtitles):

OTTO: When you think what a weight of iron is flying through the air up there. That's nothing to do with nature any more. Iron, steel, explosives and phosphorus.

MARIA: I've got used to it. That droning in the dark every night. It really makes me drowsy. When I listen to it. First it gets louder and louder. Then for a while it's constant. Then it gets quieter and quieter and my eyelids just close.

OTTO: (*watching her*) You've such lovely, firm shoulders, Maria.

MARIA: (turning from *the window*) Come to bed, Otto, you'll catch cold.

This attention to the personal details of German history (arguably at the expense of wider social affairs) inevitably provoked a great deal of debate and passionate criticism when it was first shown in Germany and abroad. The most consistent and damaging argument was that in only showing the history of the German people (concentrating on *private* rather than *political* history), *Heimat* simply provided its national television audience with a blatant act of historical revisionism. So obsessed with showing us history from a personal point of view the story seems to forget any other, prioritising a very particular and one-sided historical account. Such a project, critics argued, inevitably offered a dangerously biased view of historical events. Jim Hoberman, film critic for the *Village Voice* argued that the atrocities of German history could never be portrayed simply through ordinary and everyday events. He concluded that, 'With *Heimat* Germany is reborn' (cited by Kaes, 1989: 184). As Timothy Garton Ash puts it (ibid.):

> When you show the 1930s as a golden age of prosperity and excitement in the German countryside, when you are shown the Germans as victims of the war, then you inevitably find yourself asking: But what about the other side? What about Auschwitz? Where is the director's moral judgement?'

This sort of criticism seems difficult to defend and *Heimat* does give a very particular reading of real historical events. However, this is arguably the whole point of the project. Unlike *Holocaust*, the eleven-part serial was never an attempt to somehow acknowledge every aspect of World War II. Instead, it set out to offer a very personal

Heimat: a German history of the everyday

view of life from a very private perspective. As Anton Kaes (1989) points out, such a portrayal of the past was a deliberate attempt to get away from the 'official' and supposedly 'objective' accounts of German history. In contrast, *Heimat* attempts to tell German history 'from below', from the 'subjective' perspective of 'ordinary people'. Historians have called this approach *Alltagsgeschichte* ('the history of the everyday'), which tends to place wider political and social concerns 'in the background' in order to show history from a 'grass roots' level – the level at which most people actually experience it (see ibid: 188).[20]

Central to this argument (and its portrayal of Germany's past) is Reitz's unusual use of photography. While the majority of *Heimat* is shot in black and white (adding a sense of documentary authenticity), brief colour sequences (sometimes only lasting a few seconds) continually threaten to disturb the serial's underlining sense of realism. Unpredictable in their arrival, these colour sequences (a technique no doubt 'borrowed' by Spielberg's *Schindler's List*) seem to self-reflexively foreground the fact that these are not *real* events taking place, that they are being 'filtered' by something or someone that recalls some moments more intensely or *warmly* than others.

In the first episode, for example, Paul Simon (Michael Lesch) returns home from World War I to find his father, the village blacksmith, hard at work. When Paul (in black and white) looks through the window of the workshop, the scene of his father pounding red-hot metal at the anvil is shot entirely in colour. As the camera's point of view briefly alternates between Paul watching from outside (in black and white) and his father working (in colour), so the emotional significance of the scene to the returning soldier is underlined. In this way, the unexpected and momentary use of colour alerts the audience to the fact that this view of the past is not entirely objective, that the warm glow of his father's workshop somehow symbolises something safe and familiar to the homesick Paul.

As *Heimat* develops, so the personal nature of the history it deals with is further highlighted. For instance, the character Glasisch-Karl (Kurt Wagner) introduces every episode (apart from the first) to the audience, taking on the role of an unofficial narrator. Sitting at a table covered with old sepia photographs, this eccentric outsider briefly talks about particular characters, stories or events as he leafs through the faded images before him. While these recurring sequences crucially remind us of past storylines, the sheer act of him looking at old photographs perhaps also emphasises the artificiality of the photographic/filmic image, a representation that only signifies something now past and ultimately unobtainable. As Kaes points out, with each new episode more and more photographs fill his desk, perhaps aptly dramatising the problem we all have of ordering, selecting and representing the past (see 1989: 179).

This apparently 'subjective' view of the past reveals *Heimat*'s complex and deliberately ambiguous relationship with history. The fact that the rise of Nazism goes by almost unnoticed (so caught up are we, its viewers, like its characters, with the 'soap-like' attention to everyday existence) reveals exactly how dangerous and insidious such a regime may be. Not attempting to offer an unrealistically 'objective' or 'omniscient' version of Germany history, *Heimat* self-consciously attempts to portray how Fascism could slowly and almost 'unconsciously' creep into the very fabric of everyday German life. As such, the Holocaust is pushed to the margins of the narrative because this implicitly subjective version of the past reveals the way the German people themselves may have learnt to accept and deny the horrors taking place around them and in their name. In doing so, it gives a self-consciously contrasting view of history, particularly from versions of World War II that tend to depict German characters as intrinsically and unquestionably evil.

As this suggests, *Heimat*'s purpose is not to give *the* history of modern Germany, but to give *a* history, a history from the point of view of those who may have lived it. In this way, the serial seems intuitively in touch with contemporary historicism, particularly the notion that history is simply another discourse, and that it should never, in any circumstances, be confused with 'the past'. As Keith Jenkins puts it in *Re-Thinking History* (1991: 5):

> The past and history are not stitched into each other such that only one historical reading of the past is necessary. The past and history float free of each other, they are ages and miles apart. For the same object of enquiry can be read differently by different discursive practices (a landscape can be read/interpreted differently by geographers, sociologists, historians, artists, economists, etc.) whilst, internal to each, there are different interpretative readings over time and space; as far as history is concerned historiography shows this.

What a serial like *Heimat* achieves, then, is the ability to offer a mass audience a 'different' reading of the past, one which, it is hoped, may help to 'balance' the many histories, narratives and documentaries which have gone before and will inevitably follow. Like the German miniseries *Das Boot* (Bavaria Atelier, 1984), set on board a German submarine, it breathes life and depth back into a people whose very humanity had generally been denied by the cinema, television and literature of the past. While it may seem unforgivable that any account of World War II should marginalise the Holocaust, *Heimat* does so in order to construct a different sense of perspective to other filmic or televisual accounts of the war. These are not the Nazi monsters portrayed by countless British and American films, but normal even likeable individuals who, while their country carried out the systematic killing of millions of innocent people, carried on living relatively normal lives.

Critics like Thomas Elsaesser are not entirely won over by this argument, suggesting that *Heimat*'s 'normalisation' and 'routinisation' of Fascism mean that it is still fundamentally 'apologetic in tendency if not in intent' (1996: 160). However, it must be seen as offering a particular historical perspective, one which attempts to place the viewer in a deliberate act of identification with its characters, not in order to absolve responsibility for their actions but simply in order to understand them better. In Bakhtinian terms, a 'monologic' history is transformed into a 'dialogic' event, one that reveals history (much like language itself) as 'a shared social experience' (see Holquist, 1990: 49). As a result, history is transformed into *memory* that, by implication, reveals the complexity and not the simplicity of historical 'truth'. As Reitz himself puts it (cited in McQuire, 1998: 159):

Even now forty years after the war we are still troubled by the weight of moral judgements, we are still afraid that our little personal stories could recall our Nazi past and remind us of our mass participation in the Third Reich. That is the problem. We have so many stories that make up our past that can't be told, can't be true, that are stifling us, perhaps because they are so normal and for that reason so blind to history.

Seen in this light, the Holocaust is pushed to the margins of *Heimat* because the German people it portrays needed to keep it there. When the boy on the bicycle returns to the village he tells no one about what he has seen. The serial does not suggest that the German people were completely ignorant of the facts (whispers and rumours are apparent), but that they chose simply to push it to one side. *Heimat* portrays this national repression and, in doing so, offers one of the most revealing insights into how such atrocities can ever occur amid a people and a culture no more inherently 'evil' or 'vicious' than any other. In doing so, it flies in the face of more recent historical accounts of the war like Daniel Goldhagen's *Hitler's Willing Executioners: Ordinary Germans and the Holocaust*, which argues that the German people were, in fact, more culturally attuned and susceptible to the brutal extermination of their fellow human beings than all other European nationalities (1996: 408). In contrast, by showing the gradual and day-to-day rise of Fascism, *Heimat* implicitly asks us to *identify* with the German people and thereby forces us to ask ourselves the most difficult question of all – would we have acted any differently under similar circumstances?

Steven Spielberg's excursion into the historical miniseries with *Band of Brothers* (HBO, 2000), suggests a film-maker who is now seeking a broader canvas on which to tackle the complexities of the historical narrative – perhaps a reaction against what some critics argued were the narrative 'simplicities' of *Saving Private Ryan* (1998). What perhaps Spielberg has learnt to appreciate and critics like Wilsher fail to recognise is, that the very length and even the 'soapiness' of the serial's form (characters, as Wilsher puts it, 'falling in and out of love, committing adultery, having babies' and so on – see Introduction) makes it an ideal vehicle through which politics and history can be understood; not as mere 'fact' or 'polemic', but as *'memory'* and *'experience'*. Although both *Roots* and *Holocaust* are sometimes confusingly referred to as 'docudramas' (presumably to give their historical aspirations a little more significance and weight), they are clearly more 'drama' than 'docu'; attempts to dramatise history rather than document it. In particular, the twin characteristics of 'intimacy' and 'continuity' which the historical miniseries shares with soap opera, mean that it can *transform* history so that it gradually becomes identifiable, empathetic and discursive to a mass audience.

As such, the depictions of history offered by television miniseries like *Roots*, *Holocaust* and *Heimat*, attempt to 'adapt' the past not as a piece of traditional naturalism but as a form of subjective *'memory'* or *'emotional realism'*; a narrative that (sometimes self-consciously) engages with real historical events on a number of different realities other than simply the empirical. In this sense, all three dramas can be seen as dramatic 'adaptations', a form of *Alltagsgeschichte* that does not attempt to faithfully 'replicate' a 'reliable' historical record or source, but instead attempts to investigate, dramatise and even 'deconstruct' the historical landscape from a number of different (both 'macro' and 'micro') perspectives. As sensationalised, melodramatic and subjective as these dramas frequently are, the complex, multiple-narrative nature of the historical miniseries can be seen to actively inform a mass audience about difficult and sometimes complex aspects of history within a private narrative space. In contrast to Baudrillard's notion of the television set as 'lifeless' and 'cold', they have perhaps dramatically illustrated the powerful ability of the small screen's multiple/serial narrative to breathe 'emotional' and 'personal' life back into grand epic histories and broad historical landscapes which are so often clouded and frozen by the production and discourse of historiography itself. If, in doing so, history is dramatised, translated and adapted, then so be it. Perhaps the very notion that the past is filled with a countless number of personal perspectives is one of the most important insights that the historical miniseries can and should continue to convey.

NOTES

1. Parts of this chapter originally appeared in Creeber (2001a).
2. *Rich Man, Poor Man* was television's first hit miniseries that averaged a forty-five per cent share of the American television audience. It earned twenty-three Emmy® nominations and won three Emmy® awards, making ABC the number one network for the season.
3. In fact, *Holocaust* arguably owes a noticeable debt to Coppola's original movie, immediately suggested in the first few minutes of the drama with its lavish score seemingly inspired by the film's famous theme and its opening sequence which (like *The Godfather*) begins with a long opulent and deceptively joyful wedding sequence.
4. To my knowledge there are few, if any, books entirely devoted to the historical miniseries. The nearest we get are books that look at the representation of the Jewish Holocaust on film and television (see, for example, Kaes, 1989 and Doneson, 2002).
5. While Chomsky directed the majority of the first series, episodes three and four were shared by David Greene, John Erman and Gilbert Moses.
6. Awards won by *Roots* include: nine Emmys®: Best Limited Series, Lead Actor/Single Performance (Louis Gosset Jr), Supporting Actor/Single Performance (Edward Asner), Supporting Actress/Single Performance (Olivia Cole), Drama Series Writing, Drama Series Directing, Drama Series Film Editing, Series Film Sound and Achievement Music Composition. George Foster Peabody Award (1997) 'for dramatically exposing us to an aspect of our history that many of us never knew about but all of us will never forget'. Television Critics Circle Award (1997): Programme of the Year, Achievement in Drama, Achievements in Acting: Leading Male (Ben Vereen) Supporting Male (Edward Asner), Supporting Female (Leslie Uggams). Golden Globe® Award (1977): Best Drama Series.
7. African words are occasionally used but only to disguise 'delicate' references to parts of the body such as the penis.
8. Asner was head of the Screen Actors Guild and among other causes clashed with Ronald Reagan over US intervention in Central America.
9. The concluding night of the miniseries was deliberately meant to coincide with the thirty-fifth anniversary of the beginning of the Warsaw ghetto uprising.
10. See Doneson (2002): 189 and Shandler (1997): 154.

11. This article appeared in *New German Critique* that devoted an entire edition to the TV serial (19, Winter, 1980). 'Jewish self-consciousness in the post-Holocaust epoch' was the theme of the following edition (Rabinbach and Zipes, 1980: 3).

12. Also cited in Anton Kaes (1989): 3–31.

13. Paddy Chayefsky was the screenwriter of the highly influential single television play, *Marty* (1953). Starring a young Rod Steiger, it championed what Chayefsky famously termed 'the marvellous world of the ordinary'.

14. Instead of adhering to a dramatic narrative, *Shoah* takes the form of a documentary that consists only of interviews with actual witnesses.

15. Interestingly, Universal was reported to be interested in having a colour version of *Schindler's List* so that the film could eventually be sold to television (see Shandler, 1997: 156).

16. Also cited by Shandler (1997): 160.

17. Similarly, according to Horowitz, the 'demonisation' of the Nazi Goth, 'frees viewers from questioning their own possible collusion with racism or prejudice' (ibid: 137).

18. Part of this section first appeared in a different form in Creeber (2004a).

19. See Elsaesser (1996: 159), for a fuller discussion of this point.

20. Several successful television series (including Eberhardt Fechner's *Tadelloser und Wolf* [1974/1975]) and several documentaries were based on this tradition.

2 ALTERED STATES
'Alternative' Serial Drama

INTRODUCTION

> TV's audience was potentially more mature than the teen-skewing audience of most movies;
> the ongoing series offered narrative possibilities not available in a two-hour film; both the
> networks and cable outlets were demonstrating an occasional willingness to let television
> makers experiment.
>
> Robert J. Thompson (1996: 150)

As explored in the introduction of this book, many critics have tended to conceive contemporary television drama as generally less innovative, challenging and experimental than it once was. In particular, there has been an assumption that small-screen fiction now lacks the social or political 'seriousness' that it once enjoyed during the 1960s and 1970s. For John Caughie, British television drama from *Armchair Theatre* (ITV, 1956–74) and *The Wednesday Play* (BBC, 1964–70) era (particularly single plays such as *Up the Junction* [BBC, 1965], *Cathy Come Home* [BBC, 1966] and *The Parachute* [BBC, 1968] etc.) provided 'progressive' and socially critical interventions (or, as he terms, 'monuments') in postwar British culture. However, aided by technological developments such as multichannel television (that has broken up the British three-channel system, helping to disperse national viewing habits) and the video recorder (that has helped to eradicate television's sense of *immediacy*), newer television drama has tended to lack the political or critical potential of its predecessor. For Caughie (2000: 202):

> television drama for a time marked out a space where creativity was still rooted in the local
> and the particular, difference was still material, and viewing still mattered. In the 1990s, it
> seems increasingly difficult to separate out 'serious drama' from quality television and the art
> film, and the plays which gave, in a very specific way, the awkward shapes of immediacy to
> television, or the hard critical edges of modernism, begin to seem like distant memories.

As this suggests, Caughie tends to conceive this decline in the political potential of contemporary television drama as reflecting a deeper cultural transition from 'modernism' to 'postmodernism'. To put it crudely, the 'hard critical edges of modernism' that once typified early British television drama have been increasingly replaced by a postmodern 'playfulness' and 'relativism' that appears to lack the national focus and political 'seriousness' of those earlier dramas. Instead of acting as 'ephemeral' (although clearly politicised and topical) events that reflect a 'common culture' (perhaps most famously symbolised by *Cathy Come Home*), television drama has now been reduced to global universals, acting simply as 'commodities in the international market in images' (ibid: 18). Borrowing from Jameson's famous critique of postmodernism, Caughie argues that, 'the levelling out of difficult unities, the absorption of hard works into a generalised culture fuelled by consumption, leaves little purchase for a conception of art which both aspires to commonality and makes a material difference' (ibid: 90).

Although Robin Nelson agrees that there has been a shift in television drama towards 'postmodernism', he seems slightly less pessimistic about its lack of political or critical potential. Employing the term *'critical postmodernism'*, Nelson argues that postmodern television drama can reflect more than simply an obsession with market forces and an increased level of 'art' as 'commodity'. As a result, the apparently 'postmodern' characteristics of *Twin Peaks* become more than simply 'the mere pastiche of past styles thrown together with no other thought than to maximise [its] audience' (1997: 239). Instead, they become a critical investigation into identity, an 'interrogative text' that offers 'radical disjunction of different channels of discourse ...' (ibid: 238). Similarly, the postmodern interpretation of historical subjectivity implicit in *Our Friends in the North* still manages (in its obsession with British life and politics) to refuse 'the transnational market' (ibid: 240) while retaining the presence and possibility of 'critical realism'.

Indeed, I would go further than Nelson, suggesting that much of contemporary television drama that is interpreted and perceived as 'postmodern' (whether 'critical' or not) actually still displays many of the major elements and fundamental characteristics of modernism. For example, I would argue that *Our Friends in the North* was typically (if not *classically*) modernist, not only in its projected importance as a piece of 'agitational' television drama (see Macmurraugh-Kavanagh, 1997: 367–81) but also in its representation of national politics as integral to both personal and public life. This 'state-of-the-nation' drama clearly held all the primary characteristics of *The Wednesday Play*, a piece of 'event television' that seemed deliberately intended to reflect and respond to a localised, generational and politicised audience. As Jeremy Ridgman points out, it clearly 'shares the perspective and techniques of the 1970s' TV dramas of social comment and socialist commitment' (2000: 75), while also continuing discussion (like Trevor Griffith's *Bill Brand* [ITV, 1976] before it) into personal and gendered politics (ibid: 84–5). Seen in this light, *Our Friends in the North* seems to ironically represent the epitome of Caughie's notion of a television 'monument', a contemporary small-screen drama that still managed to retain ' a space where creativity' is 'rooted in the local and the particular' (2000: 202).

As this suggests, what determines a piece of 'postmodern' television drama is not always as clear as some critics might like to make out. For instance, although critics like Ib Bondebjerg have celebrated the postmodern aspects of *The Singing Detective* (1992: 161–80), Caughie himself declares that it is clearly 'a key work of British modernism' (2000: 177). Perhaps part of the confusion here lies in the serial's apparent attempt to reclaim authentic and personal meaning in a seemingly 'postmodern' world of spectacular semiotic excess and 'floating signifiers' (Bondebjerg, 1992: 167). However, while its surface narrative confusion (particularly its dramatic re-formation and re-interpretation of popular cultural forms like pulp fiction and popular music) appears to signify a depthless world of pastiche and frantic hybridity, the central protagonist's continual search for truth and identity within that world itself suggests a modernist sensibility at the heart of the drama that finally explains all semiotic excess within a seemingly subjective narrative structure. In other words, although Potter's protagonist appears to be at the mercy of a semiotic postmodern confusion, his continual search for a real and final solution to his fragmented identity is, in itself, implicitly modernist.

As *The Singing Detective* reveals then, it would be strange if contemporary television drama did not take on and reflect some aspects of the wider culture around it. However, this does not necessarily mean that it is always completely complicit in its reproduction – nor that we can always be sure of its interpretation. Nor does it mean that postmodernism itself cannot be inherently critical or subversive. In fact, a so-called 'postmodern' text may actually be able to go much further in its social critique than the hierarchical and intellectual limits of modernism could have possibly imagined. To simply reduce postmodernism to 'critical' or 'non-critical' theoretical terms therefore fails to really understand and appreciate its implicit deconstruction of cultural assumptions about art and commerce as a whole. As Jane Feuer puts it: (1995: 10):

> An overall distinction between good (deconstructive) postmodernism and bad (neoconservative) postmodernism is difficult to make at the level of textual analysis, especially when it is assumed that the avant-garde is always good and the mass media always bad. In this sense, TV is like architecture; we inhabit its postmodernism in our daily lives without necessarily responding to it as an art movement ... but whether that impact is complicitous with or critical of a dominant ... ideology no amount of textual analysis can determine. Indeed we may want to conclude that postmodern TV – like several other postmodernisms – deconstructs the very oppositions between commodity and art, complicity and critique.

To assume, then, that all television drama after the late 1980s is 'postmodern' is akin to suggesting, like Jim Collins, that television 'never had a modernist phase' (1992: 331) at all. While such a statement seems slightly ludicrous in the light of Caughie's detailed and skilful account of modernism in British television drama, it does reflect an increasing tendency to suggest that postmodernism is now the only cultural frame by which popular art can be conceived and understood. In fact, many critics would argue that we are at a complex moment of historical transformation and need a number of interpretative strategies and debates to understand and make sense of the world we live in. As Collins himself accepts (1992: 328):

> Although easy moralizing about postmodernism may often reveal little besides the presuppositions of the critical languages used to demonize or valorize it, the contested nature of the term – the fact that no definition of contours can ever be ideologically neutral, that description is inseparable from evaluation – reveals one of the most significant lessons of postmodern theory: all of our assumptions concerning what constitutes 'culture' and 'critical analysis' are now subject to intense debate.

What I aim to do in the following chapter is not to simply argue that particular examples of television drama are rigidly 'modernist' or 'postmodernist', but how frequently aspects of both cultural terms can be used as a means of understanding and interrogating the contemporary (and some might argue, transitional) televisual landscape. In doing so, I aim to stress how television drama can still retain a form of social critique within a seemingly 'postmodern' environment that many may assume is completely and unreservedly market-orientated. Audiences are becoming increasingly dispersed, markets are becoming increasingly globalised and market forces are becoming increasingly ubiquitous, but I hope to illustrate how there is still a space – in, what we may loosely term, 'art television' – that continues to produce politicised, localised and experimental drama that has within it a critical and inherently subversive edge. Although, by definition, 'art television' will never be in the mainstream of television practice, it does reveal the possibility of contemporary television drama to continually produce 'alternative realities' to those generally offered by more conventional narrative structures.

I hope to refute the more pessimistic claim that the majority of contemporary television drama is now politically and aesthetically conservative, illustrating how certain examples of television drama can and will continue to subvert and interrogate traditional narrative forms and ideological expectations. While the mode, production and even reception of television drama may change and evolve in a 'postmodern' environment, its potential to produce 'experimental' ways of seeing will not necessarily be eradicated, although the form, structure and style of experimentation itself may inevitably change. However, for the time being at least, it seems that the radical potential of modernist television drama laid out by the likes of Caughie and Nelson still remains an important and crucial element of its enduring success. As the examples below reveal, it may actually be a little premature to mourn the complete passing of all 'art' and 'experimental' television drama – that, while in the minority, they are still very much part of the fabric, structure and content of international television drama as a whole.

Twin Peaks (ABC, 1990–1)

> I do not mean to suggest that I have found *the* meaning of *Un Chien andalou* – or even that the film has *any* meaning. Indeed, the film's playful, tantalizing, but ultimately frustrating lack of meaning may be the very basis of its surreality.
>
> Stuart Liebman (1987: 154)

Originally the brainchild of both film director David Lynch (*The Elephant Man* [1980], *Dune* [1984] and *Blue Velvet* [1986]) and television screenwriter Mark Frost (*The Six Million Dollar Man* [ABC, 1973–8] and *Hill Street Blues*), *Twin Peaks* is now regarded as *the* consummate televisual example of postmodernism. Even the drama's very process of distribution and consumption has led critics like Jim Collins to suggest that the unique televisual event that it became (which, he argues, was promoted by the technological revolution of cable and VCR) was itself 'postmodern', unsettling any stable (or modernist) notion of television viewing (1992: 341). However, more commonly critics have connected postmodernism with the serial's tendency to disrupt any stable notion of the 'real', replacing it with a complex array of dreamlike fantasies and bizarre hallucinations. This is reflected in a hybridity of form that seemed to incorporate many different visual styles and narrative traditions, apparently taking great delight in unsettling its audience's own generic desires and expectations. According to Kathryn Kalinak, *Twin Peaks* comes from a tradition (she also cites MTV [1981–], *Miami Vice* [NBC, 1984–9], *Moonlighting* [NBC, 1985–9] and *Cop Rock* [ABC, 1990]) that deliberately distorted familiar conventions in order to 'undercut expectation, leaving viewers to face a brave new world of postmodern television without conventional channels of response' (1995: 82).

An important part of this narrative disruption has been reported to occur in the generic hybridity of the drama as a whole. While there is the famous central detective storyline revolving around the FBI investigation into Laura Palmer's (Sheryl Lee) murder, the series also displays and employs elements from a number of varied and frequently conflicting generic styles. In particular, critics have highlighted its use of the soap opera (its multilevel narrative structure and complex array of characters), the sitcom (such as the comic and bizarre antics of characters like Lucy [Kimmy Robertson] and Andy [Harry Goaz]), the horror movie (for example, the arrival of evil spirit 'BOB' [Frank Silva]), the fifties' juvenile delinquent film (especially the action in the 'Double RR Diner'), the television commercial (Special Agent Cooper's [Kyle MacLachlan] endless commentary about service), the Western (the character of Sheriff Harry S. Truman [Michael Ontkean] and the scenes at 'One Eyed Jacks') and even traces of film noir (Audrey Horne's [Sherilyn Fenn] comic pastiche of a classic *femme fatale*). In this way, the drama appears to transgress normal generic boundaries, using a complex array of parody, intertextuality and pastiche to create a heady mixture of narrative levels and generic juxtaposition (see, for example, Reeves *et al.*, 1995: 178–81).

For an example of this generic eclecticism we need look no further than the first few minutes of the pilot episode. The style of the opening montage is reminiscent of a horror movie like Stanley Kubrick's *The Shining* (1980), a story that similarly used its isolated location for emotional and dramatic effect. Indeed, the eerie solitude of the town of Twin Peaks is heightened by the overpowering presence of 'Laura's Theme' (composed by Angelo Badalamenti), an atmospheric and slightly melancholic soundtrack to the visual style that further emphasises the drama's ominously 'dreamlike' mood. Seen in this context, the tragic discovery of Laura's dead body (washed up on the shore and 'wrapped in plastic') in the first few minutes is not entirely unexpected and is evidently meant to both move and disturb its audience. Pete Martell's (Jack Nance) visible shock helps to create a deep sense of emotional involvement between character and viewer that is generically consistent with the visual and audio *mise en scène* of the narrative up to that point.

However, when Pete's tragic and distraught telephone call comes into Sheriff Truman's office, the horror style and tragic sensibility of the action suddenly and abruptly changes. 'I'm going to transfer to the phone on the table by the red chair', says Lucy to Truman in her comically high-pitched voice. 'The red chair against the wall', she confusingly explains, 'er … the little table, with the lamp on it, the lamp that we moved from the corner. The *black* phone, not the *brown* phone.' This seemingly ridiculous and irrelevant piece of dialogue (darkly comic considering the tragic circumstances, appears to be completely out of touch with the emotional intensity of the storyline so far, shattering the genre expectations that the viewer may have already assimilated).

In this way, different stylistic categories (horror, melodrama, comedy and even perhaps slapstick) are brought together in the first few minutes of the serial in a manner that is both unusual and inherently unsettling. The drama appears to employ the traditional generic tropes of the horror movie (dreamy and evocative music, a melancholy, isolated location and an unidentified corpse), but then suddenly and unexpectedly undermines this genre construction with comic and frequently absurd narrative digressions. These digressions are particularly pronounced in the presence of characters such as Lucy, Andy, Cooper and the mysterious 'Log Lady' (Catherine Coulson), whose personalities and acting styles deliberately clash with the more 'serious' sensibility of characters such as Sheriff Truman, Pete Martell or Laura's mother, Sarah Palmer (Grace Zabriskie). Similarly, the soundtrack gradually becomes disjointed, the moving 'syrupy' intensity of 'Laura's Theme' increasingly juxtaposed with a 'salacious cocktail-lounge swing' (cited by Kalinak, 1995: 85) that seems to deliberately undermine the drama's emotional depth at important moments in its narrative development.

For many critics, such generic eclecticism produces a sort of 'ambivalent parody' that is clearly 'postmodern' (Collins, 1992: 346). However, it is important to recognise that these types of stylistic effects are not exclusively the preserve of contemporary culture. Indeed, they are reminiscent of techniques such as 'montage', 'collage' and 'juxtaposition', commonly associated with aspects of the modernist rather than postmodernist tradition. For example, T. S. Eliot's *The Waste Land* (1922) incorporated allusions borrowed from 'Baudelaire, mythology, Shakespeare, Eastern religion, paganism, music hall and a host of literary predecessors in order to express contemporary life in a polyphony of cultured soundbites ...' (Childs, 2000: 98). Similar techniques were also an important element of the avant-garde, particularly avant-garde cinema of the 1920s and 1930s where, according to the film critic Susan Hayward (1996: 21):

> Genres were mixed, intercalated and juxtaposed. Similarly, the popular was fused with the experimental (mainstream cinema with counter-cinema), socio-realism with the subjective (documentary with melodrama). Working within these popular genres allowed them to extend, distort, even subvert dominant discourses.

The surrealist's appreciation of popular culture (particularly the films of Charlie Chaplin, Mack Sennett and Buster Keaton) meant that of all the modernist movements it was particularly open to this breakdown of generic hierarchies.[1] Indeed, the contrast in *Twin Peaks* between the 'serious' (such as Sarah Palmer's overwhelming grief when she first learns of her daughter's death) and the comic or absurd (such as the Log Lady's mystic 'conversations' with her piece of dry timber) is reminiscent of a movement that delighted in mixing the 'high' with the 'low' or the 'deep' with the seemingly 'superficial'. For surrealism, this type of juxtaposition was a way of creating a world that no longer obeyed the rules of rational logic. Inspired by Freud's *The Interpretation of Dreams* (1900), surrealists seemed intent on celebrating the irrational, creating in their work an aspiration to express the landscape of both the waking (conscious) and sleeping (unconscious) states. Originally taking the title of the movement from a review by Apollinaire, André Breton argued that he wanted to achieve 'the resolution of these two states, dream and reality, which are seemingly so contradictory, into a kind of absolute reality, a *surreality*' (cited by Childs, 2000: 121).

Not surprisingly, then, the surrealists were particularly fond of film's ability to mix, dissolve and edit images together, forming unexpected sequences that deliberately shocked, surprised and perplexed audiences. As the BFI's *The Cinema Book* (Cook and Bernink, 1999: 115) puts it,

> The surrealists were interested in releasing the power of the unconscious through procedures which followed the logic of dreams. [Salvador] Dali and [Luis] Buñuel used bizarre imagery and incongruous juxtapositions to create their own dreams, almost as in surrealist automatic writing.

In other words, surrealism's interest and fascination with juxtaposition seem to have been important in the way that it brought together different levels of consciousness, breaking down conventional (purely conscious) ways of seeing and experiencing the world. Famously for Breton, there was nothing more 'beautiful' than 'the chance encounter of a sewing machine and an umbrella on a dissecting table' (cited by Kuenzli, 1987: 9).

Although surrealism has now become an all-encompassing term loosely applied to any piece of art that is remotely 'strange' or 'weird', there are explicit echoes of its artistic heritage in David Lynch's work as a whole. According to the film critic Geoff Andrew, 'Like the surrealists, Lynch's work exhibits an abiding fascination with the unconscious ... [and] the inexplicable ... For Lynch, creativity is a matter not of carefully reasoned and intellectual activity, but of allowing intuition and imagination free rein ...' (1998: 40). Lynch's film-making seems to reject traditional narrative structures and the usual limitations of linear storytelling, frequently allowing chance events to determine both dramatic content and visual style. According to David Hughes, 'Ever since a bug flew into one of Lynch's unfinished paintings and stuck to the still-wet paint, the "artistic accident" has been an important phenomenon for him' (2001: 131). Indeed, according to Lynch, the idea of making BOB Laura's murderer in *Twin Peaks* only came about during shooting. Apparently Frank Silva who played BOB was originally the set dresser on *Twin Peaks*, but simply caught Lynch's eye during filming.[2]

If Lynch's methods of work are 'surreal' then so are many of his famous directorial techniques. One can also detect the use of surreal juxtaposition at work within *Twin Peaks*, frequently becoming the subject of jokes or seemingly irrelevant events and conversations. In the first episode Pete Martell rushes in on Agent Cooper and Sheriff Truman shouting, 'Fellas, don't drink that coffee! You'll never guess. There was a *fish – in* the percolator' (cited by Hughes, 2001: 109). Such an image is strikingly surreal; playing on the juxtaposition of two disparate and random objects. Similarly, when Special

Agent Cooper and Sheriff Truman visit the local bank in the pilot episode they find the head of a large moose disconcertingly placed on the table in front of them. 'Oh, it fell down', is the only explanation that is offered to the two startled policemen. Like the severed ear found by Kyle MacLachlan (who, of course, went on to play Special Agent Cooper) in *Blue Velvet*, the image is also perhaps ironically reminiscent of the famous scene (involving two rotting donkeys pulled on pianos by a struggling cyclist) from Luis Buñuel's and Salvador Dali's 1928 surrealist film, *Un Chien andalou*. Although clearly not as brutal or striking an image as in the earlier film, it does nevertheless seem to alert the audience to the fact that Twin Peaks is a town (and perhaps even a 'mind-set') where 'surreal' juxtapositions are to be expected.[3] As Cooper tells Sheriff Truman, 'I have no idea where this will lead us, but I have a definite feeling it will be a place both wonderful and strange' (cited by Hughes, 2001: 109).

This type of 'surreal' juxtaposition is continued throughout the serial by the peculiar and frequently irrelevant observations of a numerous set of eccentric characters, not least Special Agent Cooper. His police investigation certainly reveals a detective who seems to have more in common with the psychological techniques of Sigmund Freud than with traditional and logical methods of detection. At one famous point in the series he tries to finally find out who killed Laura Palmer by systematically throwing rocks at a bottle while Lucy reads out a list of possible names. As Cooper tells his bewildered colleagues, this strange process of deduction came from a dream he once had about the plight of the Tibetan people. As he explains, he awoke realising that he had 'subconsciously gained knowledge of a deductive technique involving mind-body coordination, operating hand-in-hand with the deepest level of intuition'. Cooper's unusual investigation procedures might suggest how the drama itself should be read, i.e. as a 'dream' rather than as a piece of conscious 'decoding' (see Nochimson, 1995: 146–7).

Such unusual procedures reveal Cooper's profound belief in unconscious intuition, a doctrine shared by the surrealists in techniques such as 'free association' and 'automatic writing'. Although surrealist painting is better known, a significant tradition of surrealist poetry established itself in France, in the work of André Breton, Paul Éluard, Louis Aragon and Benjamin Péret. For these writers, automatic writing enabled the writer to bypass the conscious part of the mind, tapping straight into the unconscious world of dreams and hallucinations, often finding meaning and significance in what the conscious mind would tend to disregard as unimportant, ridiculous or banal. For Breton, automatic writing produced a 'considerable assortment of images of a quality such as we should never have been able to obtain in the normal way of writing, a very special sense of the picturesque, and, here and there, a few pieces of out and out buffoonery' (cited by Gascoyne, 1970: 46).

Such a description seems strangely appropriate for a drama like *Twin Peaks*, a piece of television that appears, at times, to be precariously positioned between the various extremes of beauty, bathos and playful banality. Cooper's habit of speaking into a Dictaphone to the anonymous 'Diane' (presumably an FBI secretary, but for all we know a figment of his imagination) certainly seems surprisingly akin to methods like free association or automatic writing. Not content with recording the details of the actual murder case, he goes into exceptional detail about the town's picturesque setting, the freshness of the mountain air, the quality of service at his hotel and inevitably the state of the coffee.[4] As such, he also appears to borrow from the surrealist movement a belief that nothing is irrelevant, not even the smallest, trivial and most *ridiculous* of details.[5] Despite the seriousness of the murder investigation, Cooper clearly seems concerned with the most trivial and banal details about the town of Twin Peaks. 'This must be where pies go when they die', he famously exclaims in episode three.

Nowhere is the surreal belief in the unconscious more explicit than in Cooper's dream of the 'Red Room', its billowing scarlet curtains suggesting a psychological 'chamber' where little is expected to make any *logical* sense. Here, the Red Room's cryptic dialogue and distorted speech is contrasted with its riddle-talking dwarf (named in the credits simply as the 'Man from Another Place' [Michael J. Anderson]). His red shirt, red suit and tawdry vaudeville routine (he performs a strange little dance to some bluesy/jazzy saxophone) is similarly contrasted with classical art (the Grecian white marble statue and the 'Escher-like geometric' flooring [Nochimson, 1995: 151]), providing striking visual juxtapositions. Indeed, the Red Room as a whole could be seen as an almost perfect caricature of a surrealist painting or film, an attempt to create a bizarre world where the boundaries between the conscious and unconscious are deliberately and provocatively dissolved.

Like *Blue Velvet*, the historical indeterminacy of *Twin Peaks* (it looks vaguely like the 1950s but appears to take place some time in the present) also seems to heighten the possibility that everything in the drama is taking place in 'dream-time'. Certainly, its overriding *mise en scène* suggests a strange sense of physical juxtaposition at work. Richard Hoover was the production designer on the whole series (except for the pilot), creating a look that played with the very notion of confusing physical juxtaposition (such as the 'natural' and the 'industrial' or 'inside' and 'outside'). As Martha Nochimson puts it, 'A massive use of wood gives an outside feeling to the interiors. The interiors burgeon with dead animals and their parts – horns, shells – and nature drawings that are often photographed as if they are theatrical backdrops for the action' (1995: 148–9). As suggested by the show's famous opening montage – a dreamy dissolve between the 'natural' (a bird and waterfalls) and the 'industrial' (the work of the logging factory) – this visual juxtaposition helps to create the sense that this is a town where traditional or logical boundaries are perhaps no longer as stable as they might be. According to Mark Frost, the effect creates a 'cultural compost heap' (cited in Nochimson, 1995), a vivid description of visual juxtaposition that appears to play with images of death, decay and civilisation.

But perhaps what makes *Twin Peaks* more 'surreal' than 'postmodern' is not so much the techniques it uses (which, as we have seen, are frequently interchangeable between the two cultural conditions) but what exactly these techniques appear to tell us about the world they both reflect and help to create. As 'postmodern' as this 'polysemic' world might seem, its constant generic 'bricolage' finally reveals more than simply a *depthless* postmodern commodification. Ironically, Cooper's detective work (however strange it appears) does gradually uncover a 'truth' of sorts, a world populated by unimaginable

Twin Peaks: intent on creating a 'cultural compost heap'

evil, horror and abuse. Laura's tragic murder (and her secret life as a drug addict and prostitute) eventually reveals a world split in two – a 'conscious' and 'unconscious' universe that (as in *Blue Velvet*) is reflected in the town's strange (*sur*)reality.

In generic terms, this binary split can be viewed most clearly in the juxtaposition that exists between the homely and clean-cut life of the town's '*conscious*' veneer (reflected perhaps in its use of soap opera, sitcom or even advertising techniques) and the dark and possibly '*unconscious*' influences of the town's dangerous underbelly (evoked through its employment of genres such as horror, the fantastic and the Gothic). As Diane Stevenson implies, a binary structure runs through the drama as a whole, reflecting a world diametrically divided and intrinsically split (1995: 75):

> Through its play with the genre of the fantastic and with the kindred genre of the mystery, *Twin Peaks* gives play to different ways of assessing family violence: in terms of normal and abnormal (which ... we inherit from medical discourse), in terms of innocence and guilt (the discourse of the detective and the law), in terms of good and evil (the discourse of religion and the horror story), of outrage and redemption, and in terms of the inner and the outer, the psychological and the social, the intrinsic and the constructed.

Laura's abuse then, by her father, brings about a sudden transformation, constructing a space where all 'generic' and 'cultural' categories suddenly begin to merge, including, as we have seen, the natural and the industrial, the serious and the banal and even commonplace perceptions such as 'outside' and 'inside'. As a result, Laura's rape and murder by her own respectable and middle-class father (although possessed by the spirit BOB at the time) produces a world where traditional genres such as the 'soap opera' and the 'horror movie', the 'sitcom' and the 'detective drama' suddenly begin to dissolve into one another, where all traditional boundaries collapse and where two distinctly juxtaposed worlds dangerously collide. As suggested by her doubling (in the form of Maddy Ferguson [also played by Sheryl Lee]) and implied in Mike's (Al Strobel) poetic message to Cooper, Laura Palmer is forever caught 'between two worlds', like some persistent 'ghost' trapped within the 'conscious' and the 'unconscious' realms of American 'myth' and American 'reality'.[6]

Rather than simply reflecting the drama's 'depthless postmodernity', such a clear *binary* structure (perhaps hinted at by the 'Twin Peaks' of its title) ultimately reminds its audience that beneath the shiny and reflecting surfaces of the 'conscious' world lies the irrational, baffling and bizarre continent of the *'unconscious'*. It is this *surreal* merging of these two ('seemingly contradictory') realms that is the real concern of *Twin Peaks*. Rather than simply reflecting a soulless array of endless surfaces it suggests a world in which all categories of common sense and logic have been upturned, creating a universe that is not so much defined by its *lack* of an unconscious as one consumed by its unbearable *presence*. Laura's dead body may be found wrapped in plastic, but inside this cheap and disposable body bag we gradually glimpse a woman (and subsequently a town) with bizarre, but unmistakable depths.[7] 'Is this real, Ben?' asks Jerry (David Patrick Kelly), 'Or some strange and twisted dream?' (cited by Hughes, 2001: 109). Strange and twisted as it might seem, *Twin Peaks* displays all the signs of being a drama distinctly in touch with its own irrational and dangerous unconscious.

Added to this, it could also be argued that *Twin Peaks* did everything it could to present itself as a modernist television *'monument'*. In spite of its many similarities with serial TV, its makers used every means possible to distinguish the drama as 'art television', associating it with all the credentials of auteurist experimental cinema. Its modernist aspirations were certainly matched by an artistic agenda that attempted to revolutionise television drama, rejecting the apparently 'logical' and 'rational' parameters of conventional soap opera or the 'formulaic' series. 'Like Nothing Else on Earth: David Lynch's *Twin Peaks* May Be the Most Original Show on TV' ran the headline in *Time* (9 April 1990; cited by Collins, 1992: 334). As such, its artistic intentions were no less than those of the surrealists: to break down the boundaries of 'bourgeois culture' and construct a new, radical and startling form of representation.

As the *Time* headline suggests, some of the show's implicitly 'modernist' aspirations can also be glimpsed in the way that it marketed itself around the name of a single author or auteur, i.e. David Lynch. In this way, it tended to conceive and sell itself as the product of a single creative will rather than a piece of 'postmodern' commodification. Consequently, the series was made to look less like industry-driven television and more like an authentic 'work of art'. However, the truth was that while Lynch played a huge role in the conception and development of the series as a whole (although, during the second series he was actually more involved in his film project *Wild at Heart* [1990]), *Twin Peaks* was a huge piece of industrial collaboration.[8] But this was not something its makers (or television executives) wanted to dwell upon, preferring instead to market it as the strange and personal vision of one individual mind. So, rather than exploiting and reflecting the 'postmodern' television environment of the time, the series actually seemed to go against the contemporary cultural condition by attempting to reconstruct a more traditional view of authorship and production.

As this reveals, *Twin Peaks* actually marketed itself along surprisingly traditional (if not 'modernist') lines for a text that was apparently 'polysemic' and 'multiaccentual' by nature (Collins, 1992: 335). In doing so, it set up conventional expectations (a singular artistic vision with a rational, linear and resolvable plot, i.e. the murder of Laura Palmer) that betrayed its more 'subversive' and 'unconventional' sensibilities. Seen in this light, it could be argued that *Twin Peaks* immediately staked a claim on its own modernist credentials in order to distinguish itself from the 'commodification' of contemporary television as a whole. It attempted to turn the tendency of recent television on its head by reclaiming and renewing its own 'authorial' and 'artistic' agenda. One has only to look at *Invitation to Love*, the fictional soap opera portrayed in the drama (with its cheap sets, wooden acting and over-the-top music) to realise exactly what it was in fear of becoming.

In conclusion then, one can say that *Twin Peaks* attempted to transfer the style and sensibilities of 'art cinema' onto the small screen. However, like the surrealists, this was also perhaps partly the reason for the drama's ultimate demise. After a while, audiences found that the images that once shocked, stunned and surprised gradually began to look familiar, pedestrian and predictable (see Dolan, 1995: 30–1). This may partly explain why the show was eventually cancelled by ABC in mid-season, a continual shift in scheduling not enough to bring to an end its consistent drop in audience ratings (see Lavery, 1995: 2–3). Yet, such a history perhaps only confirms its 'modernist' sensibilities, a drama that attempted to subvert the conventional notions by which (televisual) 'reality' is conceived and represented, but ended up alienating a large majority of its audience in the process.

Riget (*The Kingdom*) (Danish Television, 1994)[9]

> Historical events resonate not merely through the archives that have been collected, but also through its gaps – the historical material that has been lost or has not been collected. For example, the oral histories of indigenous people, or the folk tales of European peasants find no place within the written historical records, but they continue to 'haunt' this record through their silences, opening up gaps within the historiographic enterprise.
>
> Danaher *et al.* (2000: 101)

Despite *Twin Peaks'* eventual cancellation by ABC, David Lynch's excursion into television had clearly helped to lessen the stigma of film directors working for the medium. Like *Twin Peaks*, *The Kingdom* (or *Riget* as it was originally known in its native Denmark)[10] was partly created and directed by a well-known film-maker, in this case the controversial Danish auteur, Lars von Trier (helped by assistant director Morten Arnfred). Von Trier was also partly responsible for creating the original story (along with Niels Vørsel and Tomas Gislason). Originally inspired by *Twin Peaks*, von Trier had observed how Lynch seemed to have been 'liberated' by television. As Jack Stevenson puts it (2002: 76–7):

> TV had allowed him [Lynch] to escape from the pressures attached to making 'a great work of art' – a feature film – and it has liberated his whole creative process. Von Trier had a great desire to do the same, to escape the oppressive apparatus of the film industry, inclusive of the burdensome financial and artistic expectations. In any case, there would be no time for perfection. This was TV and they had a mere fifty hours of shooting time to produce approximately five hours of fiction.

Surprisingly perhaps, the critics' reaction to *The Kingdom* was considerably more favourable than it was to von Trier's more controversial and experimental films. Indeed, many critics have argued that von Trier's movies, like *The Element of the Crime* (1984), *Epidemic* (1987), *Breaking the Waves* (1996) and *The Idiots* (1999), were aesthetically off-putting and distancing, earning the director the dubious title of 'Lars Von Trying'. Although the more recent *Dancer in the Dark* (2000) (a musical starring the Icelandic singer Björk) won the Palme d'Or for best film at Cannes, some critics were less than forthcoming in their praise. 'I thought it was rubbish', wrote Peter Bradshaw in the *Guardian*, '[f]or all the style and brio, there was something crudely manipulative about the story, and something facetious and shallow about the whole enterprise' (2000: 14).

In contrast, *The Kingdom* won almost unanimous praise, with the Italian newspaper *L'Unità* even declaring it better than *Twin Peaks* (see ibid: 85). Although its length and television status meant that it was disqualified from receiving prizes at the major European film festivals, it did win the Bodil in 1995. It also played to huge crowds at the Venice, Rotterdam and Berlin festivals where audiences, despite its four-and-half-hour length, frequently stood up and cheered at its end. Its fame and notoriety also reached the US where the American horror writer Stephen King is currently producing a prime-time thirteen-part adaptation of it for ABC. At the time of writing *The Kingdom 3* is currently in production.

The international acclaim of *The Kingdom* is perhaps surprising when one considers its frequently unconventional mixture of fantasy and reality, as well as its relatively limited and localised subject matter. Despite many critics' fears that increased market forces have meant that contemporary TV drama is gradually becoming more homogenised and globalised, *The Kingdom* seems to deliberately resist such trends. Not only is it sometimes difficult viewing, its subject matter seems peculiarly parochial. Its strange and frequently sensational action takes place almost exclusively within the walls of a real Copenhagen hospital (known as the Rigshospital but actually nicknamed 'Riget' – 'The Kingdom' – by the locals). In this way, the serial offers the viewer a contemporary television drama that actively goes against the apparent tide of global television practice, presenting a less than conventional television narrative centred around issues of a uniquely local nature.

Indeed, made before von Trier's allegiance to the 'back to basics' manifesto of Dogme '95, *The Kingdom* appears to reject any heavy reliance on traditional notions of realism.[11]

While the rigid 'documentary' austerity of the Dogme manifesto (see Kelly, 2000) prevents the use of such features as special lighting, post-synchronised sound, optical filters, make-up or incidental music, *The Kingdom* appears to exploit all manner of televisual effects, generic conventions and technical devices, including a specially written score by Joachim Holbek which provides all the moody atmospherics of the classic horror film. Although von Trier's ubiquitous hand-held camera adds to the serial's unsettling authenticity, the story's fantastical elements continually threaten to undermine its inherent realism. Under the art direction of Jette Lehmann, the directors employed an array of special effects to create a complex mix of fantasy and reality that destabilises any unproblematic sense of 'the real'. In its most notorious scene, for example, a nurse gives birth to a fully grown man, his head coming first as he graphically spits and screams his way into the world.

Perhaps part of the success of *The Kingdom* can be attributed to the fact that unlike many of von Trier's more experimental films it is 'centred' by the familiar conventions of television. In particular, the intrinsic familiarity of the hospital/medical drama provides an important narrative framework around which its bizarre story can carefully and gradually develop. In fact, the serial both appropriates and subverts many of the more traditional televisual genres, constantly pushing their conventional boundaries to the extreme while also relying on their recognisable form and content to deliver both meaning and expression. Its generic familiarity is also supported by the serialised structure of the narrative that allows viewers to grow intensely familiar with both its characters and settings. In particular, it seems to owe a debt to the legacy of a television series like *Hill Street Blues* (NBC, 1981–7) and that whole subgenre of television drama (von Trier cites Barry Levinson's *Homicide: Life on the Street* [NBC, 1994–] as an influence [see Stevenson, 2002: 82]) which seemed to revel in a complex number of narrative threads and subplot digressions (see Introduction). As a result, its soap opera, serial familiarity provides a narrative grounding for an audience who may otherwise have been disturbed and confused by the less conventional elements of its storytelling.

First shown on Danish television during November and December, 1994 (co-funded by DR, Swedish Television and the EU Media Programme), *The Kingdom* primarily revolves around the exploits of a clairvoyant patient, Mrs Drusse (Kirsten Rolffes) and her bungling son Bulder (Jens Okking) to exorcise the ghost of a small girl from 'The Kingdom'. During their illicit investigations they discover that the girl was horrifically murdered by her own father (and the hospital's founder) Aage Krüger (Udo Kier), a hero of modern scientific medicine from the last century. However, Drusse's paranormal beliefs meet strong opposition from the majority of the medical staff, particularly from Stig Helmer (Ernst-Hugo Järegård), a newly arrived doctor from Sweden. Although the arrogant Helmer (obviously meant to be the J. R. Ewing of the narrative) has faith only in the wonders of science, his own medical incompetence has left an innocent young girl permanently brain-damaged. In contrast, the kind-hearted Dr Krogshøj (Søren Pilmark) believes in the old woman's paranormal abilities, particularly when he reluctantly begins to fear that his lover has actually been impregnated by Krüger's ghost. Eventually, a whole number of phantoms are accidentally freed from the hospital walls, while Helmer flees to Tahiti to escape charges of malpractice.

The Kingdom appears to explore (perhaps like Lindsay Anderson's *Britannia Hospital* [1982] before it) different and varied aspects of national life via the metaphor of a medical institution. While Mrs Drusse's exploration of the paranormal uncovers the dark and hidden history of 'the kingdom', the clinical and overtly rational nature of the doctors and nurses appears to reveal a contemporary world increasingly governed by rationalism, bureaucracy and scientific intolerance. Although the logical world of the hospital carries on as normal, Mrs Drusse seems to tap into a 'spiritual' substratum that lies deep within the hospital's vaults. It is the clash between these two opposing cultures, particularly the 'spiritual' and the 'scientific' worlds, that provides much of the narrative and thematic context of the story, reflecting a building or nation that has lost touch with the rhythm and nature of its 'organic' past. In this way, the serial seems to be undermining not only the rationalism of contemporary medicine but also perhaps the rationalism of the genre of which it undoubtedly forms a part. As Jason Jacobs has put it (2003: 29):

> In Lars von Trier's mini-series *The Kingdom* – first screened in 1994 along with *ER*, *Cardiac Arrest* and *Chicago Hope* – the very formation of the new hospital drama genre seems to be under examination. Its juxtaposition of horror, soap and the uncanny enable it to create a setting and a discursive address that seems to undermine the claims of rationalist medical science that the other hospital dramas cling onto even in the face of decline and despair.

This juxtaposition between the 'rational' and irrational' world of the hospital is immediately foregrounded by the serial's unusual and striking opening sequence (which has sadly been deleted by the BlackStar DVD version that seems intent on packaging the drama as a single film rather than a piece of serial television drama). Acting almost as a prologue and cut into two distinct halves, its first section briefly describes the historical origins of the land on which this ultra new, modern hospital has been built. Against a foreground of dull human figures bathed in a sepia tint, we see a dark, damp and desolate landscape. 'The ground under the hospital is ancient marshland,' the narration explains. 'Here bleachers once soaked and worked great lengths of cloth. It was a place permanently wreathed in fog.' The sequence then shifts abruptly to the present day, represented by a montage of more conventional televisual images (close-ups of principal characters, high shots of the modern hospital, speeding ambulances etc.), accompanied by a pulsating score (all reminiscent of an American medical series like *St Elsewhere* [NBC, 1982–8] or *ER* [NBC, 1994–]). As a result, the viewer is immediately provided with two generic points of view, the land's pagan past (portrayed by its ghostly images of men and women) is immediately contrasted with the rational and scientific world of this brightly-lit Copenhagen medical institution (suggested by its imitation of contemporary television medical drama).

The very quality of the film also reflects this implicit binary structure. For while the constant use of a hand-held camera gives a decidedly contemporary feel to the serial as a whole (echoing the 'documentary' aesthetics of a modern medical drama like *ER* or *Casualty* [BBC, 1986–]), the sheer graininess of the print itself (the colour was apparently manipulated in the copying and colour-grading process) gives it a strangely 'antiquated' or sepia look. Originally shot on 16mm, von Trier also had the film trans-

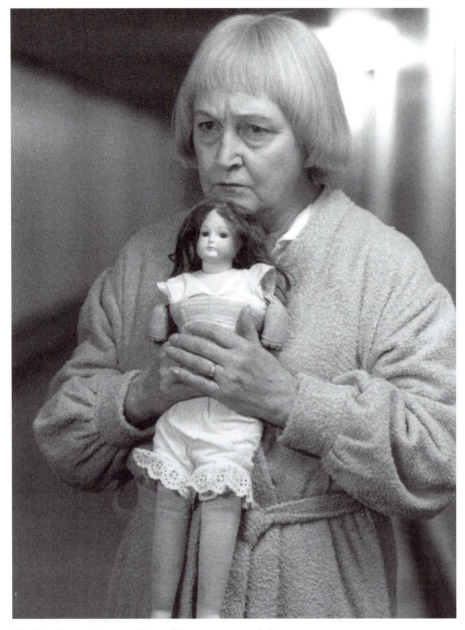

The Kingdom: a juxtaposition of horror, soap and the uncanny

ferred onto videotape before finally converting it to 35mm. This gives the serial a peculiarly 'monochromatic' and 'otherworldly' appearance, in direct conflict with its
otherwise contemporary aesthetics. This unusual combination of 'artistic' techniques and
documentary 'realism' may partly reflect the wider tension at work within the narrative
as a whole, particularly that which exists between the 'spiritual' and the 'physical' and

the 'past' and the 'present'. Although the under-lit and frequently unsteady video image has become the contemporary signifier of truthfulness – imbuing the drama with an equal amount of realism and modernity – the 'antique' or *distorted* quality of the actual print is perhaps suggestive of another world altogether. 'Perhaps arrogance and denial of the spiritual have become too much', the opening narration explains, 'for it is as though the fog has returned'.

This 'fog' is further suggested by the drama's obsession with the shadowy images of poorly defined television, CCTV and VDU screens. Directly after the opening sequence a black-and-white image fills the frame in *extreme* close-up. This deliberately shadowy and blurred representation of an ambulance by a close circuit camera is meant to enhance its 'ghostly' appeal. The grainy images of hearing scans, brain scans, ultra scans and X-ray images continue to foreground the presence of a dark 'subterranean' world, as if the doctors are literally peering into unknown realms through a dense and impenetrable (albeit technological) 'fog'. In this way, the drama's visual construction neatly reflects the cultural rupture alluded to in the opening sequence, a hidden and mysterious universe concealed beneath the surface veneer of everyday rationality.

Reflecting the structure of the opening section, the hospital itself also appears to be divided into two distinct halves, its logical and scientific upper levels offering a stark and distinct contrast to the dark and somewhat 'irrational' world housed in its lower depths. Indeed, the lower levels of the building reveal a Kafkaesque labyrinth of dimly lit rooms and a complex maze of corridors. A Down's Syndrome couple (played by real Down's Syndrome actors, Vita Jensen and Morten Rotnue Leffers) are located in the hospital's kitchens, continually washing up as they comment eerily (like a Greek chorus) on the narrative which unfolds high above their heads. Meanwhile, Dr Krogshøj has converted an area of forgotten space in the basement into his own living quarters, supplementing his wages by recycling the hospital's endless supply of waste products (including cocaine that he sells to other members of the medical staff). The hospital's all-male Masonic Lodge ('Sons of the Kingdom') also meets on one of the lower levels, with the bizarre rituals of an ancient and slightly ludicrous secret society. Indeed, after one meeting Helmer gets lost in the very bowels of the building, frantically finding his way to the roof as if he were coming up for air. Finally, running like a hidden vertebra through the whole building, the elevator shaft houses Mary, the ghost child and the innocent victim of infanticide.

This apparent split between the higher and lower levels of the building seems particularly Freudian, further enhanced by the 'Sleep laboratory' strategically placed somewhere between the upper and lower floors. As if to underline this association, one of the Down's Syndrome couple actually suggests that the events taking place around them are 'uncanny'. According to Freud's article the 'uncanny', the repressed, will often return in irrational and perplexing forms, taking on the resemblance of a 'ghostly' or 'spiritual' apparition (1958, 17: 247–8):

> We – or our primitive forefathers – once believed that these possibilities were realities, and
> were convinced that they actually happened. Nowadays we no longer believe in them, we

have *surmounted* these modes of thought; but we do not feel quite sure of our new beliefs, and the old ones still exist within us ready to seize upon any confirmation. As soon as something *actually happens* in our lives which seems to confirm the old, discarded beliefs we get a feeling of the uncanny, it is as though we were making a judgement something like this ... 'So the dead *do* live on and appear on the scene of their former activities!'

Such a statement aptly sums up one way to interpret the 'paranormal' activities apparently at work within the hospital. From a Freudian perspective The Kingdom (perhaps like the human psyche itself) seems literally *haunted* by its dark and 'unconscious' secrets. Perhaps the lower depths of the building can be seen as somehow reflecting the hospital's own misguided repression. Following this line of interpretation further, we can even detect the suggestion of what Jung might have termed a 'collective unconscious' – a mythological substratum that exists below the conscious veneer of the hospital's everyday life. According to Jung's controversial notion, a collective unconscious exists within us all, a personal storeroom of organic traditions and culture reflecting our own particular national origins. Although heavily criticised for its deterministic implications, in its simplest form it suggests that each nation has a set of archetypes and myths that are passed on from one generation to the next. As Anthony Storr has put it, 'it seems intrinsically likely that whatever parts of the mind may be considered responsible for producing dreams, visions, myths, and religious ideas should function rather similarly in different parts of the world and at different periods' (1975: 36).

As such, the hospital archives (also in its lower depths) appear to represent some form of national memory. Both the records for Helmer's recent case of negligence and those belonging to the murdered child are discovered there, as if the archive houses dark and forbidden secrets which could unlock the repressed truths about the building's (and possibly Denmark's) long and complex history. As one doctor revealingly puts it, 'All pain is hidden there'. Perhaps this dusty collection of records and medical documents comes closest to a literal representation of the national 'unconscious'. Kept strictly under lock and key (it is an archive only available to a privileged handful of professionals) it comes to represent a repressed 'memory' or 'history', a record of events that are too painful or perhaps too dangerous to be opened to the public. In a similar way, the ghosts that occupy the building seem to represent that which cannot be recorded, a forgotten past that is forever trying to erupt and finally reveal itself.

As we have seen, the narrative dynamic is played out and echoed in both the aesthetic nature of the film and in the very structure of the building itself. For the tension at the heart of the narrative is reflected in a hospital that is itself divided into a cross-section of the nation's own cultural and mythological history. As Mrs Drusse begins to uncover the secrets of the hospital's tragic past, so a national rupture begins to emerge that suggests that Denmark's current neglect of its own historical heritage may be unsettling its very foundations (quite literally in the case of the hospital). 'No living soul knows it yet', the opening narration explains, 'but the portals of The Kingdom are reopening' (see Figure 1).

Perhaps one way to understand this narrative construction is to view the drama within a Danish national context. Denmark's resolute defence of its national heritage is certainly deep-rooted in its own history. As the country's recent rejection of the euro (the single European currency) suggests, there seems to be a ground swell of opinion within modern Denmark that it has gone far enough in terms of its ever-increasing global or 'Europeanisation'. It was this very fear of absorption into other cultures that lay behind the origins of the first Danish Folk Schools (or 'People's College'), founded by Nikolai Frederik Severin Grundtvig. As the principal of such a school has put it, 'We are fighting for dear life against the culture of larger nations like Germany. They could have swallowed us. What Grundtvig did was to teach us that we had a culture of our own' (cited by Connery, 1967: 161). As a result, the serial's title may actually be seen as an implicit reminder of an older nation state, a time when Denmark's powerful empire (sometimes described as the oldest kingdom in the world) still included Sweden, Norway and Greenland. Such a wealth of cultural history certainly makes Denmark's origins particularly opulent in metaphorical significance, revealing a distant and complex national past that perhaps its scientific and sanitised present will never fully appreciate.[12]

Seen in this light, the arrival of the Swedish Doctor Helmer may partly suggest one reason why the hospital/nation seems to have become divorced from its forgotten past. Helmer appears out of place in a country whose history and culture he is unable or unwilling to understand and appreciate. Medically and politically arrogant, his obsession with business and cost-cutting (putting economic concerns before patients' health and well-being) is in stark contrast with Denmark's long-standing belief in the principles and ideals of the welfare state.[13] 'In your Danish language', he sarcastically asks his first board meeting, 'is there a word for budget?' Later he stands on the roof of the hospital to look across at Sweden and to shout names at the Danish people. He even comically comforts himself by remembering famous Swedish commodities and icons. 'Tetrapak, yes', he nods to himself, 'Volvo, yes. Pripps Blue, yes. Bjorn Borg, yes'.

As an outsider, Helmer is simply unable to appreciate or sympathise with the national psyche that the spiritualist Mrs Drusse, for instance, seems so acutely attuned to. Not brought up in Denmark, he appears to have little interest in its past life or its cultural history. 'Shat out of chalk and water' is how he vividly describes the country, a comment that crudely and comically dismisses its rich natural and cultural heritage. Sweden, by comparison, is 'hewn out of granite', a symbol of strength, power and stability. As such, Helmer perhaps symbolises Denmark's contemporary disconnection from its own historical heritage, now it is occupied and ruled by arrogant foreign interests. He even seems to provoke an earthquake while standing on the roof of the building, as if his nationalist incantations have finally caused the ground beneath the building to shift – Denmark's forgotten heritage forced to react to the ignorance and intolerance he so vividly represents.

The 'ghosts' trapped within the hospital walls suggest the return of a repressed history that has been denied by official interpretations. Such a conception of the past has perhaps been increasingly supported by recent suspicions surrounding the very notion of historical 'truth'. Rather than viewing history as a solid and unmoveable object, con-

HOSPITAL ROOF (the location for Helmer's xenophobic ranting)

MAIN HOSPITAL (sanitised wards and operation theatres)	E L E V A T O R S H A F T	'Conscious' levels: Rational, modern, scientific Documentary realism (hand-held camera)
SLEEP LABORATORY	Ghost- child, Mary	
HOSPITAL ARCHIVES ('All pain is hidden there').	E L E V	'Unconscious' Levels: Irrational, spiritual, uncanny
MASONIC LODGE (the all-male brethren, the 'Sons of The Kingdom')	A T O	Artistic abstraction (distortion, graininess)
KITCHENS (occupied by the Down's Syndrome couple)	R	
BASEMENT (Dr Krogshøj's secret apartment and recycling exercise)	S H A F T	
HOSPITAL FOUNDATIONS (the site of its pagan past and possibly its 'collective unconscious')		

Figure 1. A rough cross-section of 'The Kingdom'[14]

temporary interpretations have suggested that history itself is an ever-changing and fluid entity, one which a people must be willing to reclaim, reinvent and sometimes even reconstruct (see Chapter One). As a result of this sort of historical indeterminacy the very notion of a stable concept of national identity has become more fluid and open to interpretation. As Anthony Giddens has put it, '[t]he era of the nation state is over. Nations ... have become mere "fictions" ' (1991: 31). Such a view of history and nationhood renders the very idea of identity as something that is searched for and discovered rather than simply inherited. As Michel Foucault has put it (1991: 82):

> we should not be deceived into thinking that ... heritage is an acquisition, a possession that grows and solidifies; rather, it is an unstable assemblage of faults, fissures, and heterogeneous layers that threaten the fragile inheritor from within or from underneath ... The search for descent is not the erecting of foundations: on the contrary, it disturbs what was previously considered immobile; it fragments what was thought unified; it shows the heterogeneity of what was imagined consistent with itself.

It is these 'faults' and 'fissures' in the search for identity that *The Kingdom* seems intent on opening up. It appears to be urging 'new histories' to be written, finding ways to connect Denmark's cultural heritage (however splintered, diverse and unstable that might be) with its present self. The Down's Syndrome couple are perhaps meant to be symbolic of Denmark's 'instinctual' and 'spiritual' past, a forgotten and repressed manifestation of the country's organic and 'pagan' roots. Indeed, von Trier has been criticised for his 'romantic' perception of autism in films such as *The Idiots*, suggesting perhaps an association between the educationally subnormal and some kind of spiritual 'wisdom'.[15] Acutely in tune with the building's inner workings (they even claim to hear it 'cry'), they clearly seem to represent some kind of spiritual 'haven' or sacred realm. In a similar way, the working-class Mrs Drusse embodies the elements of an organic Danish folk culture, still in touch with the country's traditional past and literally able to connect it with its present incarnation through her paranormal mediation.

In this way, The Kingdom's complex and fragmented layered structure suggests a loosely 'archaeological' framework; its sanitised and technocratic present is revealed as only the tip of a complex and multilayered historical trajectory. The paranormal events, the two-tier structure of the building and Helmer's rampant xenophobia suggest that the hospital's instabilities are rooted in its rupture from the past. As a result, *The Kingdom* represents and dissects a national 'unconscious', exploring the role of cultural memory in the construction of both personal and national identity. While it could be argued that a similar framework might be applied anywhere in the world, the drama implies that a peculiarly intense form of cultural 'amnesia' seems to have overtaken modern Denmark, producing a country which is dangerously out of touch with its own national heritage. In particular, the drama implies that global culture, science and economics are swallowing up the specific connection that each country has with its own deep-rooted and even 'spiritual' origins.

Indeed, it soon becomes clear that *The Kingdom* regards neither the notion of national nor personal identity as anything less than unstable. For the modern insecurity at the heart of the nation is also reflected in the instability of the subject itself. In an episode entitled *The Foreign Body*, Professor Bondo has his own healthy liver replaced with a diseased organ in order to further his career and research. This provides a graphic example of the way the certainty of the self has now become as destabilised as any notion of a fixed national heritage. Medical technology not only prolongs life, it can now alter both our external appearance (eyes, lips, teeth, breasts, etc.) and our internal organs (liver, heart and hip replacements, etc.). In this way, the notion of an 'authentic' self now seems as illusory and elusive as the utopian notion of the 'organic' nation-state. Countries and bodies have both been invaded and the line between the 'foreign' and the 'authentic' is now blurred beyond distinction.

This instability of the self is dramatically reflected in the predicament of Judith (Brigitte Raaberg), the pregnant nurse who suddenly and briefly becomes 'transparent' in the last episode. 'I fear that Judith ... is a ghost', her boyfriend Dr Krogshøj tells Mrs Drusse in desperation. Perhaps Judith's paranormal impregnation by the hospital's founder, Aage Krüger, suggests a dramatic personification of the return of the (national) repressed. In this way, cultural citizenship is undermined and destabilised by past secrets and hidden histories. Until the injustices of the past are uncovered, acknowledged and exhumed, subsequent generations are forced to carry their burdens, quite literally in the case of Judith. As Benedict Anderson has argued, national identity is an 'imagined community', and differences between nations lie in the different ways in which they are imagined or created (1991). Seen in this context, Judith's body becomes the site of that imagining, the symbol of a nation whose imaginary 'rebirth' may be imminent. However, her impregnation by a figure from history might suggest a nation whose future identity is threatened by its own inability to come to terms with and lay to rest the 'ghosts' of its past.

The Kingdom then, expresses a crisis in both nation and selfhood that characterises and embodies much of the uncertainty at the heart of postmodern culture. Implicit in its construction of identity is the view that it is now made up of so many 'arbitrary' or 'imaginary' categories that any sense of a 'real' or 'authentic' self can only be illusory or simply the construction of (global) socio-scientific knowledge. As a result, contemporary identities have become increasingly transient, fleeting and ephemeral, the byproduct of categorisations that no longer appear to pertain to any local or national context. In this way, it attempts to examine identity on a number of levels, suggesting different means by which it can be constructed and perpetuated through a combination of fact, fantasy and fiction, exploring and investigating Denmark's 'imagined community' from a number of opposing and contradictory perspectives.

However, like *The Singing Detective* (which was also set in a hospital and dealt with similarly ambiguous matters of identity), *The Kingdom* appears to reveal a complex and slippery connection with both modernism and postmodernism. Although the drama, at times, implies that all identity (both personal and national) is ultimately illusory, there is still a past world buried deep within the foundations of the hospital that seems to be both real and authentic. In fact, it is the rupture between this organic Danish past/culture and its sanitised and globalised present (particularly symbolised by internationally accepted notions of scientific 'truth') that creates the cultural fragmentation at the heart of the hospital/nation as a whole. It could be argued that despite its apparently 'postmodern' portrayal of personal and national disintegration, the drama still tends to conceive the past as a real and discernible entity. Rather than a simple celebration of cultural fragmentation then, the Jungian re-invention of national symbols and cultural myths seems to suggest a modernist hunger for order and meaning in an increasingly dislocated and schizophrenic world. As Peter Childs has put it, '[f]or the modernists ... the point of using myth was to compensate for the dissatisfying fragmentation of the modern world: to create a controlling narrative that could be mapped onto, and make sense of, the rapid social changes of modernity' (2000: 198).

But perhaps there is an implicit caution within *The Kingdom* that also suggests the dangers of looking for and isolating an 'authentic' national past. As parts of Europe are savaged by civil war, it is perhaps worth remembering that ancient national beliefs can be as cancerous and as evil as they are frequently liberating and grounding. The fact that Mrs Drusse's attempt at exorcism accidentally fills the hospital with *more* uncontrollable spirits, perhaps suggests the problem of 'memory' and 'heritage' falling into dangerous (or incompetent) hands. For while a clear sense of self and nationhood can be a positive and healing power, nationalism, in its most crude and unreconstructed form, can often become a violent and destructive force. Perhaps this is the inherent warning behind *The Kingdom*, graphically expressed in its horrific final scene of a nurse violently giving birth to a fully grown man. This potent and terrifying image reveals the complex and dangerous consequences that can result from a nation's re-examination of its own dark and hidden histories: a literal embodiment of its perhaps monstrous and grotesque *rebirth*.

The Kingdom finally does not simply celebrate the fragmentary nature of the 'postmodern' experience or blindly accept the 'modernist' need to reclaim an authentic and organic past. Instead, it appears to examine and critique both cultural conditions within a narrative framework that is itself inherently ambiguous and thematically contradictory. In doing so, it reveals the power of contemporary television drama to explore the effects of globalisation without necessarily succumbing to its implicit tendency towards transnational homogenisation. While bravely localised in its concerns, it creates a complex, ambiguous, cross-generic, stylistically challenging, televisual fiction that still proudly carries on some of the radical and subversive traditions of television drama from the 1960s and 1970s. Perhaps von Trier himself implies this complex moral ambiguity at the end of each episode when he playfully and bizarrely addresses the audience. 'Should you want to spend more time with us at The Kingdom', he warns, 'be prepared to take the good with the evil'.

Cold Lazarus (Channel Four/BBC, 1996)[16]

> The multimedia are not only seen as creating more pressure on the quality of the output of mass media, whereby the 'serious' is eroded by the drive for more entertainment to satisfy the search for audiences to maximise profits, but also as a direct threat to literary culture and reading ... But perhaps more crucial is the view that the commercialisation is changing the relationship between the mass media and their audiences: no longer as citizens but as consumers.
>
> Kevin Williams (1998: 256)

The four-part serial *Cold Lazarus* was written by Dennis Potter, one of Britain's most prolific and well-respected television dramatists whose work covered the so-called 'golden age' of the 1960s through to the 'market-orientated', consumer-led economies of the 1990s. From *Stand Up, Nigel Barton* (BBC, 1965) and *Vote, Vote, Vote for Nigel Barton* (BBC, 1965) through to *Pennies from Heaven* (BBC, 1978), *Blue Remembered Hills* (BBC, 1979) and *The Singing Detective* (BBC, 1986), his work provided some of the most acclaimed and talked about drama ever to be produced for the small screen anywhere in the world. Quickly acquiring a reputation for being controversial, Potter's work continually took risks and challenged the habitual expectations of viewers. As Graham Fuller has put it (1993: xv):

> the landscape Potter occupied is the inside of the head. Where other writers have been constrained by the dramatic parameters of the 'here and now', Potter has trade-marked a number of bountiful and profoundly unsettling techniques for navigating the streams, tributaries, cross-currents and sewers that flow through his protagonists' minds. Challenging viewers' assumptions about what they are watching, he pioneered the fourth-wall-breaking, anti-theatrical techniques of non-naturalism – more out of necessity, he says, than design . . .

The circumstances behind Potter's last two screenplays are now part of television legend. Diagnosed with incurable cancer (and with only a few months to live) he appeared on Channel Four's *Without Walls* in April 1994, interviewed by broadcaster and friend, Melvyn Bragg (see Cook, 1998: 297–300 and Creeber, 2000: 129–37).[17] Memorably, he concluded this BAFTA award-winning programme by promising two new screenplays before his imminent death. Some two months later, not only were they both completed but the playwright had also influenced important areas of their subsequent production. Not just involving himself in the casting, he also insisted that both serials were to be directed by Renny Rye, responsible for earlier Potter creations, *Lipstick on Your Collar* (Channel Four, 1993) and *Midnight Movie* (BBC, 1994).[18] It is perhaps no exaggeration to say that the scripts themselves were adhered to with almost religious reverence, and the £10-million-budget helped to faithfully reproduce the finest details of location and design. But perhaps Potter's greatest coup was to have the BBC and Channel Four co-produce the two serials, each channel broadcasting a repeat of the episode first seen on the rival channel.[19]

While *Karaoke*'s (BBC/Channel Four, 1996) story of a drunken and dying television writer brought together the well-known Potter themes of sex, death and biography, *Cold Lazarus* appeared to offer a completely new departure. Set in the year 2368, this science-fiction pastiche centred on a group of British scientists intent on tapping into the memories of a cryogenically frozen head. Yet despite its futuristic setting, comically kitsch costumes and seductive sci-fi music composed by Christopher Gunning (which, according to Trodd, attempted to remind us of *Star Wars* and *Blade Runner*)[20] its conception of the future is seen unmistakably and inevitably from the point of view of the present. Greatly undervalued by its critics, *Cold Lazarus* offers a complex satire on the state of contemporary Britain. In particular, it portrays a society where Milton Friedman's monetarist economics (the type favoured by Thatcherite and even more recent 'Blairite' policies) have reduced everything to a commercial transaction.[21] Above all, the serial is

Potter's final comment on the sort of 'management culture' and its desire for 'market efficiency' which he felt was eroding the basic ideals of British life and slowly corrupting the fundamental principles of British broadcasting.

In 1989 Rupert Murdoch delivered the James MacTaggart Memorial Lecture at the annual Edinburgh International Television Festival. 'Most of what passes for quality on British television', he argued, 'is no more than a reflection of the values of the narrow elite which controls it and has always thought that its tastes are synonymous with quality'. British TV he said, was 'obsessed with class', tended to 'hark back to the past' and was dominated by 'anti-commercial attitudes'. According to Murdoch,

> the television set of the future will be a global cornucopia of programming and nearly infinite libraries of data, education and entertainment. The arguments that have recently dominated British broadcasting ... will soon sound as if they belong in the Stone Age.[22]

It came as no surprise then, that when Potter (a great adversary of Murdoch) took the stand for his own James MacTaggart Memorial Lecture in 1993, the earlier speech became the target for much of his personal contempt and passionate rhetoric. For Potter, Murdoch's commercially financed media empire symbolised the total destruction of state-funded public service broadcasting as he knew and understood it. Funded by the licence fee rather than advertising revenue, the BBC of Potter's childhood remained the very model upon which he believed British broadcasting should still be founded. Above all, he seemed concerned that the increased commercialisation of both television and radio would finally eradicate the unique power of British broadcasting to both 'educate' and 'inform', as well as 'entertain' (Potter, 1994: 45):

> I would not dispute for one wayward whistle or cackle that the BBC of my childhood was not paternalistic and often stuffily pompous. It saw itself in an almost priestly role. But at a crucial period of my life it threw open the 'magic casement' on great sources of mind-scape at a time when books were hard to come by, and when I had never stepped into a theatre or a concert hall, and would have been scared to do so if given the chance.

It is with this background in mind that *Cold Lazarus* is best understood. Set four hundred years in the future, it takes Murdoch's broadcasting practice and philosophy to its most logical and extreme conclusions. Potter's media mogul is David Siltz (Henry Goodman), a vacuous American and the president of UTE ('Universal Total Entertainment'). Siltz is the most powerful man in a wholly privatised world, intent on transforming the entire planet into a global entertainment industry. 'He's like the ... Tsar of all the Russias', a character observes, 'Genghis Khan's a better analogy' (Potter, 1996: 271), replies another. As Potter told Bragg, this is his dramatisation of a Murdoch-type figure, whose own global entertainment empire already stretched across the UK, US, Germany, Asia, Latin America, Australia and the Pacific Basin.[23]

Siltz's media empire is even more global, but the type of programming it offers is essentially limited. Above all, his entertainment business is driven by the all-consuming need to keep audiences *watching*, regardless of the quality of the programmes they receive. 'If I lose nought point two of an audience in any of my shows', he declares, 'we calculate we lose nought point *three* of advertising revenue . . .' (ibid: 232). Seat sensors tell his programme-makers exactly how the viewer or 'interactivator' is viewing. 'We know', he explains, 'when a killing or a fuck or a droplet from the tear duct is needed' (ibid: 231). Such a vision of the world reflects Neil Postman's *Amusing Ourselves to Death: Public Discourse in the Age of Show Business* (1985), a nightmarish vision of a media-saturated planet. According to Postman, the future will not resemble Orwell's *Nineteen Eighty-Four* where terror is the ruling edifice, but Huxley's *Brave New World* where people 'are controlled by inflicting pleasure' (1985: viii).

Siltz's fellow marketer is Martina Matilda Masdon (Diane Ladd) who, like him, is a symbol of a world which has allowed the pressures of economic forces not only to control people's dreams, but also their bodies and minds. She is the head of a powerful pharmaceutical company that has recently produced a Prozac-like drug to obliterate anxiety. As a result, she asks Siltz if she could sponsor a television programme specifically designed to produce the highest level of fear, thereby ensuring the greatest demand for her new product. '[Y]ou gotta make a whole damn zillion of folks mighty *anxious*', she tells him, '[a]nd that's where your TV and VR . . . comes in' (Potter, 1996: 243). A combination of Margaret Thatcher and the Wicked Witch of the West, she seems to spend most of her time being massaged by semi-naked, muscular, young men and admonishing her employees for going over budget. 'You've tilted tit-up into overspend,' (ibid: 205) she cries in frustration at her demoralised British scientists.

Cold Lazarus: a nightmarish vision of the new broadcasting age

However, as we gradually discover, a group of scientists are in the process of unearthing a form of 'media' no longer conceived by such a commercially obsessed industry. They have in their possession the head of Daniel Feeld (Albert Finney) (the same character from *Karaoke*) which had been cryogenically frozen at his death in 1994. In contrast to the sort of inane and revenue-led programming currently on offer from Siltz and sponsored by the likes of Masdon, Daniel's fragmented memories from the late twentieth century (which they are able to project onto the 'living wall' of their laboratory) conjure up images of an immensely human and organic world. As a result, Daniel's recollections of a postwar, working-class childhood offer a distinct contrast to the media-manipulated world of the future. His memories even provoke some of them to be more critical of the present, forcing them to ask why, as one of the scientists puts it, 'we can't mingle and touch and hope in the way our forefathers and mothers used to do?' (ibid: 307).

Daniel's memories are familiar even to the most casual of Potter's viewers. The Forest of Nead (a re-arrangement of the name of Potter's own childhood Forest of Dean), with its chapel, dance halls and dense woodland, portrays, as the script puts it, 'another land', one infinitely more 'natural' than Britain's dehumanised and commercialised future. As elsewhere in Potter's work, this postwar, working-class community somehow embodies Britain's own 'land of lost content'.[24] With its coal mines and working men's clubs there is the sense of a world that, despite its narrowness of horizon and expectations, was fundamentally more 'organic' and 'authentic' than Britain in 2368. The British scientists of the future can only look on bewildered by this reminder of a time when comradeship, courtship, citizenship and community were the staple ingredients of British life. As Daniel and his future wife sit talking on the grass near Wordsworth's Tintern Abbey, so the beauty and innocence of a rural British summer comes drifting across the centuries, highlighting the urban isolation at the heart of their future dystopia.[25] Not surprisingly, one scientist spies an opportunity to use Daniel's memories for their own salvation. '[I]f we wear our VR helmets', she excitedly explains, 'we will live for hours at a time in the *real* past, the *authentic* past ... and perhaps escape' (ibid: 204).

In this way, *Cold Lazarus* suggests that Britain is in danger of losing touch with its past. Not perhaps the history of empire or monarchy, but the organic history of its people and folk traditions. Mirroring themes in *The Kingdom* (see above), there seems to have been a national or cultural 'repression' which has allowed Britain to forsake some of its most treasured beliefs and culture. The first thing one notices is that the scientists are a mixture of ethnic groups, suggesting a multiculturalism perhaps at odds with Daniel's 'authentically' British memories. Indeed, four hundred years into the future and Britain no longer 'exists as a political entity' (ibid: 237). As a result, Daniel's memories act as a reminder of what Britain has lost; a glimpse of 'Eden' before the Fall. 'Oh, we have so much to learn or relearn from the past', a scientist explains, 'Daniel Feeld ... could have been our ... teacher!' (Potter, 1996: 243). And, as elsewhere in Potter's work, Daniel's distorted and fragmented memories (projected onto the 'living wall') illustrate how the past, present and future can never be successfully separated from each other, that each depends on the other for its own particular meaning and significance.

Potter's serial then, dramatises the potential dangers of a world obsessed with and controlled by the entertainment business, a business in every sense of the word which cares more for present and future profit than preserving the cultural and social traditions of the past. Put crudely, it dramatises the contemporary conflict between a form of public service broadcasting which possessed and dictated a national, historical and cultural identity (represented here by Daniel's 'authentic' memories), and Murdoch's market-led form of broadcasting (here represented by Siltz's global entertainment empire) which has dispensed with any such cultural mission in the pursuit of increased advertising revenue. As Anthony Weymouth (1996) explains, such a division can be understood in terms of a 'modernist' and 'postmodernist' divide. As Weymouth puts it (Weymouth and Lamizet, 1996: 11–12):

> According to some contemporary thinkers, public service broadcasting was conceived within the final phases of what has come to be known as the 'modernist era'. By this they mean that PSB developed in a time of clearly defined national identities as well as of strongly held views of historical destiny (i.e. Marxist and capitalist theory). It is currently a *fin-de-siècle*, postmodernist argument to assert that such cultural and ideological certainties, which gave the states of Western Europe their sense of mission, were illusory. If this is the case, then a large part of that illusion ... was reinforced by the media and by public service broadcasting in particular.

Cold Lazarus offers a deliberate and conscious critique of contemporary broadcasting in particular and 'postmodernism' in general.[26] The serial constructs a nightmarish and satirised vision of a world in which so-called 'postmodernism' has overwhelmingly triumphed, displacing any notion of historical identity or even *'reality'* as simply illusory or ideological. 'Postmodernism', Fredric Jameson writes, 'is what you have when the modernisation process is complete and nature is gone for good ...' (1991: x). However, in this future dystopia *'nature'* and *'reality'* come back (via Daniel's memories) with a vengeance, and threaten to disrupt the entire premise of people's distorted and media-saturated perceptions. This can help explain why many viewers were apparently not convinced by Potter's knowledge and understanding of the science-fiction genre. *Cold Lazarus* was an attempt to parody perhaps the most 'postmodern' of all genres to re-assert the very notion and possibility of 'truth' and 'reality' that so many contemporary science-fiction dramas attempt to destabilise.[27] From this point of view, one can see Potter's final screenplay as offering a conscious subversion of a science-fiction dystopia like *Blade Runner* (Ridley Scott, 1982), by providing, at its very centre, an *actual* and *authentic* sense of 'history' which Scott's 'replicants' (with their implanted memories) so conspicuously lack.[28]

As one might expect then, Potter's narrative does uncover a group of activists intent on returning a sense of *'truth'* to this morally decentred world. Deriving their title from an acronym of 'Reality or Nothing', the RONs (with their 'power base' in England) are a terrorist organisation intent on overthrowing the media-saturated society, preferring 'reality' to the mindless mass entertainment on offer from Siltz's global media empire.

So it is that Daniel's memories (particularly in their seemingly chaotic disregard for chronology, almost mimicking Potter's own style)[29] offer the RONs an antidote to the media-manipulated world of Britain's future. Although limited in their resources, they do finally free Daniel's head from its virtual imprisonment and even manage to kill Siltz, dramatising Potter's own deeply held wish to inflict a similar demise on Murdoch. As Potter (1994: 14) told Bragg,

> I'd call my cancer, the main one, the pancreas one, I call it Rupert, so I can get close to it, because the man Murdoch is the one who, if I had the time – in fact I've got too much writing to do and I haven't got the energy – but I would shoot the bugger if I could.

Like *The Kingdom* then, here is a treatment of personal consciousness that offers a parallel with human history – denial or repression being as unhealthy for a particular society, nation or community as it is for the individual. Whether national or personal, in Potter's drama repression will amount to distortion, psychosis and finally mental and physical breakdown. This could also be interpreted as setting itself directly against the popular conception of postmodernism that has tended to proclaim 'the end of history'.[30] According to the historian Eric Hobsbawm (1994: 3),

> [t]he destruction of the past ... is one of the most characteristic and eerie phenomena of the late twentieth century. Most young men and women at the century's end grow up in a sort of permanent present lacking any organic relation to the public past of the times they live in.

Perhaps, then, this is the dilemma of the British scientists, *literally* forced to live in a postmodern 'permanent present', in a society which has lost all sense of its national identity and historical destiny. However, cast adrift in this totally privatised world, Daniel's projected memories provide the final reminder of what has been lost, a form of British 'broadcasting' which is still able to fulfil its basic requirement to act as a public service, a 'keeper of folk memory' and the 'guardian of the national conscience' (Weymouth and Lamizet, 1996: 11).[31]

It is this essentially 'modernist' vision of broadcasting that clearly lay behind Potter's unusual request that *Karaoke* and *Cold Lazarus* be shown both on the BBC and Channel Four. Such a demand was surely an attempt to take British broadcasting back thirty years, to recreate the so-called 'golden age' of British television drama. In particular, the move can be seen as an attempt to reconstruct the circumstances of the BBC's *Wednesday Play* when the whole country seemed to be watching this new 'national theatre'.[32] Indeed, both serials yearn for a mythical past, nostalgic for an 'innocent' and 'simpler' world whose notions of identity and community were seemingly more stable and secure. Daniel's 'folk memories' offer a last glimpse of this forgotten world, a reminder of a time when Britain (at least, in comparison with the present or the foreseeable future) was apparently united in a shared vision and a common goal. In contrast, the commercialised and 'postmodern' world offered by digital broadcasting (producing the possibility of five hundred television channels) suggests a national fragmentation which threatens to destroy the sort of cultural cohesion which the BBC may have once symbolised.

Although *Cold Lazarus* failed to receive the sort of critical acclaim lavished upon some of Potter's earlier work, perhaps it does finally act as a 'fitting memorial' for a writer and a public figure who continued to champion and defend the founding ideals upon which British broadcasting and perhaps even postwar British society were established. As bizarre and outlandish as it might at first seem, Potter's last screenplay offers us a chilling critique of British television and politics as they stood facing an uncertain and turbulent future.

Although Potter's work, as a whole, may generally be seen as a reminder of the more 'radical' and 'subversive' television drama of the 1960s and 1970s, *Cold Lazarus* suggests that relevant and critical television drama is still being made. Rather than simply accepting the apparently 'commodified' landscape of postmodernism, examples of television drama in the 1990s could still be found that critically interpreted, subverted and re-imagined the contemporary world they portrayed. Although television commissioning, production and even consumption has clearly changed over the last thirty years, this does not necessarily mean that TV drama cannot still offer 'alternative realities' to the more formulaic, genre-based television that so many critics condemn. While, as explored in the next chapter, genre itself does not have to be an inevitably 'conservative' restraint, there is still clearly a place for 'art television', drama that tries to transcend and transform traditional ways of seeing. Like *Twin Peaks* and *The Kingdom* before it, *Cold Lazarus* revealed the power of television drama during the 1990s to critically respond to and engage with some of the most important social, political and personal dilemmas of the age.

NOTES

1. 'Modernity', according to Salvador Dali, 'does not mean ... Fritz Lang's *Metropolis*, but a hockey pullover of anonymous English manufacture; it also means comedy film, also anonymous, of the silly nonsense type' (cited by Kuenzli, 1987: 8).

2. In fact, Lynch (if his account is to be entirely believed) was only made certain of his decision to make BOB Laura's murderer when a previously unconnected shot was shown to have accidentally reflected Silva in a mirror. This moment of chance was according to Lynch '*perfect*'. But, as the director later explained to Chris Rodley, he 'still didn't know what in hell it meant' (Rodley, 1997: 164). It was only when ABC insisted on an alternative ending of the pilot for foreign markets (an extended version of the episode was released directly onto video in the UK as a stand-alone Lynch feature film [see Hughes, 2001: 116]) that BOB's part in the murder was finally confirmed. As Lynch told the *Los Angeles Times*, 'We needed a resolution, so I made a resolution. I just sort of took off and got into a very strange world. I was free to do whatever I wanted for the alternate ending, so I, uh got into something that was very strange indeed' (cited by Hughes, 2001: 116).

3. Seen in this light, perhaps the bizarre opening sequence of a moose casually walking through an empty town at the beginning of *Northern Exposure* may be seen as both *homage* to *Twin Peaks* and a similar acknowledgment of its own 'surreal' elements.

4. Cooper's often quoted mantra, 'Damn fine coffee – and *hot*' is actually a steal from Deputy Chester in *Gunsmoke* (CBS, 1955–75).

5. Lynch has even confessed to using a similar technique in his own paintings. 'More ideas come out of that and it becomes really unbelievable. By trying to remove yourself you can see some fantastic things sometimes' (cited by Rodley, 1997: 18).

6. The poem in full reads: 'Through the darkness/Of future past/The magician longs to see/One chants out between two worlds/FIRE/Walk with me' (cited by Lavery, 1995: 148).

7. The long-running magazine devoted to *Twin Peaks* (and all things Lynch) is actually called *Wrapped in Plastic*. It celebrated its fiftieth issue in early 2001. See <www.wrappedinplastic.com>.

8. Although the pilot episode was co-written by Lynch and Mark Frost and directed by Lynch, this combination was to prove rare for a series that was, by any standards, a highly collaborative production. Out of thirty episodes (including the pilot), Lynch directed only six, with a total of twelve directors involved in the series as a whole (including Tina Rathborne, Lesli Linka Glatter, Caleb Deschanel, the actress Diane Keaton and Mark Frost's nephew Scott Frost). There were also eight writers involved in the series including Lynch who co-wrote four episodes (if one includes his input to the storyline of episode eight), and Mark Frost who wrote ten episodes with various writers including Lynch, Harley Peyton, Robert Engels, Barry Pullman and Tricia Brock (episode seven was unique in that it was both written and directed by Mark Frost alone). For a detailed filmography see Lavery, 1995: 196–258 or Hughes, 2001: 119–31.

9. This section first appeared, in a different form, in Creeber (2002b).

10. *The Kingdom* was known in Germany as *Geister* and in France as *L'Hôpital et ses fantômes*.

11. Von Trier co-founded Dogme in Copenhagen on Monday 13 March 1995. It involved a set of principles that were intended to create a new form of 'honest' cinema. Along with Thomas Vinterberg and two other Danish directors, they produced 'The Vow of Chastity', a set of ten filmic principles which would dictate the way that Dogme films should be made and look. According to the manifesto, these films should go back to the very basics of film-making. As the original statement explains, 'The camera must be hand-held. Any movement or immobility attainable in the hand is permitted. (The film must not take place where the camera is standing; shooting must take place where the film takes place.)' Added to this, 'genre movies' were not acceptable, there was to be no superficial action ('murders, weapons etc.') and the time and place in which the film evolves must be 'here and now'. Finally, directors should receive no credit, an apparent attempt to bring about the end of auteur cinema. See <www.Dogme95.dk>.

12. Denmark ruled Sweden until 1523, Norway until 1814 and incorporated Greenland as a province in 1953. The ancient tradition of the Danes was certainly founded on a rich and elaborate wealth of fables, myths and sagas. Even the arrival of Christianity initially did little to suppress a culture that had its own unique traditions and complex religious beliefs. According to one historian, 'As late as the beginning of the twelfth century there were many inveterate pagans in Denmark, and for hundreds of years the churches were enmeshed in a tangled web of paganism, Christianity, faith and superstition' (Rying, 1967: 6).

13. 'The Scandinavians pay some of the highest taxes in the world. Taking all direct and indirect

taxes into account, approximately fifty per cent of the average man's earning go to taxes' (ibid.: 74).

14. This diagram is meant to give nothing more than a very rough impression of the different levels of the hospital. Clearly it is difficult to be precise about the *exact* location of certain activities.

15. For further discussion of the criticism surrounding von Trier's use of autism, see *Playing the Fool: Von Trier on* The Idiots, a documentary shown in the UK on Channel Four, 19 August 2000.

16. This section first appeared in a different form in Creeber (1998b).

17. 'Dennis Potter – An Interview with Melvyn Bragg', *A Without Walls Special*, was broadcast by Channel Four on 5 April 1994. Such was the demand for a transcript of the interview that Faber & Faber published it a few months later (see Potter, 1994). A Channel Four video of the interview was also subsequently released.

18. When, after Potter's death in June 1994, the serials' producer Kenith Trodd tried to have Rye replaced by a more experienced director (some rumours had Martin Scorsese up for the job) the wishes of the dead dramatist still managed to triumph.

19. Such a feat may have been partly influenced by the fact that Alan Yentob (Head of BBC1) and Michael Grade (the then Chief Executive of Channel Four) were well-known Potter fans, but it also paid testament to Potter's immense standing in television and his endless powers of persuasion. *Karaoke* was principally the responsibility of the BBC, while Channel Four took responsibility for *Cold Lazarus*. *Karaoke* was therefore shown first on BBC and repeated on Channel Four, while for *Cold Lazarus* this running order was reversed.

20. See Kenith Trodd's sleeve notes to the soundtrack of *Karaoke and Cold Lazarus* (Channel Four and BBC Records).

21. Milton Friedman (born 1912) is an American economist, particularly associated with the concept of monetarism and a forceful advocate of free market capitalism.

22. All quotations from the lecture are cited by 'John Heliemann: Can the BBC Be Saved?' (<www.wired.com/wired/2.03/features/bbc.html>). For a review of the lecture see 'Home Truths', *Broadcast*, August 1989. For futher information on Murdoch see 'The Rupert Murdoch Information Page' on <www.cusn.edu/~kab42291/>.

23. Murdoch has now controversially spread his empire towards China. In the UK, Murdoch owns the *Times*, *Sunday Times*, *Sun*, *News of the World*, *Times Educational Supplement*, *Times Higher Educational Supplement*, *Times Literary Supplement*, *Times Scottish Education Supplement*, *Trader*, *Sky Television*, *Sky News*, *Sky Movies*, *Sky One*, *Eurosport*, *Sky Radio*, as well as several publishing houses and a number of other operations.

24. This is a quotation from A. E. Housman's *A Shropshire Lad*, a section of which Potter recites with great pathos at the end of *Blue Remembered Hills*.

25. Potter's work abounds with Romantic allusions. The name of Emma Porlock (one of the leading British scientists) may also refer to Coleridge's writing of *Kubla Khan* in which the poet is awoken from an opium dream 'by a person on business from Porlock'.

26. Potter made no bones about his dislike of the term 'postmodernism'. 'In the long, grey, ebb tide of so-named Post-modernism', he wrote in 1984, 'pseudo-totalitarian, illiberal, and dehumanising theories and practices lie on top of the cold waters like a huge and especially

filthy oil slick' (Dennis Potter [1984]), *Waiting for the Boat: On Television*, Faber & Faber: London: 26).

27. According to Chris Baldick, postmodern fiction such as Thomas Pynchon's *Gravity's Rainbow* (1973) and Vladimir Nabokov's *Ada* (1969) 'employ devices reminiscent of science fiction, playing with contradictory orders of reality or the irruption of the fabulous into the secular world' (1990: 175).

28. In *Blade Runner* (a film generally regarded by critics as typically 'postmodern') the 'replicants' (androids who are apparently 'more human than human') are provided with memory implants which artificially give them a sense of their own history and individual identity. However, as a number of them gradually find out, their identity is fundamentally illusory and artificially induced.

29. Because Daniel's memory does not present events in a logical and chronological manner, we are given the past through a series of typically Potteresque 'flashbacks' and 'flash forwards'. The distortion of memory is also emphasised by Daniel appearing as a child yet played by a fully grown man, a technique Potter originally employed in *Stand Up, Nigel Barton* and *Blue Remembered Hills*.

30. This phrase has been used by several contemporary commentators to suggest that the project of a 'single' history has come to an end. See, for example, Francis Fukuyama (1992).

31. According to Anthony Weymouth, public service broadcasters have been '[a]cting simultaneously as entertainers, interpreters of events, and ... ', offering '... to the peoples of Europe a mediated reflection of themselves as national communities'(Weymouth and Lamizet, 1996: 11).

32. It was for *The Wednesday Play* that Potter began writing television drama. In Britain in the early 1960s there were only two television channels (BBC2 was introduced in 1964), making it much easier for a television programme to become a 'national event'.

3 SERIAL KILLERS
Murder, Masculinity and the Reinvention of the Crime Genre

INTRODUCTION

> Throughout history people like us had to use existing structures and make them work for us as best we can. If forced to work in a particular genre, then we must try to subvert it, or put new wine in old bottles, or find other ways of creating 'Trojan Horse drama'.
>
> Tony Garnett (cited by Cooke, 2003: 162)

Genre is a French word meaning 'type' or 'kind'. Put crudely, genre studies argue that literature, theatre, film and television can be broken down into different 'types' or 'kinds', i.e. a group of texts can be linked together by similar generic characteristics. In theatre, different genres might come under the headings of 'tragedy', 'farce' and 'melodrama'; in cinema they might include the 'musical', the 'Western' and the 'horror film'; while in television we might find 'soap opera', 'situation comedy' and 'news and current affairs' (see Creeber, 2001c). Few theorists would argue that these categories are rigid constructions, accepting that many texts might not fit into only one or any category at all. In fact, generic hybridisation and the creation of subgenres (such as 'tragicomedy' in theatre or the 'docusoap' in television) is a fundamental and necessary part of the process by which genres continually adapt and evolve over time (see Turner, 2001). However, most critics agree that genre classification is a fundamental way in which audiences organise and understand both media and art forms. As Steve Neale puts it (2001: 1):

> In many cases, of course, it is likely that audiences will have some idea in advance of the kind of film (or play or programme) they are going to watch or, if their preferences dictate, to avoid it. They will have done so on the basis of information supplied by advertising, by reviews and previews, perhaps a title (*Singin' in the Rain*) or by the presence of particular performers. They are therefore likely to bring with them a set of expectations, and to anticipate that these will be met in one way or another.

Consequently, genre-based texts have often been treated with suspicion by many critics, their formulaic narrative structures somehow suggesting an overly manufactured and manipulative text (see Feuer, 1992: 145). Films, plays or programmes that appear to adhere to a rigid generic format may therefore be seen as intrinsically less experimental, innovative and challenging than other less genre-based texts. In the *Film Genre Reader*, for example, Barry Keith Grant writes that genre movies are 'commercial feature films' that established 'the popular sense of cinema as a cultural and economic institution, particularly in the United States, where Hollywood studios early on adopted an industrial model based on mass production' (1986: ix). This connection with industrial mass production is revealing, implicitly suggesting that genre-based Hollywood, i.e. 'commercial' rather than 'avant-garde', films are processed (mainly for 'economic' reasons) much as a factory might produce tins of baked beans or cars.[1] This may explain the dismissive perception many people seem to have about television as a whole, regarding it not as a medium of artistic integrity but one that endlessly revamps and renews tried and tested formats.

Despite these perceptions, audiences clearly seem to respond to the recognisable forms imbedded in many genres. As Nicholas Abercrombie puts it, '... part of the pleasure is knowing what the genre rules are, knowing that the programme has to solve problems in the genre framework, and wondering how it is going to do so' (1996: 43). This is certainly true of the police or detective drama on television. From the days of *Dixon of Dock Green* (BBC, 1955–76) and *Dragnet* (NBC, 1952–8), through to *Murder, She Wrote* (CBS, 1984–6) and *Inspector Morse* (Central, 1987–93), much of the joy of watching these types of shows is knowing and expecting the kind of formula it will follow.

In a traditional detective story, the viewer will expect an 'enigma' to be enacted or revealed at the beginning (usually a serious crime, most commonly murder). This is generally followed by a police or detective investigation that comes across a number of clues, suspects and frequently one or two diversions ('red herrings') to heighten and develop the narrative suspense. The drama will then come towards its conclusion when the police or detective reveal 'who done it'. Finally, resolution is achieved with the capture and arrest of the criminal(s). As the literary critic Jonathan Culler explains, the success of this resolution also depends on the plot being explained within the bounds of logic and rationality (1975: 148):

> The detective story is a particularly good example of the force of genre conventions: the assumption that characters are psychologically intelligible, that the crime has a solution which will eventually be revealed, that the relevant evidence will be given but that the solution will be of some complexity, are all essential to the enjoyment of such [texts] ... It is only at the level of the solution that coherence is required: everything deviant and suspicious must be explained by the resolution which produces the key to the 'real' pattern ...

However, generic texts can also produce pleasure by upsetting and contesting such expectations. As seen in the previous chapter, much of the enjoyment of *Twin Peaks* stemmed from its refusal to fulfil the narrative requirements of the traditional detective story. It began predictably enough in classic detective genre style with the discovery of a dead body (Laura Palmer) and the arrival of a detective (in the form of FBI Special Agent Cooper). However, both the methods of deduction employed by the detective (for example, his bizarre use of dream analysis and Tibetan philosophy) and the revelation of the murderer as Laura's father (possessed by the evil spirit BOB), refused to adhere to the conventional notions of logic and rationality upon which the detective story is traditionally founded. However, it is interesting to note that once Laura's murderer had been revealed, the audience ratings began quite a steady decline (see Lavery, 1995: 2–3). Although viewers had been led to believe that they were watching a detective story, when the central enigma (i.e. 'Who killed Laura Palmer?') was resolved, audience interest quickly waned (see Dolan, 1995: 30–50). What this suggests then, is that, although viewers are frequently happy to have their generic expectations undermined, when that generic subversion becomes too pronounced, many viewers will abandon the narrative trajectory altogether (see Chapter Two).

As this suggests, a primary element by which genre produces pleasure is by both fulfilling and undermining viewer expectations. If all detective stories were identical then the genre would soon become redundant. However, if there is too much interference with generic expectations then frequently the narrative dynamics by which pleasure is produced are in danger of being lost altogether. So while subtle variations of the police or detective genre are desirable – such as, putting the detective in a wheelchair (*Ironside* [NBC, 1967–75]), replacing male detectives with female detectives (*Cagney and Lacey* [CBS, 1981–8]) or revealing who did the crime at the beginning of the story rather than at the end (*Columbo* [NBC, 1971–7]) – many of the traditional elements of the genre must remain intact if the viewer's generic pleasure is not to be completely removed.

However, this is not just a matter of changing generic tropes in order to retain a sense of novelty (although that is crucial). Genre reinvention is also an important means by which art and the media can reflect and respond to changes in cultural practice and public opinion at large. While we may have once accepted the notion of the policeman as a friendly, trustworthy and kindly figure at the time of *Dixon of Dock Green*, by the 1970s and 1980s audiences needed and demanded programmes like *The Sweeney* (ITV, 1975–82) and *Hill Street Blues* that depicted the police as ambiguous, fallible and sometimes even dishonest figures. Genres develop over time to keep pace with and sometimes even influence public attitudes and opinions. As Leo Braudy has put it (cited by Lavery, 1995: 13):

> Genre films essentially ask the audience, 'Do you still want to believe this?' Popularity is the audience answering, 'Yes'. Change in genre occurs when the audience says, 'That's too infantile a form of what we believe. Show us something more complicated'. And genres turn to self-parody to say, 'Well, at least if we can make fun of it for being infantile, it will show how far we've come'. Films and television have in this way speeded up cultural history.

In this chapter then, I aim to show how genre is not simply the domain of 'mass-produced' and 'formulaic' television drama. Despite the fact that a more 'market-orientated' television landscape generally produces and demands more genre-specific programmes, I will argue that there is always room within generic-based forms to produce new, challenging and original texts. While some critics argue that genre-based programming follows a strictly predictable and repetitious format, I aim to show how subtle variations of genre can also help to keep those genre conventions fresh, relevant and even socially challenging. In order to keep this discussion focused and within certain genre boundaries I will therefore concentrate my analysis on the 'crime genre'. Although the crime genre includes such a varied array of programmes as the police and detective show, the gangster drama and the police procedural, I hope that it enables this particular discussion to draw parallels and comparisons between other generic-based dramas in a useful and insightful manner. However, although this discussion may be specific to these particular types of programmes, I hope it can be applied more generally to the notion and interpretation of contemporary television genre as a whole.

Prime Suspect (Granada, 1991–)[2]

> – what kind of tales did men tell men,
> She wonder'd by themselves?
>
> Lord Alfred Tennyson, *The Princess* (Tennyson, 1969: 749)

Prime Suspect is a British crime drama that, on its surface, concerns the hardships and difficulties a woman officer faces in the traditionally masculine world of the London Metropolitan Police. Like its television predecessors – *Police Woman* (NBC, 1974–81), *The Gentle Touch* (ITV, 1980–4), *Juliet Bravo* (BBC, 1980–5) and *Cagney and Lacey* – its female detective encounters institutional and personal discrimination in her day-to-day duties; forced to fight both criminals and entrenched male chauvinism in her pursuit of justice and equality. Written by Lynda La Plante and directed by Christopher Menaul, the first *Prime Suspect* miniseries (consisting of two, two-hour episodes shown on consecutive evenings) was made by Granada Television and originally broadcast in Britain on 7 and 8 April 1991. Renowned for its high-production values, it continued and developed many aspects of the original police genre while also breaking new ground in its graphic realism and its close attention to squalor, violence and police practice.

La Plante's first big hit as a writer came with *Widows* (1983), a successful British television series about a group of women who turn their hands to bank robbery. *Prime Suspect* similarly inverted a traditionally masculine story/genre, placing a woman at the head of a homicide team in pursuit of a sadistic serial killer. As part of her research, La Plante shadowed a real-life female Detective Chief Inspector (DCI), observing autopsies, interviewing killers and getting to know her subject over a matter of months (see Hayward and Rennert, 1996: 108–9).[3] Played by Helen Mirren, the fictional DCI Jane Tennison quickly became something of a modern icon, her unusual mixture of ambition and vulnerability producing a complex female character that quickly set a benchmark for the portrayal of women on the small screen.

According to La Plante, the reason she started writing was because she quickly became frustrated with the type of roles she was being given as a television actress. As she told Sean Day-Lewis, 'The process of television casting is so strange. You could play Ophelia at the Royal Shakespeare, or star as Hedda Gabler at the National, and when you went up for a television part they would … invite you to read the two-line part of a prostitute from Liverpool anyway' (cited by Day-Lewis, 1998: 81). Indeed, it was playing a prostitute (preposterously called 'Juanita') in London Weekend's female police series *The Gentle Touch*, that decided La Plante, as she puts it, 'to write something better' (ibid: 81).

Seen in this light, perhaps Jane Tennison's investigation into the prostitute serial killer George Marlow (John Bowe), may partly be seen as a critical exposé of a type of genre that La Plante felt demeaned and devalued its female characters. In fact, on close viewing one can begin to see that the drama begins typically enough, as many crime films and television police shows had done in the past, only to have its traditional genre conventions gradually and subtly undermined and investigated by the presence of its female protagonist.

At its start then, there seems little to distinguish *Prime Suspect* from a host of television crime stories from the past. In particular, fans of *The Sweeney*'s Jack Regan (John Thaw) will certainly recognise the masculine figure of DCI John Shefford (John Forgeham), a tough, macho and hard-living detective, his bullying and belligerent persona an Identikit picture of previous fictional male detectives. 'Fished' out of a nightclub at two in the morning, he typically arrives at the scene of the crime dishevelled and puffing on a large cigar. As Regan was tightly bonded to his younger partner George Carter (Dennis Waterman), so Shefford also seems closer to his righthand man Bill Otley (Tom Bell) than his own wife and son (whose birthday we see him celebrate only on the telephone). Like the long-suffering Frank Haskins (Garfield Morgan) in *The Sweeney*, Shefford's superior also has difficulties containing his detective's unorthodox style of policing.

The Sweeney: hard-boiled TV detectives

While Alan Clarke traces such a portrayal back to Clint Eastwood's 'man with no name' (Clarke, 1986: 220), the critic Geoffrey Hurd goes back further to suggest an even longer literary and filmic ancestry. According to Hurd (1981: 61):

> the bureaucratic, authoritarian, father-figure of Haskins, and the sibling, pupil-figure of Carter serve, in their different ways, as supports that sharpen the image of Regan as the tough individualistic, freebooting cop, an image that finds its fictional heritage in the 'hard-boiled' detectives of American crime writers and the gangster thriller movies of the 1930s and 1940s.

Shefford then, is meant to embody the hard-boiled, film-noir hero that, as Frank Krutnik points out, involves 'an emphatic process of masculinisation', creating a breed of men who are 'tough, cynical, epigrammatic' and 'controlled' (1991: 42). Like Jack Regan before him, he is bluntly spoken, fundamentally proletarian and contemptuous of all social pretensions. 'Right', he tells Otley at the police station, 'his girlfriend states he was at home the time that Della Mornay was murdered. Tough bitch and won't be budged. Plus that lawyer got her out of here faster than a fart.' Inevitably, he helps create a strong homosocial environment inside the station, a world seemingly fuelled by wisecracks, cans of lager, sandwiches and cigarette smoke (later, a boxing match is arranged in his honour). When we discover that he was sexually involved with the prostitute whose murder he is currently investigating, he joins a long list of detectives for whom work and pleasure were often dangerously mixed.

To complement Shefford's 'hard-boiled' persona, Christopher Menaul's direction of *Prime Suspect 1* is suitably 'neo-noir' with its dark streets, low-key lighting and claustrophobic settings. The opening of the drama sees Shefford arrive at the scene of the murder; the wet urban location, cramped interiors and dimly lit street are certainly reminiscent of the genre as a whole. Set in silence without an opening soundtrack, the murky shadows, the frequently inaudible dialogue and the butchered female corpse would not seem out of place in a contemporary 'neo-noir' film like *Chinatown* (Polanski, 1974) or *Se7en* (Fincher, 1996). Even the opening extreme high-angle long shot suggests a noir world where people are at the mercy of dangerous and overpowering forces. As Place and Peterson suggest in their analysis of the genre, such a shot is the 'archetypal noir composition . . . an oppressive and fatalistic angle that looks down on its helpless victim to make it look like a rat in a maze' (Place and Peterson, 1996: 68).[4]

This noir sense of oppression is perhaps emphasised by the serial's initial use of washed-out colours, particularly the proliferation of stark grey, pale green and the occasional dingy yellow. Only when Shefford and Otley dress for the examination of a corpse do they wear white, but even then the colour looks faded rather than brilliant. Before arriving at the autopsy room they are briefly framed by a small rectangular window as they talk into a telephone, the thick reinforced glass giving them both a murky or submerged appearance that suits the opening's dimly lit aesthetic. Similarly, when Marlow's aggressive wife (Zoë Wanamaker) first answers the door to the police, she is shot like a typical 'moll' or 'vamp', the dark shadows that frame her face suggestive of dangerous and clandestine worlds. Indeed, it is this distinctive use of light and darkness which, according to Place and Peterson, most distinguishes the visual motifs of film noir (1996: 66):

> Unlike the illumination of high-key lighting which seeks to display attractively all the areas of the frame, the low-key noir style opposes light and dark, hiding faces, rooms, urban landscapes – and, by extension, motivations and true character – in shadow and darkness which carry connotations of the mysterious and unknown.

The use of a shaky hand-held camera (probably a Steadicam) also adds to the graphic and unsettling sense of realism. Following Shefford up the stairs of the murdered prostitute's flat the lightweight camera is left to emphasise the shadowy claustrophobic interior of the cramped stairway and lonely bedsit. Similarly, Steven Warbecks' score is suitably understated, gradually building from the silence of the opening credits into an ominous background 'pulse' which adds to an underlying sense of anxiety.

Added to this implicit sense of an earlier noir sensibility is, of course, the name of the suspected serial killer, George Marlow. By giving him such a strikingly similar name to that of Raymond Chandler's hard-boiled detective (only an 'e' is missing at the end of his surname), La Plante seems to be suggesting the story's explicit connection with film noir and the 'hard-boiled' tradition as a whole. The name Marlow (also without an 'e') also implicitly connects the serial with Dennis Potter's *The Singing Detective*, a piece of television drama also concerned with misogyny, detection and the dark nature of male sexuality (see Creeber, 1998: 149–89). Indeed, on close inspection, it is striking how many psychological similarities these two characters actually share. In particular, both possess an unusually close relationship with their mother and an unhealthy view of the opposite sex.[5] Written by Guy Hibbert, *Prime Suspect 4: The Scent of Darkness* picks up on these implicit connections. It is here that we discover the root of George Marlow's sexual anxieties for, like Potter's protagonist, he accidentally witnesses his mother's sexual adultery in early childhood. Like Potter's Marlow, it is a traumatic event that will determine much of his life, particularly his twisted view of and relationship with the opposite sex, leading to an unhealthy obsession with prostitutes.[6] In an argument with her partner, Tennison even explicitly refers to Potter's earlier drama. 'She might be a lousy detective', she cries, 'but she was a good shag. The Shagging Detective!'

There is also mention of an unseen DCI Hickock. The similarity between this name and that of a famous British film director is also hard to ignore, especially when one considers that a film like *Psycho* (Hitchcock, 1960) has become a classic case study of feminist film theory.[7] Like Potter, Hitchcock's use of fetishised and violent images of women was also frequently set within a deeply Oedipal and masculinised narrative point of view. As John Caughie has put it, 'In [Potter's] peculiar and obsessive mixture of guilt and redemption, repression and excess, sexual fear and sexual aggression, he seems at least psychically related to that other great English artist with his roots in modernism: Alfred Hitchcock' (2000: 176). What these implicit allusions to an earlier masculine tradition of writing suggest, is that *Prime Suspect* is explicitly and self-consciously aware of the type of narrative and genre tradition with which it is engaged. In particular, it plays on and alludes to television and cinema genres of the past, re-negotiating and re-investigating the means by which the classic crime story (as a traditional narrative form) has tended to construct notions of gender, genre and masculinity. Jane Tennison may not completely clean up Chandler's 'mean streets', but she does gradually accumulate enough evidence to put Marlow in the dock, forcing the jury (and, in the process, the audience) to finally reflect on his (and perhaps even the genre's) crimes against women.

How *Prime Suspect* gradually begins to investigate this earlier genre tradition is in the slow arrival of Jane Tennison into this typically masculine environment. At first she is pushed to the margins of the story, observing but never participating in this seemingly traditional narrative. When Shefford and two male colleagues accidentally join her in an elevator, Tennison is literally pushed to its rear; obscured from the view of the camera and almost physically obliterated by the male bodies. Shefford intensifies this domination by staring at her briefly but intimidatingly, laughing to his colleagues as she makes her way out. Later we see her isolated figure staring out of a window as Shefford and his band of men get in a car to arrest their suspect. We watch from her point of view as the car screeches its way out of the depot in a sequence reminiscent of the type of car chases that so characterised *The Sweeney* and *Starsky and Hutch* (ABC, 1976–81).[8]

In contrast, Tennison is initially placed within her domestic space, seen preparing dinner for her partner and anxious about the arrival of his young son from a previous marriage. But her name has possible literary allusions that suggest that the true nature of Tennison's role will be gradually revealed. The poet Lord Alfred Tennyson was the author of *The Princess* (1848), a tale of androgyny and women's rights which, as the literary critic Rebecca Scott puts it, 'concerns the enforcement of women's expulsion within the framework of male homosocial exchange' (1996: 19). For it is this female 'expulsion' from a tight-knit homosocial world which is the real subject of *Prime Suspect*.

When Shefford suddenly dies of a heart attack the case is, at her insistence, reluctantly handed over to Tennison who had been consistently overlooked in the past. As the pale and dying Shefford is carried out of the station on a stretcher, she is seen walking in, as if the genre were being handed over like a 'baton' from the old school to the new. As a result, her difficult and uncomfortable position within the narrative can be seen partly as the space through which two opposing generic forces fight it out for dominance and possible control. While her investigation calls into question the very attitudes and procedures that characterised Shefford's handling of the case, it also highlights the problems and the fundamental inequalities of a genre that Shefford and Marlow are meant to represent. In this way, Tennison's investigation of the serial murders becomes an explicit investigation of genre, her determination to solve the Marlow case both an attempt to reveal the dynamics of an inherently masculine tradition and an attempt to assert and redefine her own feminine power and control.

This 'deconstruction' of the traditional masculine narrative is alluded to visually even before Tennison's acceptance of the murder case. Her short blonde hair, lightly coloured suits and ubiquitous white blouse seem to act as an immediate contrast to her generally black-suited and dark-featured colleagues. Even her partner's ex-wife seems surprised by her feminine and relatively casual appearance, expecting her to be in uniform. 'I should have worn a flat hat', is Tennison's sarcastic reply. While we see nothing of Shefford's home, Tennison's is bathed in golden brown and orange, fresh flowers and bright lights offering a stark contrast with the drama's opening low-key lighting and dingy aesthetic. This shock of colour and light is emphasised when Tennison accidentally drops chocolate cake on her white blouse, suggesting the difficulties of combining the rigour of a career with her traditionally feminine role, but also transforming her official dress into an object of domestic use and pleasure.

Nowhere is the contrast between these two worlds more pronounced than in Tennison's first anxious confrontation with the policemen she has inherited from Shefford. In vivid contrast to her light brown suit and white blouse, nearly all the men are dressed formally in black suit and tie (although it is not made clear, it seems to be the day of Shefford's funeral). Like extras from a Tarantino film they provide a dense wall of masculine resistance, embodying the sense of 'darkness' and 'shadow' which so characterised film noir and more recent gangster movies like *Reservoir Dogs* (Tarantino, 1992). In this way, the visual aesthetic initially and convincingly constructed by the serial's opening fifteen minutes, is subtly and carefully undermined by Tennison's emergence. While her constant cigarette smoke may suggest iconographic echoes of the classic *femme fatale*, her short blonde hair and her association with light and pale-coloured clothing suggest a female figure who is determined to dismantle the visual stereotypes of the past. Although her character offers a clear danger to male power, her visual image is not of the dark 'spider woman', but of a confident and assured heroine whose bright and illuminating appearance refuses to be contained by the traditional restrictions of the male text.

If Tennison refuses the role of classic *femme fatale*, then so do the other 'working women' she encounters. Indeed, the fictional prostitutes in *Prime Suspect* are a long way from the sort of stereotypical 'vamps' and 'whores' that characterise male fantasy.[9] For while Dennis Potter's prostitutes tended to simply symbolise the dark and twisted psychology of his central male protagonists, La Plante attempts to bring a greater realism to her women generally. Tennison is even mistaken for a prostitute in the course of her investigations, suggesting an implicit identification between this group of women and this confident female detective.[10] Ironically, Detective Otley's repeated description of Tennison as a 'tart', further enforces this implicit relationship. In contrast, Shefford's all-male team tend to dehumanise the prostitutes, seeing them simply as informants, sex objects or 'slags'. 'We clean the streets up', says one policeman, 'and back they come like rodents.'

However, Tennison's ability to perceive the victims as 'real women' (an insight gained by La Plante's meetings with real prostitutes in the course of her research), enables her to glean unique insights into the Marlow case. She appears to connect and empathise with the women in a way unimaginable by most of the men. As a real policewoman told Mary Eaton, 'We got on very well with the girls, I think because we saw the female aspect of it ... we could identify with them being in a real predicament' (1995:

171). Indeed, it is her refusal to stereotype or objectify both the living and dead prostitutes she encounters that gradually distinguishes Tennison from an earlier genre tradition, and which also finally helps her to solve the case. As Yvonne Tasker puts it (1998: 94):

> Helen Mirren's character ... succeeds in part because she deems prostitutes worth speaking to and values their dead bodies (as worth investigating). The prostitute is more than simply a backdrop to the crime narrative, recurring as a central figure who articulates in class terms the confluence of working woman and sexuality, returning us to the complex connotations of the 'working girl'.

In this way, *Prime Suspect* goes a considerable way in carefully unravelling the very dynamics through which the traditional male narrative appears to be initially motivated and maintained. Indeed, Tennison's detective techniques explicitly uncover and reveal the dynamics by which the murder case (as partly representative of a wider masculine genre) is decoded and gradually deconstructed. Her understanding and respect for the prostitutes and her refusal to turn them into sexualised or objectified objects, finally enable her to solve the crime and perhaps even re-interrogate the genre in which she unconsciously acts. In contrast, the male detectives belong to a tradition of detection that is no longer able to successfully uncover the true identity of the murderer or the victims.

Yet despite these feminist aspirations, *Prime Suspect* was criticised for its inability to actually re-invent or subvert the inherent dynamics of the traditionally masculine police series. Writing in 1987, Gillian Dyer voiced concern about the female cop show generally, arguing that 'Women police series are not necessarily progressive and that the "feminism" is usually personalised and depoliticised ...', failing to 'question the aesthetics and conventions of the male crime series through which meanings are in part realised' (Baehr and Dyer, 1987: 10). In particular, attention has been paid to Jane Tennison's apparent 'masculinisation', as if the price of her success has been at the expense of her 'femininity'; the traditional male crime genre left virtually undisturbed by a woman detective who acts 'like a man'. As Mary Eaton puts it, 'Close inspection shows that the triumphs achieved by Jane Tennison are brought at a high price; a successful detective but not a successful woman' (1995: 175).

Indeed, Tennison famously swears, drinks and smokes, her ruthless determination to crack the murder case bordering on an aggressive and almost 'masculine' obsession. At one point she continues to interview the father of a murdered girl when it is obvious that he is in no state to answer questions; her male companion is forced to physically pull her away from the grief-stricken man. Reminiscent of Shefford, even the birthday of a close family member is quickly relegated in importance to her police work. Arriving late for her own father's party, she becomes angry and abusive when she discovers that he has failed to properly record her first television appearance. Like numerous male detectives before her, she also seems unable to sustain a successful home life or relationship, the job finally becoming more important than any other aspect of her life. In this way, Tennison appears, on the surface, to be a very different (*feminised*) detective, but on greater scrutiny is acting no differently than her male predecessors. According to Charlotte Brunsdon, the drama thereby carries out a careful 'balancing act' which inscribes (1998: 232):

> a story about sexual discrimination, with its implicit liberal/feminist address, into what we might call the smoking-and-drinking end of the television police genre, with its explicitly tabloid and masculine address ... the series explicitly addresses fans of the crime genre through its condensation of procedures and reworking of familiar tropes. Like Jane's lads, some large part of the audience is assumed to be drinking lager and smoking while watching.

But Tennison is arguably more than simply Philip Marlowe or Jack Regan in drag. Although apparently 'masculinised' by many aspects of her career, it is her fundamentally *feminine* traits that gradually bring about the end of Marlow's killing spree. Indeed, the success of Tennison's detection is carefully attributed to traditionally feminine characteristics, evidently not accessible to her male colleagues.

She solves the Marlow case using not only masculine aggression and determination, but also feminine insight. As Brunsdon points out, Tennison's understanding of female clothing and the crucial evidence she discovers by taking time to have a drink with the prostitutes, is vital to solving the murders. Similarly, her female constable's insight into the relevance of the victim's false nails also helps (see Brunsdon, 1998: 223–4). Indeed, it is arguable whether Marlow's wife finally opens up to Tennison because of her gender, asking to be left alone with her to reveal incriminating evidence. As this reveals, Tennison actually relies on both her traditionally 'feminine' and traditionally 'masculine' skills and characteristics in order to crack the case. Open to both a 'masculine' and 'feminine' point of view, the case is eventually dealt with more satisfactorily than if only one particular mind-set was employed.

For, although Tennison may be prepared to forsake aspects of her femininity when necessary, she clearly and quickly enforces limits when not. 'My voice suddenly got lower?' she sarcastically asks a male colleague who insists on calling her *sir*. 'Maybe my knickers are too tight? Listen, I like to be called Governor or the Boss.' While it would be naive to suggest that the choice of the actress Helen Mirren to play Tennison was not based partly on her attractiveness, it did make the character less easy to stereotype or dismiss as simply 'butch' and 'unfeminine'.[11] Indeed, so concerned were the producers with her retaining her 'feminine side' that whole scenes were actually dropped which, to La Plante's dismay, were thought to make her too 'masculine'.[12]

In this respect, an interesting comparison can be made between Tennison and a female character like Clarice Starling (Jodie Foster) in *The Silence of the Lambs*, directed by Jonathan Demme and also released in 1991. Like Tennison, Starling is a woman-hero or, as Carol J. Clover puts it, a 'Final Girl', whose ability to transcend traditional femininity plays a crucial role in her eventual victory against the 'male monster' (see Clover, 1999: 234–50 and Staiger, 1999: 214). Indeed, the adjectives used to describe Starling by publicity material for the film ('gutsy', 'tenacious', 'sturdy', 'tough', 'resourceful', 'persistent', 'ambitious' and 'driven') could easily be (and have been) applied to Tennison (cited by Staiger, 1999: 222).

Prime Suspect: an investigation into gender and genre

But do such portrayals necessarily 'masculinise' characters or do they reveal ways in which traditional mainstream television and cinema can successfully interrogate gender identities? Ironically, Foster's public 'outing' during the film's release may unintention-ally echo Otley's sexist description of Tennison as a 'dyke', as if a strong female character cannot, by definition, possibly retain her heterosexual desirability (ibid: 210–11). For critics like Amy Taubin, a hugely popular film such as *The Silence of the Lambs* suggests that sexuality and sexual 'role fantasies *can* be exhumed and examined, and that their meanings can be shifted' (cited by ibid: 217). According to Julie Salmon, Starling is simply 'an attractive woman of unexceptional size doing what used to be thought of as a man's job. ... She is a rare heroine, a woman who goes about her work the way men do in the movies, without seeming less a woman' (cited by ibid: 217).

If, as such narrative implications suggest, the real 'prime suspect' of La Plante's screenplay is the classically masculine narrative; then it must be seen as dramatising a bold and far-reaching generic struggle. By breaking into the homosocial world from which she was once denied, Tennison does not simply take on the 'language of the lads' (Brunsdon, 1989: 234), for the process is clearly a two-way exchange. The large bouquet of flowers she is presented with at the end of the serial suggests that she has won the respect of the men she leads *on her own terms*, not by simply becoming *one of them*. Ten-nison may be more 'hard-boiled' than many of her female predecessors, but it is her *difference* from the men which gradually helps her to solve the case and decode the very genre that she so skilfully inhabits. As much as some critics might dislike many of the 'masculine' characteristics she is forced to adopt as a successful woman in a principally male domain, it reflects a world in which traditionally gendered stereotypes are now perhaps as outdated and outmoded as the image of the community policeman in *Dixon of Dock Green*. If Tennison's project is to re-investigate the 'hard-boiled' tradition of the past, then it should come as no surprise that in doing so she must both assimilate and deconstruct parts of the very genre she so carefully employs.

As a result, the gender reversal offered by Tennison's role as detective suggests a world where the whole dynamic of the traditional masculine narrative is not only undermined but also transformed. She symbolises a visual contrast to Shefford's 'mean streets', a figure free of masculine anxiety and sexual angst, she offers a glint of light into a world traditionally bathed in darkness. When she celebrates the conviction of Marlow with her male colleagues, the fizzy champagne covers her and all the male officers with white froth and light, the flowers she is given are a symbolic triumph of the 'natural' and the 'feminine' over the 'urban', 'masculine' and neo-noir world she inevitably inherited. 'Personally', says Potter's Philip Marlow in *The Singing Detective*, 'I don't want to walk down no mean streets, not me. But there's no money in picking bluebells – Am I right? Or am I right?' (Potter, 1986: 246). Tennison is not interested in picking bluebells either, but the men she leads do finally reward her with flowers, both for her success as a police officer and in recognition of her femininity. In doing so, she inevitably takes on aspects of the genre she has inherited but also appears to transform and reinvent it for a contemporary audience whose idea of the police genre was in desperate need of transformation.

Cracker (Granada, 1993–6)[13]

> Feminism pathologised masculinity in a way hitherto unprecedented, and lay at its door guilt and responsibility for everything from nuclear war and pollution, to rape, incest and high heels.
>
> Rowena Chapman (1988: 226)

Cracker first appeared on British television screens on ITV in 1993, running periodically until the last one-off special in 1996.[14] Usually divided into two-part or three-part storylines (there were ten complete stories in total), the series quickly built a regular audience of around fourteen million and won numerous awards, Robbie Coltrane picking up a BAFTA for Best Actor for his portrayal of Edward 'Fitz' Fitzgerald two years running. Originally written and conceived by Jimmy McGovern, the drama has generally been regarded as his creation. However, although he provided the scripts for the whole of the first series, stories from the second series and the one-off special were also written separately by Paul Abbott (originally a producer on the series) and Ted Whitehead.[15] But whether written by McGovern, Abbott or Whitehead (a long line of directors included Michael Winterbottom, Andy Wilson and Roy Battersby), the series was praised for its attempt at re-interpreting the traditional male detective and, in particular, his re-positioning within a contemporary and increasingly morally ambiguous world.

First broadcast only three years after *Prime Suspect*, *Cracker* also came out of a time of transformation for the conventional crime drama. However, while *Prime Suspect* controversially inserted a female senior police officer into the terrain of the traditional detective series, *Cracker* seemed intent on re-instating the hard-drinking, hard-living male protagonist back at the centre of this traditionally masculine genre. By tackling subjects such as racism, homosexuality, rape and serial killing, it quickly achieved a reputation for dealing with controversial and socially uncomfortable subjects. And it was probably the enigmatic figure of Fitz (not only his confrontational interrogation of male psychology but also the troubled terrain of his personal life) that became the primary focus of the drama. Not a traditional detective, his role as a forensic psychologist was to present psychological profiles for the Greater Manchester Police Force. Indeed, it was his almost 'Holmesian' ability to get inside the head of a criminal that made him such an ambivalent character; a detective who, one suspects, used his own dark turmoil to understand how to decode or 'crack' the mind of a murderer.

In many ways, Fitz is the dramatic personification of the traditional male detective. Middle-aged and overweight, he has an illicit affair with a female colleague, his wife walks out on him, he drinks six to seven bottles of whisky a week, smokes fifty to sixty cigarettes a day and is a compulsive gambler. 'I like the lows', he explains in a rare trip to Gamblers Anonymous, 'they make the highs seem even higher. Peaks and troughs, mountains and valleys, give me that any day to the long, straight, flat boring road ...' (*To Say I Love You*). Although he seems equipped with a deep-rooted moral compassion, a razor-sharp wit and a prodigious intellect, his appetite for danger and self-destruction is the epitome of traditional masculinity. As Fitz himself so succinctly puts it, 'I drink too much. I smoke too much. I gamble too much. I *am* too much' (*Brotherly Love*).

Although more accurately defined as a police procedural (i.e. he generally works alongside the law rather than outside it), the character of Fitz could be described as the embodiment of the traditional 'hard-boiled' detective. Like *Prime Suspect*'s John Shefford, he is a tough and disillusioned individual, a man who confusingly blurs the distinction between the 'good' and the 'bad' guys. Revealingly, he has a poster of Humphrey Bogart on his wall at home, the cinematic incarnation (he played both Chandler's Philip Marlowe and Dashiell Hammett's Sam Spade) of the hard-boiled tradition. As Edgar Morin points out, Bogart's character suppressed 'the opposition of the odious ex-gangster and the good-policeman-arbiter of justice, proposing instead a new confused and confusing type ... half good, half bad' (1960: 25–6). Not surprisingly, then, Fitz appears to share as many characteristics with the criminals he brushes up against as with the police he works alongside. As Bob Millington points out, such ambivalence was an integral part of the police and detective genre as a whole. According to Millington, in shows like *The Sweeney* (1997: 1603):

> storylines frequently blurred the sharp distinctions that are normally drawn between good and evil characters in crime melodrama. Regan and Carter were shown inhabiting the same sleazy world as the criminals, mixing with low-life to obtain their leads, and adopting the same vernacular. Both law-enforcers and law-breakers indulged in womanising and heavy-drinking ... [using] physical violence to achieve their objectives.

Cracker: a re-investigation of the hard-boiled detective

Like his male predecessors, Fitz is certainly willing to take the law into his own hands
when the police threaten to undermine his fanatical pursuit for truth and justice. When,
in the first story, he is unceremoniously thrown off the case he insists on continuing his
detective work outside the official police investigation. And as Regan had DCI Frank
Haskins to fight and rebel against, so Fitz has DCI David Bilborough (Christopher
Eccleston), a detective whose surname's resemblance to the 1989 Hillsborough disaster
possibly suggests the sheer incompetence at the heart of the British police force.[16] When
Bilborough talks of 'only doing his job', Fitz complains of 'smelling gas ovens and six
million burning corpses' (*To Be a Somebody*).

   As one would expect, Fitz also sacrifices aspects of his personal life for his professional
commitments. According to Alan Clarke, Regan 'never had any time for his wife and his
family, his work always had to come first . . .' sacrificing 'his personal family for the greater
good of us all' (1986: 229). Similarly, Fitz's private life is an unadulterated mess. In particular, his relationship with his wife inevitably suffers as he spends much of his time
(and their money) either at the casino, the dog track, betting office, in the slot machine
or the pub. 'Bitch, harridan, witch . . .' he shouts at her when she finally leaves him,
angrily throwing a 'House for Sale' sign through the rear window of her car (*The Big
Crunch*). The father of two children (a third is born during the second series), he also
clearly sacrifices parenthood for his work and his other addictions, seemingly unable to
face up to the realities of his adult commitments.

   Like his hard-boiled predecessors, Fitz is devoid of any profound or substantial set of
religious or moral beliefs, a modern 'agnostic' in a world apparently bereft of any sig-

nificance or meaning. In particular, he seems to have turned his back on his own religious upbringing. In *Brotherly Love*, for example, the sexual hypocrisy of Catholicism is revealed in a complex plot that mixes Catholic repression and guilt with a number of gruesome serial killings. 'I knew you'd be Catholic', he tells the killer who pays prostitutes to dress up like Shirley Temple. 'Innocence, virginity, Catholicism . . . You have to find somewhere to dump all that lust, all that filth.' Yet despite his angry rejection of faith, the serial reveals a man still not completely free of its powerful and subliminal grip. 'I take it you're a lapsed Catholic', a priest tells him, 'Why? Because you're so serious in your mockery.'

In this context, Fitz is a contemporary personification of the traditional hard-boiled sleuth, a pessimistic and stubborn individual who walks those dark mean streets carrying a festering void where once he carried faith. Cynical, streetwise and faithless, he possesses a heavy, world-weary resignation to the innate inequalities of human life, relying almost wholly on reason to understand and decode the world around him. In this way, he can be seen as an almost perfect embodiment of the 'old' or 'traditional' detective, a 'pre-feminist', *Bogartesque* embodiment of masculinity, sacrificing the personal side of his life for the endless pursuit of truth and his own selfish and hedonistic obsessions.

However, it is apparent early on that this typically hard-boiled detective is forced to live in a world that Bogart would not easily have recognised. In particular, Fitz is forced to deal with a contemporary environment in which traditionally male and female identities are in the process of radical transformation. It is this new landscape of gender relations that Fitz seems particularly ill at ease with, bluntly described by his colleague Jane Penhaligon (Geraldine Somerville), as a 'self-loathing, misogynistic, arrogant sod' (*The Mad Woman in the Attic*). He certainly seems to possess a less than complimentary view of feminism generally. 'I'm greatly in favour of women's movements', he sarcastically explains in *Men Should Weep*, 'I just hate it when they lie there'. In fact, he criticises 'women's studies' early on in the first story, *The Mad Woman in the Attic*, perhaps itself an ironic reference to Gilbert and Gubar's groundbreaking piece of feminist criticism from the late 1970s.[17] As he angrily tells one of his wife's friends having spent the whole dinner drinking double whiskies:

> So you pay this woman three pounds an hour to clean your house so you can go out and teach 'women's studies' for twenty pounds an hour. You don't think that's just a teeny wee bit hypocritical? There's you up on the podium talking about equality, freedom, feminism and she's at home with her arm half way down your lavatory!

The narrative conflict in *Cracker*, then, partly erupts out of Fitz's frequently clumsy attempts to deal with a world altered by feminism. He is surrounded by strong women who constantly criticise his conventional masculine characteristics. Unlike the traditional detective's spouse (audiences, for example, famously never got to meet Mrs Columbo) his wife, Judith (Barbara Flynn), is a strong and powerful figure in the story. Although apparently in love with Fitz, she stands up to him time and time again, refusing to let him get away with his selfish and destructive behaviour. Indeed, her constant rowing with her errant husband proves a crucial and recurring theme in the narrative trajectory as a whole. In *Best Boys*, for example, she forces Fitz to take his new-born child to work when she fails to cope, granting us the pleasure of seeing this overweight sleuth bizarrely feeding his baby with a bottle at the scene of a murder. Eventually she leaves him and goes into therapy, having an affair with her therapist in the process.

Fitz's relationship with his younger, female colleague, Jane Penhaligon, also forces him to try to understand gender relations in an even more contemporary arena. Interestingly, DS Penhaligon shares the same Christian name as her predecessor in *Prime Suspect*, perhaps suggesting a strong, assertive and determined woman.[18] When, for example, she discovers that Fitz is back with his wife, Jane takes advantage of the fact that he doesn't drive to put her foot down on the accelerator and stare at *him* rather than at the road, forcing him to beg her to stop. It is a symbolic gesture that reveals the apparent power and aggression of this younger female. In the first story there is even an explosive encounter between Penhaligon and Fitz in an elevator, reminiscent of the scene in *Prime Suspect* when Tennison is pushed to the rear of an elevator by the dominating presence of John Shefford and his team of male detectives (see above). However, in *Cracker*, Fitz dramatically presses the elevator's emergency button, thereby forcing them to stop between floors. This provocative action literally enables a confrontation to take place between the seemingly 'hard-boiled' sleuth and his younger female colleague, suggesting perhaps the narrative's desire to have Fitz confront this brave new world of liberated women.

Jane's later violent and shocking rape by her colleague, Jimmy Beck (Lorcan Cranitch), confronts the genre issues at the heart of the drama as a whole (as she points out, Fitz's ability to *force* himself into the mind of another person makes him something of an 'emotional rapist' himself [*To Be a Somebody*]). Acting as her own detective (on Fitz's advice, Jane follows up clues such as identifying the type of aftershave worn by her attacker), she finally takes matters into her own hands when her boss fails to act on her accusations. Surprising Beck alone in his flat, she makes him lie on his back, straddles him, forces a seemingly loaded gun into his mouth and tells him to '*suck it*'. This overtly sexualised demonstration of dominance attempts to re-enact the rape, but now places her in the position of power and control. It is an act that subverts the conventional dynamics of the hard-boiled detective, forcing the traditionally 'passive' woman and 'active' man to finally swap places. In this way, Jane consistently puts her self 'on top' or 'in the driving seat' in order to deal with men on an equal footing, a younger woman who is meant to put traditional male values into confusion.

Interestingly, the majority of the crimes investigated by Fitz are the rape and murder of young women. Frequently personal and particularly gruesome, these violent crimes (including Penhaligon's savage rape) act as important symbols of what men can do to the opposite sex, a dark reminder perhaps of the warnings provided by first-wave feminists of the 1960s and 1970s. Rather than identifying such attacks on women as the product of a few psychologically deranged men, radical feminists argued that rape and sexual violence was an inherent (if not biological) component of masculinity itself. As John MacInnes points out, in such a context traditional masculine virtues (those typically associated with the hard-boiled detective) gradually become disturbing and evil vices (1998: 47):

> What were once claimed to be manly virtues (heroism, independence, courage, strength, rationality, will, backbone, virility) have become masculine vices (abuse, destructive aggression, coldness, emotional inarticulacy, detachment, isolation, an inability to be flexible, to communicate, to empathise, to be soft, supportive or life-affirming) . . .

Seen in this context, Fitz dramatically embodies the problems and anxieties that the contemporary male has in accepting and coming to terms with a new version of masculinity. He is forced (partly by his job as a forensic psychologist and partly by his own archetypal characteristics) to continually confront the darkest recesses of the male psyche, particularly in the light of a new 'feminist' agenda. The crime genre particularly has him struggling to accept this new world, a traditional hard-boiled detective compelled to confront a new 'feminist' terrain, one in which the traditional boundaries of 'male' and 'female' identity have become increasingly blurred.

Nowhere is this cultural struggle more apparent than in the way that *Cracker* forces the hard-boiled detective to enter the traditionally 'feminine' world of the domestic space. Rather than clearly separating what Alan Clarke refers to as the 'masculine' world of work and the 'feminine' world of home (1986: 229), Fitz is violently pushed into the domestic sphere, his private life is a *central* element of each storyline. Indeed, this sleuth is reluctantly but constantly made to confront matters of a personal nature, forced to deal with a pot-smoking adolescent son, an estranged daughter, a raped mistress and an unhappy wife.

As a result, *Cracker* appears to create much of its narrative tension by incorporating and juxtaposing two distinct narrative genres. As Graeme Burton points out, *Cracker* particularly combines 'the psychology of crime drama' with 'soap characteristics' (2000: 208), constructing a traditional male sleuth and forcing him to face up to the personal and emotional dynamics more commonly associated with soap opera. While horrific murder, rape and violence do take place, the narrative seldom has Fitz studying autopsies or photographs of ravaged female flesh in the same obsessive manner as *Prime Suspect*'s DCI Tennison (see above). Instead, we tend to see him in the betting office, the pub or the casino, maybe dragged to a scene of a crime with a hangover but only staying long enough to produce a quick (albeit remarkably accurate) deduction. If, as Marion Jordan argues, the 'social realist' setting of British soap opera should be 'commonplace and recognisable (the pub, the street, the factory, the home, and more particularly the kitchen)' (1981: 28), then *Cracker* is as much *Coronation Street* (Granada, 1960–) as it is *Chinatown*, as much *Crossroads* (ITV, 1964–88) as it is *Columbo*.

In the opening of the first story, for example, we immediately encounter the hard-boiled detective's uneasy arrival into the domestic sphere. When Fitz comes home looking for money to pay a waiting taxi, the director Michael Winterbottom has a hand-held camera frantically follow him through the chaos of the family maze. The unsteadiness of the camera certainly gives us a sense that Fitz is unable to fully nego-tiate the unfamiliarity of the domestic space, grabbing his bottle of whisky as if it were the only familiar landmark in an unpredictably foreign terrain. This feeling of alienation is further increased by his children's failure to acknowledge his presence, his attempt at communication drowned out by pop music, television and domestic lethargy. Revealingly, Fitz's son is watching the British soap opera *Coronation Street*, perhaps an implicit sym-bol of the 'feminised' world that his father finds so difficult to enter or accept. 'I'll put my foot through that thing' his father angrily tells him as he spies the television with a mixture of rage and suspicion. In this way, we immediately view Fitz as a character unable to cope with the 'soap opera' dimensions of the domestic space, a seemingly hard-boiled sleuth whose own home is a bigger mystery to him than any of the crimes he is employed to investigate. Yet, it is a world he is *forced* to confront and explore, made to face nar-rative situations that his generic predecessors would have traditionally refused to enter or even acknowledge in any depth.

Consequently, *Cracker*'s genre slippage into the domestic world of 'soap opera' is sug-gestive of a traditionally 'masculine' genre being forced into areas normally associated with more traditionally 'feminine' terrain. According to Jane Root, traditional British soap operas like *Crossroads* portrayed 'a women's world, dealing almost exclusively with women's problems and women's stories' (Root, 1986: 67). As a writer on *Brookside* (Chan-nel Four, 1982–2003) for seven years from 1982 to 1989 (providing eighty episodes in total) Jimmy McGovern was aware of the more 'feminised' conventions of the genre. However, as Root pointed out at the time, *Brookside* could be distinguished from other British soap operas of the period by its obvious 'masculinisation'. As Root puts it (ibid: 72):

> *Brookside* is clearly separated from previous British soap operas by powerful, complex male
> characters and masculine stories. Men like Bobby, Barry and Damon Grant and Billy
> Corkhill are very different from the gentlemanly heart-throbs of *Crossroads*. A large number
> of *Brookside*'s plots centre on these men, and their desires and aspirations.

As this reveals, then, McGovern is a writer who feels comfortable mixing traditionally 'feminine' and 'masculine' genres together, perhaps even a writer for whom the mixing of such genre conventions is an important means by which traditional notions of male and female identity can be broken down. Revealingly, McGovern remembers that his scripts for *Brookside* were conceived during 'the height of the feminist movement' (cited by Day-Lewis, 1998: 63). As such, the mixing of more 'masculine' issues and debates within a traditionally 'feminine' genre can be seen as an attempt to articulate the changes taking place in traditional gender patterns as a whole. Talking of *Brookside*'s Bobby Grant (Ricky Tomlinson) (who went on to play DCI Wise in *Cracker*) and Sheila Grant (Sue Johnston), McGovern told Melvyn Bragg that the difficulties behind their relationship lay in the totally separate worlds they lived in. 'I think in his world', he explained, 'it was the world of men, and issues, and the trade union, but in her world . . . it was about faith as well, and family. And there was bound to be a clash ...' (cited by Bragg, 1996). In this way, the *gendered* conflict at the centre of the drama is articulated through the *generic* clash set up by the narrative as a whole.

It is not surprising therefore that McGovern has described Fitz as an 'extension' of Bobby Grant (see Day-Lewis, 1998: 67), both *Brookside* and *Cracker* incorporating a generic conflict between traditionally 'feminine' and 'masculine' narrative genres that reflects a much wider transformation in gender roles as a whole. Both men are certainly at the frontline of the *'feminisation'* of their world, desperately trying to cling onto a set of (traditionally masculine) beliefs and traditions that are gradually and carefully being eroded. When Fitz enters the 'private' world of the home (as he does with surprising frequency), he is forced, like his predecessor Bobby Grant, to confront the limitations and boundaries of his hard-boiled persona; finally made to face up to a world of family, intimacy and emotional responsibility.

'My life's a mess', he finally confesses to Judith in *The Big Crunch*, 'I've fouled up. Emotionally, I'm incompetent.' Although such characteristics are typical of the hard-boiled sleuth, it is not a confession you would expect to hear coming from the mouths of Bogart or Regan, and certainly not one they would easily make to their wives or girlfriends.

The sheer size of the Glaswegian actor Robbie Coltrane (originally a stand-up comedian) adds a further element of instability to the traditional conception of the hard-boiled sleuth. While the unhealthy lifestyle of such a figure is legendary (smoking, drinking, late nights, womanising etc.), here the very damage Fitz may be inflicting on his health can be glimpsed, as it were, on his hugely overweight physique. As much as he may want to hide behind a hard-boiled façade, the extent of his weight problem means that it is difficult for the audience not to feel that behind his witticisms and wisecracks lay an infinitely more vulnerable figure. Revealingly, McGovern was originally critical of Coltrane's casting in the role. Indeed, the much slimmer Robert Lindsay (previously the star of *GBH* [Channel Four, 1991], written by McGovern's fellow Liverpudlian Alan Bleasdale) was an early suggestion (see Day-Lewis, 1998: 69). Although, as McGovern told Bragg, 'in my mind it was always John Cassavetes, an English John Cassavetes' (see Bragg, 1996).

Through Coltrane, however, we are forced to confront the reality of Fitz's over-indulgence in a way that may not have been as pronounced if an actor with a more 'conventional' build had been cast. His obvious obesity vividly reminds us of the real (and not the mythical) consequences of his lifestyle. As such, the sheer size of Fitz's body threatens to 'demasculinise' him, preventing him from running, driving or even womanising in the traditional sense. Interestingly, some of these very characteristics were restored in *Fitz* (ABC, 1997), the American version of the show which included the rather slimmer Robert Pastorelli even driving himself around.[19] In this way, the 'masculine' world of *Cracker* is interrogated further; the classic hard-boiled detective forced to confront the traditionally 'feminine' world of sickness, disease and depression (see Yeates, 2000). 'What is it? This sadness, this void in your life?' a suspect asks Fitz in *The Mad Woman in the Attic*. Although our sleuth typically replies by laughing, drinking a large scotch and lighting another cigarette, it is a question that the narrative (by pushing him into uncharted, traditionally 'feminine' terrain) is perhaps implicitly forcing him to acknowl-edge and perhaps even address. Certainly not an archetypal 'new man', Fitz nonetheless displays traditionally 'feminine' characteristics (empathy, intimacy and his interest in per-sonal psychology) that distinguish him from his traditional hard-boiled predecessors.

In this way, we can begin to view *Cracker* partly as an attempt to reinvent the crime genre from a masculine perspective after more 'feminised' police dramas like *Prime Suspect*. While *Prime Suspect* attempts to completely dispense with the traditional hard-boiled detective and replace him with a newer, more 'feminised' and perhaps even more 'politically correct' figure, *Cracker* can be regarded as the 'return of the repressed', an attempt to bring back the hard-drinking, Bogartesque, hard-boiled detective and force him to re-negotiate and make sense of the contemporary world around him. While *Prime Suspect* conveniently has the cigar-chomping, chauvinistic DCI Shefford die of a heart attack in the first few minutes of the serial – thereby allowing Tennsion (not without resistance) to take over the reins of the genre – McGovern has Fitz stubbornly stay around, forcing any 'feminist' rewriting of the genre to take place *with* him and *around* him. In this way, the traditional hard-boiled hero is forced to confront a whole new agenda of narrative possibilities, compelled to acknowledge the personal problems in his life and address areas of private experience not usually associated with his generic terri-tory. But he does so without losing the very characteristics that made the hard-boiled detective what he is, in other words, by not rewriting the genre (or its central protagon-ist) beyond all recognition.

Cracker's implcit critique of *Prime Suspect* may even be implicitly alluded to by the name McGovern chose for his central protagonist. If *Prime Suspect*'s Jane Tennison is an implicit reference to Alfred Lord Tennyson (connecting the drama with 'feminist' themes found in poems such as *The Princess* [1848]), Fitz's full name may well be an implicit reference to one of Tennyson's closest friends and contemporaries, Edward Fitzgerald (1809–83), whose personal interests included a 'lifelong love of crime, murder trials and low life' (Martin, 1985: 235). Indeed, Tennyson even dedicated a poem to his friend whom he addresses in the first line as 'Old Fitz' (see Tennyson, 1991: 313). Revealingly, Fitzgerald actually became a forceful critic of Tennyson's later work. Appropriately enough, he was particularly critical of *The Princess* which 'he instinctively disliked' (Martin, 1985: 148). For Fitzgerald, the poem was little more than 'elaborate trifling' and he regretted the way that Tennyson's 'idle, selfish, and unheroic way of life' had 'wasted away the heroic poet-ical faculty' (cited by ibid.). It was a criticism of Tennyson's work which Fitzgerald clearly attributed to the poet's own 'passive' lifestyle, perhaps a hint that its 'feminist' themes were perhaps not 'macho' enough for Fitzgerald's own Byronic way of life.

However, this reading of *Cracker* may also reveal one of the fundamental problems that the serial has in terms of being radically progressive. While the serial clearly inter-rogates the traditional male crime genre by exploring and portraying areas more typically associated with the personal issues of soap opera, it is arguable exactly how successful it is in completely transforming its inherently masculine characteristics. In fact, many of the women in *Cracker* tend only to 'react' to the men they encounter rather than act inde-pendently. Penhaligon's gradual emergence in the narrative, for example, is initially triggered only by her relationship with the primary male protagonist, a partnership that may mirror rather than subvert many of the inherent inequalities between traditionally 'feminine' and 'masculine' power. Their relationship could even be seen as simply re-inventing the traditional partnership between hard-boiled cop and innocent young protégée; even placing Jane within a relationship that some viewers might regard as abusive (he is married, considerably older and a skilled psychologist).

This is not to say that *Cracker* does not attempt to investigate traditionally gendered categories, but in its obsession with its central male protagonist and its generic interrogation of masculinity, the women in the narrative act mainly as a means for his own self-analysis. Although it may be difficult to imagine a young, attractive woman like Penhaligon falling for the slovenly, overweight, middle-aged drunk that is Fitz (in a moment of rage she even blames him for her rape, arguing that men would look at her with him and think she was 'easy'), the relationship does allow the narrative to explore the central dynamic between the 'old' and 'new' schools of fictional detection. 'Beck's no good to me', Fitz tells Bilborough, 'Panhandle knows the way I work. Beck's too old-fashioned, too *Starsky and Hutch*' (*The Big Crunch*).

In this way, *Cracker* investigates matters of masculinity, but does so primarily from a traditionally 'masculine' point of view. The desire to transcend the conventional dynamics of a (male) buddy cop show like *Starsky and Hutch* is apparent, but Jane is never really accepted as an equal partner and clearly plays the apprenticeship role in both her professional and even her personal dealings with Fitz. As Fitz never actually leaves his wife for Jane, so he never wholly leaves the safety of the hard-boiled tradition, a sleuth prepared to test and experiment with traditional forms of masculinity but perhaps never willing to transcend them completely. It is a cultural dilemma that Rowena Chapman explains with reference to the phenomenon of the 'new lad' (1988: 235):

> the new man represents not so much a rebellion but an adaptation in masculinity. Men change, but only in order to hold on to power, not to relinquish it. The combination of feminism and social change may have produced a fragmentation in male identity by questioning its assumptions, but the effect of the emergence of the new man has been to reinforce the existing power structure, by producing a hybrid masculinity which is better able and more suited to retain control.

Despite these shortcomings, *Cracker* can still be seen as an important development in the generic evolution of the television crime series as a whole. Its attempt to take on and acknowledge many of the changes brought about in traditional notions of masculinity, makes it a crucial and revealing drama for all those interested in matters of gender and representation in contemporary television. Although its reinvention of genre may not be entirely successful, it is an interesting example of the way the crime genre itself attempted to take on and explore a world transformed by changes in traditional notions of masculine and feminine identity. 'Life needs a bit of risk', Fitz characteristically tells Judith in *To Say I Love You*, 'a bit of Bogart and Hepburn in *The African Queen*'. 'I prefer Fitz and Judith on the straight and narrow', is her typically world-weary reply.

The Sopranos (HBO, 1999–)[20]

> I saw television take over cinema. I saw TV executives moving into movies. I saw the
> pandering, cheerleading, family entertainment shit dominate everything. Low attention span
> stuff. It all came from TV. TV ruined the movies . . .
>
> David Chase (cited by Rucker, 2000: 133)

Originally created by David Chase, *The Sopranos* premiered on the American premium
cable channel HBO in January 1999. Although it was first turned down by the Fox Network, CBS and ABC, it become one of the most successful television dramas of all time,
quickly pulling in ratings of over ten million viewers (see Carter, 2000: 36) and soon
attracting considerable praise from a number of distinguished American critics (see
Holden, 2000). According to Ellen Willis, the show was '[t]he richest and most compelling piece of television – no, of popular culture – that I've encountered in the past
twenty years . . . a meditation on the nature of morality, the possibility of redemption,
and the legacy of Freud' (2002: 2). It has also attracted its fair share of academic criticism, with a number of recent books (see Lavery, 2002 and Gabbard, 2002) devoted to
the series. Although it has received strong disapproval (most notably from those who
denounced it for what they believed to be its offensive depiction of American-Italians
(see Lavery, 2004: 189), and by those who were appalled by what they saw as its misogynist tendencies (see Lauzen, 2001), critics have also praised its sophisticated
re-articulation of the gangster genre as a whole.

    The Sopranos revolves around Tony Soprano (James Gandolfini), a depressed New
Jersey Mafia boss who appears to find it increasingly difficult to live with and negotiate
between the two 'families' in his life. These two families are his middle-class, suburban,
nuclear family at home (consisting of his wife Carmela [Edie Falco] and his two children, Meadow [Jamie-Lynn Sigler] and Tony Jr [Robert Iler]) and his mobster 'family'
at work (a group of Mafia hoodlums with their headquarters in the *Bada Bing* strip club).
When he begins to suffer regular panic attacks he (reluctantly) visits a psychiatrist (Lorraine Bracco), hoping that he can be relieved of a condition that would compromise his
leadership in the Mafia world. As even this very crude description suggests, *The Sopranos* is a generically sophisticated television serial that combines elements of sitcom and
soap opera with components of the crime and gangster genre. As such, it is difficult (if
not impossible or even desirable) to reduce *The Sopranos* to one thematic strand or even
generic exploration. However, its critique of the contemporary gangster movie is one of
its most striking features, an implicit examination of genre that resonates in many of its
most pronounced moral and aesthetic implications.

    It is obvious even to the most casual of viewers that *The Sopranos* self-consciously pos-
itions itself (however ironically) as part of a long and illustrious generic tradition. As
Caryn James points out, 'One man has a car horn that blares out the first bars of *The
Godfather* theme; another routinely impersonates Al Pacino as Michael Corleone' (2000:
29). Implicit even in areas such as casting, the drama seems intent on offering reminders
of an earlier cinematic heritage. The actors Dominic Chianese (Uncle Junior) and Tony

Sirico (Paulie Walnuts) were both in *The Godfather Part II* (Coppola, 1975); Sirico, Vincent Pastore (Salvatore 'Big Pussy' Bompensiero), Lorraine Bracco (Dr Jennifer Melfi) and Michael Imperioli (Christopher Moltisanti) all appeared in *Goodfellas* (Scorsese, 1990); David Proval (Richie Aprile) was in *Mean Streets* (Scorsese, 1973); and James Gandolfini played a gangster in *True Romance* (Scott, 1993) (see Pattie, 2002).[21] There is even an explicit nod to *Goodfellas* when Christopher shoots a shop assistant in the foot, recalling a scene in the earlier film when Imperioli received similar treatment from Joe Pesci. Martin Scorsese even makes a brief appearance in episode two of the first series. 'Marty!', shouts Christopher as the director walks into a nightclub, '*Kundun*, I liked it!'

This implicit referencing to an earlier genre tradition is paralleled by Tony Soprano's own longing to return to a forgotten era. 'Out there it's the 1990s', the Prozac-munching mobster tells his children, 'in here, it's 1954'. In particular, this depressed Mafia boss seems obsessed with the standards and the values epitomised by an earlier generation of gangsters. 'He never reached the heights like me', he says of his father, 'but in a lot of ways he had it better. He had his people – they had their standards. They had pride. Today what have we got?' (Chase, 2001: 16). As this suggests, Tony appears to believe that the world of organised crime is less 'noble' and 'respected' than it once was. It is a view reflected in a documentary about the Mafia that he watches on TV with his crew at the beginning of episode two. 'You know the hey-day … the Golden Age … of the Mob?' explains a Mafia expert, 'it's over. And they ain't coming back.'

However, this notion of a 'golden age' could refer as much to the dramatic universe Tony inhabits as it does to the reality of the mob itself. For the contemporary gangster movie seems to be distinctly different in style and content to its predecessors. Interestingly, the TV documentary goes on to suggest that the Mafia itself is partly to blame for its own decline, particularly for turning its back on the 'rules which once served the old Dons so well'. Such a statement could equally refer to a *genre* that has perhaps similarly rejected its own heritage, disregarding the set of moral 'standards' and aesthetic 'rules' that governed it in the past. Seen in this light, Tony's depression is symptomatic of a character who unconsciously feels he exists at the wrong end of a long and illustrious tradition (literally in the form of the mob and metaphorically in the form of the gangster genre). '[L]ately I've been getting the feeling that I came in at the end', he muses. 'The best is over' (ibid).

Tony Soprano certainly appears to represent an earlier *genre* tradition, a world that still remembers the 'rules' and the 'standards' that once 'served the old Dons so well'. This might most famously refer to the so-called 'golden age' of the modern gangster movie, particularly Francis Ford Coppola's classic portrayal of the Mafia epitomised by Marlon Brando's (and Robert De Niro as his younger self) inherently old-school Don Vito Corleone.[22] According to Carmela, Tony 'watches *The Godfather Part II* all the time'. On his new (recently stolen) laser disc, she adds, '[h]e says the camera work looks as good as in the movie theatre' (ibid: 30). Consequently, Tony's choice of film and his specific appreciation of the genre reflect a particular *cinematic* tradition, a time when the gangster movie clearly felt at home with the 'glamour' and 'spectacle' of the big screen.

The Sopranos: television and cinema collide with dramatic consequences

This belief that the gangster genre is most at home on the big screen is not unique to Tony. In fact, many film critics have argued that Coppola's gangster movie was made primarily for cinema, and therefore can never be fully appreciated on the small screen. As Anton Wilson puts it, the visual subtlety of *The Godfather* is something that can only really be appreciated on the big screen (or perhaps Tony's laser disc that apparently simulates the 'movie theatre' experience). According to Wilson (cited by Wasko, 1994: 167):

> Coppola created the magnificent 'underworld' texture by extensively exploiting the shadow
> detail capability of film. Most of the action in many of the interior scenes existed in the
> lowest regions of the exposure curve. In my opinion this subtle feel of the texture was lost
> when the film appeared on television as the medium could not cope with the range of
> exposure, especially the shadow details.[23]

As this suggests, Tony's character appears to epitomise the 'golden age' of the modern gangster genre, one that seemed inherently at home on the *big* rather than the *small* screen.[24] It is no wonder that his character now finds it difficult to adjust to contemporary life – his role in a television gangster serial somehow 'downgrading' his own cinematic aspirations, forcing him to take on roles and characteristics that the previous generation of big-screen gangsters would have frowned upon. In particular, Horace Newcomb argued that the small screen (especially through its use of close-up and medium shots) achieves a more *personal* and *intimate* view of the world than the 'spec-

tacle' and 'expansiveness' of cinema (1974: 243–64).[25] Seen in this light, Tony's tragic
predicament can be viewed as an essentially cinematic creation desperately trying to con-
form to the apparently *intimate* dynamics of television. Looking like extras from *The
Godfather*, he and his crew are deposited uncomfortably into a world of soap operas,
docusoaps and confessional talk shows – forced to take their personalities beyond their
traditional genre boundaries. 'Let me tell you something', Tony tells Dr Melfi angrily,
'today everybody goes to shrinks, and counselors. Everybody goes on *Sally Jessy Raphael*
and talks about their problems' (Chase, 2001: 32).

Arguably, then, Tony's long-running battle with therapy implicitly parallels the narrative's own struggle with the personal requirements of television. Frustrated by the constant
need to express his feelings, this Mafia boss is not simply resisting the contemporary preoccupation with self-analysis, but is also struggling to adapt to television's obsession with
the *private* and *personal* dynamics of human experience. It comes as no surprise, then, that
he frequently longs to escape from this frustratingly 'intimate' world and return to the traditional conventions of classical Hollywood. 'Whatever happened to Gary Cooper, the
strong silent type?' he asks Melfi. '. . . He wasn't in touch with his feelings. He just did
what he had to do' (see Chase, 2001: 32). In this context, it is clear that Tony's fear of intimacy is not just a symptom of his psychological condition, but is also perhaps an inevitable
reaction against his own generic confinement (see Donatelli and Alward, 2002).[26]

In contrast, Tony's impetuous nephew, Christopher Moltisanti, represents a new breed
of both gangster and gangster movie. There is definitely a generation gap between uncle
and nephew, Tony obviously feeling that Christopher has been spoilt, citing his new $60,000
Lexus automobile as an example of a generation that has generally been over-indulged (see
Chase, 2001: 19). It is no surprise that Christopher holds very different views from Tony
about how the contemporary gangster (and the contemporary gangster genre) should act
and look; having little time for 'old-school' conceptions of the mob. Indeed, brought up
on a steady diet of television, videos and computer games, he is clearly 'a soldier of the
MTV generation' (Holden, 2000: 129) rather than a symbol of the 'golden age'. As this
might suggest, Christopher's perspective on the cinema reflects the cultural attitude of a
whole new generation. Although obsessed with film (he is unsuccessfully writing a screenplay based on his experiences in the mob), his local video store is as near as he actually gets
to the cinematic experience. 'I love movies. You know that', he tells his girlfriend. 'That
smell in *Blockbuster*? That candy and carpet smell? I get high off it' (Chase, 2001: 103).

As a symbol of this new 'video store' generation, Christopher reflects the contemporary genre's more violent and perhaps increasingly 'amoral' sensibilities. He certainly
seems unable to disconnect movies from real life, frequently reacting self-reflexively to
volatile situations. 'This is *Scarface* final scene', he shouts at Tony and the crew, 'Fucking bazookas under each arm – say hello to my little friend'. However, his older
colleagues seem unimpressed by his uncontrolled bursts of anger. 'Always with the scenarios', Pussy comments sarcastically. As this implies, this new 'video store' generation
simply fails to appreciate many of the more subtle ingredients of the 'classic' gangster
movie. Even when Christopher travels to Naples with Tony and the crew, he spends most
of his time in his hotel room doing drugs, missing a rare chance to see and experience

his ancestor's homeland. Not surprisingly then, he also seems unable to fully grasp the details of his own cinematic heritage, even managing to misquote from Coppola's original masterpiece. 'Louis Brassi sleeps with the fishes', he recites at the disposal of a body. '*Luca* Brassi. *Luca*' (my emphasis, ibid: 36), Pussy angrily corrects him.

Christopher's disconnection from 'old-school' gangster movies like *The Godfather* is also suggested in his association with contemporary film-making. In episode seven of the second series (*D-Girl*), he meets up with film development girl Amy Safir (Alicia Witt) and real actor Jon Favreau (played by himself). Clearly affluent and sophisticated, this Hollywood pair set out to manipulate the young mobster (and the gangster script he is trying to write) to help them with their next project.[27] As Amy tells the aspiring screenwriter, 'Mob theme stories are always hot'. Later, both she and Favreau become visibly excited when Christopher tells them about real experiences he has had, secretly hoping to appropriate some of his memories for their own movie.[28] One particular tale is inspired by a horrifically burned woman walking into the diner where they are having lunch. As Christopher explains, she was the victim of a gangster who didn't realise, until they were having sex, that she was a transsexual. In retaliation, Christopher explains, he bought a can of acid and burnt '*everything*'. He poured it on 'her arms, on her face . . . on her *prick*!' Favreau is visibly shocked; literally forced to confront the reality of a type of violence he prefers to think about only in cinematic terms. However, the hard-nosed Amy is simply concerned that the story lacks cinematic originality and mentions *The Crying Game* (Jordan, 1992). 'This is a *true* story,' Favreau has to quickly remind her.

In this way, the exploitative ingredients of the contemporary gangster movie are satirised, its tendency to package violence as aesthetic 'entertainment' contrasted with the horrific *realities* of Christopher's brutal real-life experience. Indeed, for many critics, the contemporary gangster movie is representative of a new type of exploitative cinema, what some have termed a '*new brutalism*' that has tended to divorce its depiction of violence from any moral or wider social context. Julia Hallam and Margaret Marshment argue that rather than constructing 'narratively adequate motivations . . . for violent acts', these films tend to portray murderers who are not apparently motivated by any 'narrative causality' (2000: 225). As a TV psychiatrist says of Mickey and Mallory (the postmodern Bonnie and Clyde of *Natural Born Killers* [Stone, 1992]): 'They know the difference between right and wrong. They just don't give a damn.'

No surprise, then, that Amy claims to have worked with film director Quentin Tarantino, perhaps the most well known and celebrated auteur of this new breed of genre. As film critic Geoff Andrew puts it, 'Tarantino does not appear to be concerned with the moral implications of the film; rather, it is primarily a stylish variation on traditional genre conventions, designed to thrill, shock, amuse and surprise . . .' (Andrew, 1998: 323). As Hallam and Marshment put it (2000: 92):

> By the 1980s and the 1990s, the gangster film's roots in any antecedent discourse of social reality is largely obscured by 'high concept' aesthetics that foreground stylistic excess, its entertainment value articulated through accrued layers of generic self-reflexivity and intertextuality.

Interestingly, many critics argue that central to the visual style of this 'new brutalism' is its gradual movement away from the aesthetics of the cinema towards adopting the techniques and visual style of television. While film critics like Peter Cowie have praised *The Godfather* (Coppola, 1972) for epitomising the 'classical style' of modern film-making (1997: 209–23), newer gangster movies such as *Reservoir Dogs*, *Pulp Fiction* (Tarantino, 1994) and *Lock, Stock and Two Smoking Barrels* (Richie, 1998) have often been associated with the type of 'cartoon imagery' and 'MTV aesthetics', more usually associated with the small screen.[29] Quentin Tarantino's own much-hyped employment in a video store perhaps most famously suggests such a trend, revealing a writer, director and actor as openly influenced as much by the small screen as the big. As Roger Avary (Tarantino's friend, co-worker and co-writer of *Pulp Fiction*) points out: 'We were the video store generation, right after the film school generation, the first generation of people who wanted to be film-makers who had grown up alongside computers, videos, the information highway' (cited by Botting and Wilson, 2001: 7).

As this suggests, then, Tony and Christopher reveal gangster characters at different ends of the same genre spectrum. Both are corrupt, dangerous and violent individuals who represent a fundamentally different set of 'moral' and 'ethical' values. While Tony's 'traditional' sensibilities appear to represent Coppola's old 'film school' generation (and the 'moral' associations of Don Vito Corleone), Christopher encapsulates the new priorities of Tarantino's 'video store' generation (particularly its obsession with 'comic-book' violence and its appropriation of the forms and aesthetics of television). Seen in this light, *The Sopranos* offers the viewer an implicit critique of the 'new brutalism' that critics feel characterises the contemporary gangster movie, engaging both film and television techniques in order to reflect and comment on the current state of the gangster genre as a whole.

This critique of the newer type of gangster movie is suggested in the way that *The Sopranos* deliberately turns away from the principal aesthetics of 'new brutalism'. For example, the serial frequently and self-consciously returns to Coppola's earlier style of film-making, borrowing the director's famous technique of cross-cutting between scenes of extreme violence and domestic warmth (see Holden, 2000: xiii) to give an important 'moral' context to the story as a whole. Perhaps the most striking example of this technique comes at the end of *The Godfather* when the innocence of a family christening and a number of brutal murders are carefully edited together. As Michael Corelone renounces the devil in his role as godfather to his sister's child, so his role as a Mafia godfather is graphically foregounded by the cold-blooded murder that we see carried out in his name. Similarly, the end of episode three (*Denial, Anger, Acceptance*) of *The Sopranos* mixes the killing of Brendan (Anthony Desando) and the mock execution of Christopher with a choral recital from Meadow's school concert, thereby foregrounding (and putting into crisis) the two morally opposed worlds that Tony inhabits. Later, Brendan's bullet through the eye is even described as a 'Moe Greene Special', an explicit reference to the murder of a character at the end of Coppola's movie.

A similar technique is loosely applied to the whole of episode four (*College*) of the first series. When Tony visits Maine with his daughter Meadow for a college tour he accidentally comes across a notorious 'rat' now living under the pseudonym of Fred Peters (Tony Ray Rossi). As a result, the normality of this everyday trip is suddenly juxtaposed with a bloody tale of Mafia revenge. As with Brendan's death, Tony's brutal strangling of 'Fred' from behind is reminiscent of a scene from *The Godfather*, the infamous murder of Luca Brassi (Lenny Montana). Such a treatment of violence is meant to unsettle viewers, forcing them to contemplate the different facets of Tony's life and personality. As if to reinforce such a reading, Tony himself spies a plaque on a wall while waiting for Meadow to be interviewed by one of the colleges: 'NO MAN CAN WEAR ONE FACE TO HIM-SELF AND ANOTHER TO THE MULTITUDE WITHOUT FINALLY GETTING BEWILDERED AS TO WHICH ONE MAY BE TRUE (Nathaniel Hawthorne)' (cited by Chase, 2001: 91).

In this way, rather than allowing Tony's Mafia persona to dominate the narrative point of view, the viewer is given a number of contrasting perspectives (father/parent/husband/mobster). This complexity of characterisation is seldom witnessed in newer gangster movies such as *Reservoir Dogs*, where colours even replace the names of the principal characters. As Stephen Prince puts it (1998: 241):

> Tarantino is drawn to violence because he knows it as a movie style, and it is one that he finds compelling. The style itself is the subject and form of his work. Accordingly, he has not moved to explore the psychological and emotional dynamics of violence in terms that might reference life apart from the movies.

A similar approach can be detected in *The Sopranos'* use of music. Although the serial frequently employs popular music, the songs generally lack the catchy intensity of those that so often punctuate more recent examples of the genre. Indeed, the low-key beat of Nick Lowe's 'The Beast in Me' or Elvis Costello's 'Complicated Shadows' is in direct contrast with the frenetic dance beat of *Pulp Fiction's* 'Jungle Boogie' (Kool & the Gang) or the infectious pop of *Reservoir Dogs'* 'Stuck in the Middle with You' (Stealer's Wheel). Consequently, the choice of music tends to avoid constructing the sort of rapidly edited sequences that have become associated with the 'new brutalist' cinema. Instead, the serial's use of music frequently helps to create a mood and an atmosphere reminiscent of Coppola's famously languid pace; perhaps even echoing the classical eloquence of Nino Rota's memorable theme tune to *The Godfather*.

For instance, the first episode of the second series (*Guy Walks into a Psychiatrist's Office* …) begins with the lazy and melancholic tones of Frank Sinatra performing Ervin Drake's classic 'It Was a Very Good Year'. As the song plays, we are given a long and leisurely paced selection of apparently unconnected scenes. Sequences such as Livia (Nancy Marchand) lying motionless and depressed in her hospital bed, Carmela baking at home, Silvio trying on a new pair of shoes, Anthony Jr self-consciously combing his hair and Tony and Paulie making love with their girlfriends/prostitutes, provide an essentially 'domestic' montage. However, the music fails to extenuate or exaggerate the pace of the action (as George Baker's 'Little Green Bag' famously does at the opening of *Reservoir Dogs*). Instead, Sinatra's unhurried and mournful ballad (played in its full four and a half minutes) heightens the scene's leisurely construction, deliberately slowing down the story's narrative pace and transforming the spectacle of the modern gangster genre into an essentially domestic and intimate display.[30]

This leisurely pace and sense of intimacy is further heightened by the serial's deliberate excursions away from the traditional world of the gangster genre. In particular, the psychiatry sessions deliberately hold up or defer the more 'action-led' elements of the drama. Relatively static (at least, compared to the 'high concept' techniques favoured by newer examples of the genre), the emphasis is on dialogue, close-ups and human interaction, employing what many critics regard as some of the most basic ingredients of television drama (see, for example, Jacobs, 2000: 7–8). Indeed, these scenes are more reminiscent of the conventional TV chat show or the 'head-to-head' political interview than they are of the contemporary gangster or action movie. In this way, the therapy sequences self-consciously fragment the serial's narrative dynamic, forcing the viewer to stand back for a moment from Tony's exotic (and perhaps essentially 'cinematic') lifestyle so that they can briefly distance themselves from the genre's historically seductive appeal.[31]

The first (pilot) episode, for instance, opens with Tony sitting alone and in silence for a full twenty seconds in Melfi's waiting room. Once in her office, it is another thirty seconds before she finally breaks the silence, a bravely austere opening for a pilot episode of a gangster serial.[32] Compare this, for example, with the hectic opening sequence of *Lock, Stock and Two Smoking Barrels* or the famously seductive credit sequence of *Reservoir Dogs*.[33] Later in the episode, Dr Melfi interrupts one of Tony's recollections to get, as she puts it, 'some ethical ground rules out of the way' (Chase, 2001: 19). This interruption similarly breaks up the narrative pace of the action, while the rock soundtrack that accompanied Tony's violent memory is suddenly replaced by the abrupt silence of Melfi's office. In this way, the therapy sessions unexpectedly force the viewer to take time out from the traditional attractions of the gangster genre, providing a possibly 'ethical' and spatially contrasting perspective from which to view the events taking place. As a result, the typically high-powered conventions of the genre are temporarily suspended, the audience given a brief moment away from its visual and audio excitement.

In this way, *The Sopranos* implicitly reflects the use of the psychiatry narrative as employed in a television serial like *The Singing Detective*.[34] In a manner seldom matched by cinema, the sheer breadth of the television serial enables the slow and *gradual* process of psychotherapy to be more realistically represented and explored (see Introduction). Like Dennis Potter's equally reluctant patient in *The Singing Detective*, it is a relatively long while before Tony's therapy appears to have any effect at all (a technique not affordable in the relatively limited time span of the cinema). It is not until episode seven, for example, that we are given our first direct glimpse (in the form of a flashback) of his childhood. As a young boy in 1967 we see him discover (for the first time) his father's involvement in the mob, accidentally witnessing him and his Uncle Junior 'beat the crap' out of a man from the neighbourhood.

Interestingly, the way this scene is shot is strikingly reminiscent of the childhood trauma at the heart of *The Singing Detective*, when Marlow (as a young boy) accidentally comes across his mother having sex in the woods. Like Marlow, Tony stands at the foot of a tree, voyeuristically witnessing the action from a concealed spot, both repulsed and excited by what he secretly sees.[35] The echo of this famous scene perhaps implicitly pays *homage* to the depth of characterisation that the cumulative narrative of a television serial like *The Singing Detective* can achieve. Tony is ultimately struggling with the claustro-phobic dynamics of television, but, (despite its apparently limiting restrictions), may ironically gain a greater understanding of himself (and perhaps the genre in which he unknowingly exists) through serialised drama's *gradual* excavation of character, desire and perhaps even unconscious motivation.[36]

Tony Soprano is sexist, homophobic and unashamedly racist, but in his journey through psychoanalysis we learn some of the reasons for his complex condition (a psychological journey that, as we have seen, is seldom equalled by the 'new brutalist' cin-ema). We are given the means by which we can start to unravel the moral, historical and personal dynamics by which this character has arrived at such a complex and neurotic state. *The Sopranos* does not pretend to resolve these problems for Tony, indeed, in the process of therapy few real changes seem to have been made either to his mental health, lifestyle or personal views. However, the serial does attempt to examine its own narra-tive desires, asking difficult and uncomfortable questions that simultaneously harness and investigate the genre that Tony both inhabits and ultimately subverts.

It is undoubtedly ironic that *The Sopranos* attempts to do all this in the very medium that it implicitly set out to examine and critique. However, by incorporating both elements of television and cinematic practice into its essentially hybrid form, it forces the viewer to confront the very means by which the narrative is produced, contained and finally received. In this way, David Chase and his team of writers and directors have created a form of drama that transcends traditional genre boundaries, but still retains the moral framework upon which the gangster genre was originally (if not ambiguously) based. By critiquing the very medium it both utilises and exploits, *The Sopranos* ironi-cally produces a complex and sophisticated narrative structure that simultaneously denigrates and celebrates its own potential and artistic possibilities. Above all, then, it can be seen as an investigation of genre, not only an attempt to 'modernise' the portrayal of the mob, but also an attempt to look back longingly at a genre that was once perhaps more morally stable and secure than it can ever be today. In doing so, *The Sopranos* reminds us of the power of television genre to continually reinvent itself, revealing its tendency not only to repeat and rehash the old, but also its unique ability to occasion-ally create a new dramatic universe altogether.

NOTES

1. As Henry Ford famously explained, you could have the Model T Ford in any colour 'as long as it was black'.
2. This section first appeared in a different form in Creeber (2001a); parts of it may also be found in Creeber (2004d).
3. The policewoman in question was DCI Jackie Malton. See Roberts, 1991.
4. For a discussion of the visual style of film noir see Cameron, 1994: 25–30. For a concise description of neo-noir, see Cook and Bernik, 1999: 187.
5. As children, both George and Philip accidentally come across their mothers having sex with

a strange man. While Philip witnesses the event while climbing trees in his beloved forest, George stumbles across the 'primal scene' looking for his mother under a seaside pier. When Marlow's mother in *The Singing Detective* realises what her boy has seen she commits suicide, leaving Philip riddled with guilt and psychologically (and perhaps even physically) scarred. As a result, both male characters develop profound problems with women, ultimately resulting in a tendency towards misogyny and a guilty obsession with prostitutes (Potter's official biographer even suggests that this 'obsession' was not just confined to fiction [see Carpenter, 1998: 292]). Not surprisingly perhaps, both characters appear to suffer from some form of Oedipus complex. George even covers his victims with the perfume his mother wore that fateful night. Indeed, it is the mention of his mother that suddenly breaks down his convincing act of innocence, finally revealing his violent, vicious and psychopathic temper.

6. Even the name of the journalist who sets out to prove Marlow's innocence has ironic implications. Called Mark Whitehouse, the allusions to Potter's long-time television adversary Mary Whitehouse, is unmistakable. As President of the 'National Viewers' and Listeners' Association', Mrs Mary Whitehouse was a strong opponent of Potter's work, in particular his portrayal of sex. She accused his 'adaptation' of *Casanova* (BBC, 1971), for example, of 'lewdness and gross indecency' (cited by Creeber, 1998: 159).

7. *Psycho* is probably one of the most written about films ever. But perhaps a classic reading of the film can still be found in Raymond Bellour (1979), 'Psychosis, Neurosis, Perversion', *Camera Obscura*, nos 3/4: 105–32.

8. Such was the power of the car chases in these shows at the time that British police chief Kenneth Oxford once complained that it led to police officers 'driving like bloody maniacs' (cited by Lewis and Stempel, 1999: 322).

9. According to Christine Gledhill's analysis of *Klute* (1971), the female prostitute, like the traditional *femme fatale*, often becomes the embodiment of all that men fear and desire in women and so must be dealt with accordingly.

10. Such a connection is by no means unusual in film and television. The pilot episode of *Cagney and Lacey* finds both policewomen on 'john detail', reluctantly dressing up as prostitutes in order to entrap kerb crawlers. Lacey even tries to establish a prostitutes' union in an attempt to improve their working conditions. Such a connection suggests that both symbols of womanhood are strangely united in their transgression of traditional feminine behaviour (see Tasker, 1998: 94–5).

11. Indeed, some years later, and in her fifties, Mirren was chosen to lead an advertising campaign for Virgin Airlines which focused primarily on her legs. Clearly attempting to catch the 'male gaze', she physically demonstrated the leg-room available in Virgin aircraft.

12. Apparently some scenes were cut from La Plante's original script because the producers thought she was 'cold' and not very 'warm to men'. In particular, a scene in which Tennison roughly questions a victim (see Hayward and Rennert, 1996: 108–9).

13. This section first appeared in a different form in Creeber (2002a).

14. When Coltrane asked to leave the show after the second series he accepted the offer to do one-off specials, hence *White Ghost* (1995), a two-hour edition set in Hong Kong.

15. Series one of *Cracker* followed a format of two two-part serials and one three-parter, all of

which would later be repeated in 'film-length' edited versions. For the second series, it was extended to nine episodes – three stories of three episodes each (hence the need to employ other writers). Paul Abbott was originally the producer of the series, but went on to write hugely successful dramas such as *Clocking Off* (BBC, 2000–3) and *Shameless* (Channel Four, 2004). *Cracker* famously caused controversy in 1995 when an extra fifteen minutes of the first episode threatened to push *News at Ten* to 10.15pm. Eventually ITV were told by their franchise that the episode had to be moved to a Sunday night to avoid re-scheduling the news.

16. The British Hillsborough football stadium disaster in 1989 resulted in ninety-six Liverpool supporters losing their lives. According to Sean Day-Lewis, 'The disaster occurred through police incompetence and indirectly, it is very arguable, through current police attitudes to football supporters' (Day-Lewis, 1998: 67–8). McGovern first made the tragedy part of a storyline in *Cracker*'s *To Be a Somebody* and would later go on to to make a drama-documentary about the tragedy simply called *Hillsborough*, in 1996 for ITV. It is perhaps also worth mentioning that Bilborough is a Manchester United fan (seen in the scarves, posters etc. on his office wall), the arch-enemy of Liverpool Football Club. Not surprisingly, then, Bilborough is finally murdered by a homicidal Liverpool supporter who sets out to seek revenge for the 1989 football tragedy (*To Be a Somebody*).

17. See Sandra M. Gilbert and Susan Gubar (1979).

18. Like Tennison, Jane Penhaligon certainly seems to have reached an impenetrable 'glass ceiling', her application for promotion quickly turned down by the traditional Bilborough. Although a Detective Sergeant, she seems to be mainly relied upon to break bad news to bereaved families. 'You're good at that sort of thing', Bilborough tells her, 'I've had plenty of practice', she cynically replies. Later, at a meeting with the same grief-stricken parents her official authority is further undermined by being told to get the mother a glass of water (*The Mad Woman in the Attic*). Perhaps 'Panhandle' (Fitz's sarcastic nickname for her and the American slang for begging) suggests the way she is forced to constantly 'beg' from the men who inevitably hold the reins of power.

19. Starring Robert Pastorelli as Gerry Fitzgerald, *Fitz* wasn't a huge success either in the UK or the US and was eventually cancelled. The character was substantially changed while other characters were simply dropped or rewritten beyond recognition. Cutting complex three-part stories like *To Say I Love You* down to an hour did not help.

20. This section first appeared in different form in Creeber (2002c).

21. The casting of Lorraine Bracco as Tony's psychiatrist is particularly interesting, appearing to deliberately call attention to and invert her previous role as the long-suffering wife of Mobster Henry Hill (Ray Liotta) in *Goodfellas*. Apparently Bracco assumed that she would be simply asked to play Tony's wife, thereby 'repeating' her previous role (Holden, 2000: 126). The actress also had a child by actor Harvey Keitel, adding to the complex intertextual play at work within the serial as a whole.

22. As an old-school Mafia don, Don Vito is disgusted by the modern spread of narcotics and refuses an invitation to get his 'business' involved in dealing drugs. This refusal eventually leads to a Mafia war that results in his attempted assassination.

23. It is worth noting that Wilson puts the 'underworld' feel of *The Godfather* down to Coppola's direction. However, its photographer, Gordon Willis, has suggested much of the

dark lighting he provided in the interior shots was simply an attempt to conceal the poor quality of Brando's make-up (see Ettedgui, 1998). Curiously we never discover Tony's view of *Goodfellas*. When Father Phil asks Carmela where her husband stands on the film, a suspected burglar immediately interrupts them. (Father Phil's shocked reaction to the gun that Carmela instantly acquires also offers a clear juxtaposition between his reaction to 'screen' and 'real' violence.) Similarly, when Meadow tells Tony that her friends think that the Mafia is 'cool', he seems shocked and surprised when she suggests the reason is *Goodfellas*, apparently oblivious to *The Godfather*.

24. Of course, Tony is also a fan of the original gangster movies from the 1930s and 1940s. However, his pleasure in watching these movies seems implicitly different to his appreciation of more contemporary movies like *The Godfather*, appearing to be moved more by their 'innocent' view of gangster life. In the second episode of the third series, for example, we see him watch *The Public Enemy* (Wellman, 1931) on a number of occasions, clearly enthralled by its 'simpler' view of urban life, particularly James Cagney's unconditional love for his mother.

25. This notion of intimacy appears in most early discussions of the medium. See, for instance, John Ellis, 1982: 132.

26. Surprisingly perhaps, the creator of *The Sopranos*, David Chase, seems to hold a similar view to television as Tony's . . . 'All my life I wanted to do movies', he explained to Bill Carter in the *New York Times*. 'I just resented every moment I spent in television . . . for me it was always cinema, cinema, cinema' (cited by Carter, 2000: 90). Despite previous credits to his name such as *The Rockford Files* (NBC, 1974–80) and *Northern Exposure*, Chase seems to regard television as cinema's poor cousin, unable to ever capture its magnitude and visual spectacle. 'There's so much more to the movie experience', he told the British journalist Alex Blimes, 'music and pictures and rhythm. I miss that' (cited by Blimes, 2000: 169).

27. Christopher's screenplay is rather comically called, 'You Bite, I Bark'.

28. Their next film is to be called *Crazy Joe*, based on the life of the real gangster, Crazy Joe Gallo. Visibly turned on by his mob connections, Amy begins an affair with Christopher that she obviously has no intention of continuing beyond her hotel room.

29. Indeed, *Lock, Stock and Two Smoking Barrels* was recently made into a British television series, to cash in on its big screen success. According to Vincent Canby (Wasko, 1994: 166),

> Since the videocassette recorder has become, in effect, the second run of the theatrical film, there has been a televisionization in the look of movies. An interesting number of today's theatrical movies give the impression of being photographed almost entirely in the close-ups and medium shots that register best on the small screen.

30. Likewise, Sinatra's infamous association with the Mafia (the character of Johnny Fontane in *The Godfather* was rumoured to be based on the singer and actor) further reminds the viewer of an earlier genre tradition – a world before the 'amoral' onslaught on the new 'brutalised' gangster movie, perhaps epitomised by the more contemporary rhythms of rock, pop and funk.

31. For example, critics have chastised *The Godfather* for implicitly mythologising and glamorising the mob. In 'Myth & Meaning: Francis Ford Coppola and Popular Response to

The Godfather Trilogy', David Ray Papke has explained how the director was first amazed when people seemed to be *attracted* to many of the elements of the original movie. In particular, he was reported to be shocked that viewers thought he had intentionally 'romanticised' Michael Corleone (Al Pacino). This was in stark contrast with his own belief that Michael was represented 'as a monster' by the end of the movie (1996: 9). Ironically, the Mafia itself also seemed to be among some of the film's most enthusiastic supporters. As Papke points out, 'According to anonymous reports, the old-fashioned and largely abandoned custom of kissing the hands of powerful Mafia leaders revived because of its portrayal in the film' (ibid: 6). Indeed, according to the British journalist Ben Macintyre, recent transcripts of wire-tapped conversations from within the Mob show that *The Sopranos* itself is now similarly beginning to affect the behaviour and discourse of the real Mafia, with mobsters discussing the drama and repeating the characters' own hang-ups and concerns. According to Macintyre, 'What these and other Mafia tapes show is not just that art mirrors life, but that the life of the mobster is in some ways controlled by art' (2001: 24).

32. Compare their portrayal, for example, with the psychiatry sessions in a movie like *Analyze This* (Ramis, 1999), a film (often compared with *The Sopranos* because of its narrative similarities) where there is still a great deal of action and slapstick even in the meetings that take place between patient and psychiatrist.

33. Although the serial's own credit sequence employs both fast editing techniques and rock music (Alabama 3's *Woke up This Morning*), it is frequently brought to a sudden halt when the drama itself begins, an inversion of Tarantino's familiar technique, where banal conversation usually precedes a dynamic opening credit sequence.

34. This is not the first time the serial has been compared with *The Singing Detective*. 'In its leisurely use of the form', Caryn James has argued, 'it is strangely like *Brideshead Revisited*, *The Singing Detective* and *I, Claudius*' (James, 2000: 26).

35. Like Potter's Marlow, Tony's mother is a powerful and domineering woman. Indeed, the similarities between the two women are significant, not least their strangely Oedipal relationship with their young sons (Livia even threatens to poke out Tony's eyes with a fork during one of the flashbacks to his childhood). Earlier in episode four of the first series Tony dreams he is in Dr Melfi's office, a woman he is sexually attracted to. After watching Silvio and a lap dancer have sex in the waiting room he turns back to Melfi. However, as she turns around it is revealed to be his mother in the chair. (To make the connection with British television drama even more pronounced, Livia is also the name of the ruthless, scheming wife in *I, Claudius*, although it was also significantly the name of Chase's own mother). For a consideration of the role of the mother in *The Singing Detective*, see Creeber, 1998: 166–78.

36. It is perhaps worth noting that both these television dramas refer to the act of singing in their titles. It is as if these quintessentially masculine genres (film noir in the case of *The Singing Detective*) were being forced to take on board the more 'feminine' characteristics traditionally associated with genres such as the soap opera or the confessional talk show. While 'singing' is sometimes used as street slang for the act of 'grassing' to the police (or even, appropriately enough, *confession*), the surname Soprano refers to the female or adolescent section of a choir (an indication perhaps of the drama's own examination of a genre more commonly equated with the tenor or the mature male voice generally).

4 LIFE POLITICS
Friendship, Community and Identity in 'Soap Drama'

INTRODUCTION

> As it turns out, this emphasis on capturing the 'stuff of real life' by exploring contemporary gender conflicts struck a deep chord not only in the viewing audience it was targeted toward, the baby boomers, but in the larger culture as well. . . . Writing for the Jewish literary magazine *Tikkun*, Jay Rosen claimed that *thirtysomething* functioned as a kind of 'consciousness raising' for its audience by showing how personal problems are rooted in larger social conditions.
>
> Margaret J. Heide (1996: 150)

I was perhaps unusual among my male adolescent friends for actually preferring the first half of *The Deer Hunter* (Cimino, 1978). Cut into two distinct sections, the film begins with a group of close-knit, working-class friends preparing for and attending a huge community-centred wedding. In contrast, the second half follows the same group of male friends as they fight in the Vietnam War. Despite the excitement and danger of the war scenes (particularly the notorious Russian roulette sequences), I found myself wanting to return to the small-town dynamics of Pennsylvania, to find out how life was treating the folks back home. What I did not fully realise at the time was that the 'soap opera' elements of the drama had perhaps engaged me more completely than the war narrative.[1] This became even more apparent when one of my friends suggested intriguing insights into the personal dynamics of the group of friends portrayed. For example, there seem to be hints from the start that the bridegroom Steven (John Savage) is not the father of the child carried by his pregnant bride, but that the father is actually the loud-mouth Stan (John Cazale). This sort of personal detail made repeated viewing of the film strangely addictive as I gradually pieced together the intimate milieu of the small-town lives so convincingly portrayed.

What a film like *The Deer Hunter* seemed to tap into and even pre-empt was a tendency among contemporary audiences to want to watch close-knit social groups leading and struggling with lives similar to their own. Perhaps as family and community life became more fragmented and unsettled in the contemporary world, viewers longed to explore the dynamics by which social networks were formed, maintained and occasionally destroyed. In the 1970s and early 1980s big-screen melodramas like *The Godfather*, *Scenes from a Marriage* (Bergman, 1973) and *Ordinary People* (Redford, 1980) engaged with and reflected an apparent thirst for contemporary stories that revolved around the private and personal details of a single family. This was also reflected in the television miniseries from the same period with serials like *Rich Man, Poor Man*, *Roots* and *Holocaust* all employing close-knit family ties to examine wider social and frequently historical concerns (see Chapter One).

Meanwhile, films like *M*A*S*H* (Altman, 1970), *Husbands* (Cassavetes, 1970) and *Diner* (Levinson, 1982) seemed intent on reflecting and exploring the intimate dynamics of 'families' made out of close friends, colleagues and small communities. Taking many of the characteristics of TV serials and soap opera (*Scenes from a Marriage* was originally a six-part television miniseries and *M*A*S*H* would, of course, become a long-running TV sitcom [CBS, 1972–83]) films such as these reflected a growing interest in the intricate dynamics of kinship. In particular, their obsession with friendship was set directly against a world where blood and family ties were increasingly uncertain and unstable.

The culmination of this type of drama (one that explicitly focused on the contemporary dynamics of friendship with an explicit attention to the private and personal sphere) was heralded by *The Big Chill* (Kasdan, 1983). In many ways the film seemed almost 'soap operatic' in its obsession with the private lives and close relationships of its central characters. It focused its interest on a small group of baby-boomer friends grappling with maturity and the pressure and demands that come with adult responsibility. Beginning with the funeral of one of their group, the film takes place during only one weekend, is set primarily within a single house and involves only a very limited cast.[2] The film was surprisingly small-scale and dealt with personal and intimate concerns against an infectious and nostalgic soundtrack from the 1960s (reflecting the 'counter-culture' period of their youth). Timely references to running shoes, jogging, camcorders and TV celebrity made it particularly contemporary while its examination of how a generation went from revolutionary politics to comfortable 'yuppiedom' allowed it to tease with and hint at wider social issues and concerns. Although some critics found its guilt-ridden self-analysis infuriatingly narcissistic, others seemed entranced by its ability to examine contemporary life and politics through the group dynamics of a single set of friends.

The success of a film like *The Big Chill* revealed how willing audiences were to watch increasingly intimate and frequently ordinary lives portrayed in explicit detail on the big screen, particularly if their stories of contemporary friendship somehow commentated on and reflected their own. No surprise, then, that television soon spied an opportunity to develop and cash in on the success of this developing style of drama. Most notably, *thirtysomething* (ABC, 1987–91) borrowed many of the narrative concerns and debates of *The Big Chill*, concentrating as it did on the lives of a group of friends struggling to balance the heady idealism of their youth with the harsh realities of marriages, kids and careers in their thirties. Created by Edward Zwick and Marshall Herskovitz, *thirtysomething* (the winner of thirteen Emmys®) frequently took the most nondescript events in people's lives (one episode, for example, revolves around Michael's [Ken Olin] inability to pick up after himself) and reveal their significance in the social dynamics of contemporary life. Other more powerful storylines revolved around the death of Michael's father (from cancer) and the diagnosis of Nancy (Patricia Wettig) with ovarian malignancy, but all paid close attention to the personal intricacies of this small group of friends and the emotional landscape of their private lives. As with *The Big Chill*, such inward self-examination did not suit all tastes but its attempt to portray the minutiae of personal existence was unmistakably groundbreaking. As Robert J. Thompson explains (1996: 132):

> Zwick defended what he called the show's 'mandate of smallness', which was committed to looking right under our noses for the material of great American drama. His partner [Marshall Herskovitz] concurred, saying 'I believe strongly that if you go into any home, office, gas station or factory in America and get close enough to those people, you will find that they are incredibly upset about incredibly minor issues ... The so-called petty issues become the major issues in people's lives'. The audience's ambiguous feelings towards the show may have stemmed from the fact that although it validated the quotidian aspects of their lives, it also confronted them with a sometimes dark and existential treatment of those lives.

This interest in so-called 'petty issues', combined with the social dynamics of friendship, helped define a new form of contemporary drama. Films like *Peter's Friends* (Branagh, 1992), sitcoms like *Friends* (NBC, 1994–2004) and *Sex and the City* (HBO 1998–2004), TV dramas like *This Life* (BBC, 1996–7), *Cold Feet* (ITV, 1998–2002), *Our Friends in the North* (BBC, 1996) and *Queer as Folk* (Channel Four, 1999–2000) arguably reflect a new subgenre, one that incorporates and combines important elements of soap opera, drama, comedy and comedy drama. Even TV serials like *Twin Peaks* (ABC, 1990–1, see above), *Northern Exposure* (CBS, 1990–5) and *Eerie, Indiana* (NBC, 1991–2) could be said to have been influenced by this new style of drama, their interest in small-town life and close-knit communities and friends echoing the type of preoccupation with private exist-ence more commonly associated with traditional soap opera (see *Twin Peaks* above). Indeed, much of contemporary TV teen drama, like *Buffy the Vampire Slayer* (WB, 1997–2001), *Dawson's Creek* (WB, 1998–2003) and *Charmed* (Spelling Television, 1998–), addresses similar concerns, the continuous nature of the series and serial allow-ing greater room for their cumulative narratives to explore both story and character complexity – but always from the perspective of their private and emotional lives.[3] As Rachel Moseley puts it, 'Teenageness is a significant "in-between" period, and teen drama deals with the stuff of adolescent anxiety: friendship, love, sex and impending adulthood' (2001: 42).

For the purpose of this chapter I will suggest that the term 'soap drama' may best describe this mixing of various television genres. Indeed, in many ways this new type of television drama employs many of the characteristics of soap opera, in particular, its use of close-up (of people's faces) in order to convey intimate conversation and emotion, its concentration on dialogue rather than visual image to impart meaning, and its tendency towards quickly edited scenes as a way of mixing and bringing together a number of varied and multiple storylines. Like soap opera, its serial form tends to resist closure and its use of time tends to parallel actual or contemporary time (see Fiske, 1992: 179–80).

In doing so, this generic hybridisation seems to illustrate Wilsher's (1997) fear that television drama is generally becoming obsessed with soap opera's interest in personal life rather than investigating questions of 'power and politics'. However, this chapter will argue that the very hybridity of 'soap drama' means that, while utilising soap conventions, the form can also break the genre boundaries upon which traditional 'soap opera' is traditionally made and understood. By employing 'soap' characteristics, these dramas tend to construct an instantly recognisable and familiar world, but do so in such a manner that the traditional forms of representation employed by soap opera are frequently pushed to the limits or even implicitly called into question.

In other words, this chapter will argue that 'soap drama' both employs and subverts soap opera conventions and expectations, relying on its continuous familiarity while also deliberately unsettling and subverting those narrative assumptions and genre expectations. Of course, this does not mean that all 'soap drama' is radically or politically progressive (there is, for example, a clear difference in the political/historical aspirations of a serial/series like *Cold Feet* and *Our Friends in the North*) but that the form (partly because of its post-watershed scheduling) can allow the radical subversion of traditional genres to take place. As Jane Feuer points out, the very structure and style of a show like *thirtysomething* located it within the tradition of daytime soap opera (see 1995: 111–14). However, the way that it played around with modes of 'anti-realism', its radical employment of intertextual referencing and its elaborate construction of fantasy also made it comparable, at times, to various examples of experimental or 'art cinema' (ibid: 92).

Yet what is perhaps most potentially radical from 'soap drama' is not its difference from soap opera but its unmistakable similarities. In particular, the growth of 'soap drama' like *thirtysomething*, *This Life* and *Cold Feet* could actually reveal a growing interest in and awareness of 'micro' as opposed to 'macro' politics. In other words, these 'soap dramas' reveal an explicit concern with the personal and private 'politics' of everyday life rather than concentrating on grand political issues and wider socio-economic debates. For, while 'soap drama' may prioritise the 'personal' over the 'political', it could be argued that it does so in such a way that the political nature of the personal (particularly around issues of identity [*This Life*], sexuality/gender [*Queer as Folk*, *Sex and the City*] and community/nationhood [*Our Friends in the North*, *The Kingdom*]) is explored and examined more powerfully and thoroughly than ever before.

Interestingly, both *The Big Chill* and *thirtysomething* explore such questions, interrogating the relationship between the 'personal' and the 'political' and the relationship the two may now have with 'everyday life'. Indeed, the contrast between the politically revolutionary 1960s (typified by its characters' youthful interest in wider socio-political concerns such as 'freedom' and 'equality') and their current preoccupation with personal and domestic affairs (relationships, family and careers) reveals a generation reinvestigating the nature and conception of political action. While both sets of characters may feel somewhat guilty for now ignoring the grand political crusades of their youth, the 'politics' of everyday life now seem more urgent, relevant and important than ever before. What both dramas seem to suggest then, is that, since the 1960s, 'politics' itself

thirtysomething: celebrating the everyday

has become something that can no longer be disentangled from personal life. Further-more, they could even suggest that the grand political crusades of the past may have actually been a means of hiding and curtailing more pressing personal/emotional concerns. Certainly the characters that seem to have come to terms with this fact (Harold [Kevin Kline] and Sarah [Glenn Close] in *The Big Chill* and Michael and Hope [Mel Harris] in *thirtysomething*) appear to have matured the most, accepting that with age comes a form of personal commitment and responsibility that grand political manifestos can frequently (and even conveniently) ignore.

For many critics this personalisation of the political landscape can partly be traced back to the rise of feminism and the realisation that politics can never be satisfactorily disconnected from everyday life, that almost everything in 'ordinary life' has elements of the 'political' within it. As Jane Shattuc puts it (1997: 92):

> With the women's movement, power and domination came to been seen as pervading of life. Liberation slowly moved from the national to the institutional to the personal arena where the study and understanding of political oppression surrounded the relationship of the 'individually experienced and the collectively organised' sense of politics. Everyday culture became the new battlefield: the politics of the daily experience became the language of the 1970s and 1980s.

According to the sociologist Anthony Giddens, such a cultural shift in the nature of politics can be explained as the difference between 'emancipatory politics' (i.e. the struggle of society to free itself from oppressive customs and traditions) and 'life politics' (the moral and ethical responsibilities of the self which inevitably take place primarily on an individual and day-to-day level). While one is concerned with wider social justice (perhaps epitomised by the cultural revolutions of the 1960s), the other is more concerned with personal freedom and the moral/political construction of self-identity (see Giddens, 1991: 215). What this suggests is that there has been a shift in the very nature of what 'politics' may actually mean to a contemporary audience. It would therefore be surprising if the apparent shift towards 'life politics' suggested by critics like Giddens was not somehow seen and reflected in television drama, a place where 'politics' has traditionally been assimilated and represented for a mainstream, popular audience.

In this chapter then, I will examine in detail three different examples of 'soap drama', explaining how their varied narrative structures explore and examine the political nature of contemporary personal experience. In doing so, I will concentrate in particular on the nature of identity and subjectivity, exploring issues such as gender and sexuality that, although not classed as explicitly 'political', involve crucial and important notions of 'life politics', 'lifestyles' and the social construction of the self. For, while these dramas may not address traditionally 'political' issues, they still manage to dramatise and engage with the social and sociological concerns of an age now currently in the process of transforming what is meant and understood by the very notion of politics itself.

This Life (BBC, 1996–7)

> What to do? How to act? Who to be? These are all focal questions for everyone living in circumstances of late modernity – and ones which, on some level or another, all of us answer, either discursively or through day-to-day behaviour.
>
> Anthony Giddens (1991: 70)

The first series of *This Life* appeared in Britain on BBC2 in 1996, the second and last series arriving a year later in 1997. This 'soap drama' was based around a group of five young solicitors, conveniently sharing a house in South London, and concentrated on the trials and tribulations of both their professional and personal lives. While an explo-

sive wedding of one of the housemates did provide a climatic ending of sorts at the conclusion of the final episode of the second series, the drama came to an end because it
was not re-commissioned, rather than brought to a deliberate conclusion, making it more
a series than a conventional serial. However, while it clearly mimicked the
continuous, open-ended and flexi-narrative form of the traditional soap opera, its producer Tony Garnett (a veteran of British television drama from the early days of *The
Wednesday Play*), seemed intent on giving the series a limited life span. His decision not
to commission a third series was partly due to his fear that it would have only produced
narrative repetition.[4]

Originally written by Amy Jenkins (the daughter of British political columnist Peter
Jenkins), who was a legal clerk herself before becoming a writer, *This Life* was more
interested in the personal experiences of its characters than their professional lives.
Indeed, it seemed to revel in the day-to-day details of ordinary existence, its characters
falling in and out of love, breaking up, committing adultery, dealing (or not) with friend-
ships and so on. It seemed to offer an almost perfect example of what critics like Wilsher
refer to as contemporary TV drama's privileging of personal life over questions of politics and power. Indeed, for many critics, this 'middle-class' soap did little to question or
explore the 'real' social issues at the heart of contemporary Britain, preferring instead to
concentrate on the private (frequently lurid) lives of a group of privileged, good-looking, young graduates. As *The Scotsman* put it at the time, 'The dreaded yuppie has
returned, rising from its unsealed designer tomb to haunt us once more ... Jenkins
has created some of the most immediately detestable stereotypes possible' (cited by
McGregor, 1997: 126).

Lez Cooke's revealing analysis (2003) of the style of *This Life* supports the claim that
the series appeared to deliberately privilege its characters' personal lives. Rather than
being shot on traditional film or video, its makers used digital Betacam, a relatively new
form of camera that was not only considerably cheaper to use but also allowed for a
greater sense of mobility and versatility. This technical choice (based as much on economic as aesthetic considerations) was partly responsible for the distinctive style of the
programme as a whole.[5] Shooting on Betacam demands little preparation (crucially no
extra lighting is generally needed), allowing actors to move freely about and forcing the
camera operator to follow the action rather than dictate it.[6] This not only means that
shooting time is dramatically decreased but that the actors can dominate a scene, putting
greater emphasis on dialogue and character than with more traditional methods of filming. In particular, it means that the camera can concentrate on the merest of looks,
signals and gestures that are exchanged between actors.[7] As Garnett told Cooke, 'For
me the screen is about a close-up and I hate the way most television drama and most
movies are shot because they're all sort of boring mid-shots with too many people in
them. The only landscape that really interests me is the human face' (cited by 2003:
183).

Revealingly, the series often begins its action with a number of close-ups before any
establishing shots are employed, sometimes even allowing establishing shots to come in
at the end of a scene rather than at the start. Consequently, action and location is (quite

literally) pushed into the background and the subject of *This Life* becomes the characters themselves. As Cooke puts it (2003: 181):

> What is immediately striking about the drama is its energy, the fact that it moves along at a very fast pace while still enabling the viewer to get involved with the characters and to identify with them. This is made possible by a combination of rapid, elliptical editing, which maintains a fast narrative tempo, hand-held camera work, which helps to give the drama much of its energy and vitality, and close-up photography, which draws the audience into an empathetic engagement with the personal and professional experiences and dilemmas of the characters.

The aesthetic style of *This Life* means that we get to know these characters in a surprising amount of detail. We witness them swearing, arguing, fighting, drinking (often in excess), getting stoned, snorting cocaine, taking Ecstasy, having (heterosexual and homosexual) sex, committing adultery, dealing with sexual issues and diseases, talking about their problems, gossiping, going to therapy, going to the loo, having a bath or shower (sometimes with a 'friend'), competing with rivals at work, dealing (or not dealing) with their visiting relatives and generally trying to balance (frequently unsuccessfully) their professional and personal commitments. Indeed, both the style and the content of the drama are focused on the ordinary, everyday minutiae of contemporary life. And this (despite its middle-class bias) was a life that many viewers were willing to relate to or empathise with, a set of characters that probably reflected (to varying degrees) many of their own habits, attitudes, opinions and experiences.

Yet *This Life* was no ordinary soap opera where the characters tend to portray the broad demographic of a particular community. Instead, this group of young individuals represented a new and emerging generation. What was particularly striking about the series was its characters' relationship with the contemporary world, one where the certainties of the past were fast becoming redundant. It reflected the personal landscape of a group of young people who had rarely seen their lives represented realistically on television. As Jenkins puts it (2003):

> I wanted to give a voice to my generation, because they've never had one on television. We decided there would be certain themes to *This Life*. We wanted to reflect that this generation is the first who didn't expect to do better than their parents; who can't afford to buy property; who find it very hard to get a job; and who are not threatened by casual drug use. There's a new cynicism – or morality – about relationships because so many of us have seen our parents split up. *This Life* isn't about these issues, but they are there in the background.

One can perhaps detect this attempt to give voice to a new generation towards the end of the first episode when two of its protagonists guiltily admit to finding the Beatles 'boring'. Although a seemingly small and trivial confession, it is a significant and symbolic moment that distinguishes these characters from their parents. In fact, *This Life* reveals a world where the old ideological crusades of the 1960s (such as free love, political activism, the Civil Rights movement and drug-induced enlightenment) are long gone. Instead, these young characters are left to deal with many of the consequences and harsh realities that have arisen out of the idealism, utopianism and 'emancipatory politics' of that decade – including AIDS, drugs (hard and soft), unstable relationships, work insecurity and the general lack of anything to really believe in.

This Life offers a critique of the baby-boomer generation. In direct contrast to *thirtysomething*, this 'twentysomething' (as it was often referred to) drama offered a chance to see how children born during the 1960s and 1970s were actually dealing with the world they had inherited from their socially 'liberal' parents. While their parents' generation may have been driven by political and social certainties, their children seem to be devoid of any such conviction. In contrast, they live in a contemporary landscape where little is certain and the ideologies by which they may have once understood the world are increasingly fragile and illusory. 'I don't have any theories, I'm not really into them', Egg (Andrew Lincoln) tells his interview panel in the opening minutes of the first episode. 'I only mean to say that they don't work, do they? I mean, that much is clear by now. You can't do anything about crime, like you can't do anything about the rain.'

As this suggests, *This Life* reflects a world in which young people are no longer turning to the emancipatory politics of the past to make sense of their lives. In particular, it depicts a contemporary landscape in which young people are faced with an increasingly confusing set of choices, where nothing (particularly careers, relationships, gender roles, attitudes/beliefs and even sexual orientation) are secure. While increased freedom (arguably a byproduct of the cultural revolution of the 1960s and 1970s) may have resulted in greater opportunity and personal choice, it has also produced a greater level of anxiety, apprehension and overall confusion. Instead of looking for social or political certainties, these characters appear to have turned their focus towards their own identities (Egg, for example, puts a great deal of passion and energy into football), the only means by which they can establish or preserve any sense of personal identity in an increasingly uncertain world. 'It's chaos out there', Warren (Jason Hughes) tells his therapist in the very opening line of the first series. 'Out there I can't do anything about anything. I can't change anybody else. But in here (*he points to his head*), in here I can decide what it's going to be like for *me*.'

In *Modernity and Self-Identity*, sociologist Anthony Giddens argues that this preoccupation with the self is a fundamental characteristic of 'late modernity'. For Giddens, it reveals a generation for whom the construction of certain 'lifestyles' is partly a 'political' act. For while the self-reflexive construction of the self is almost irrelevant in 'traditional' societies (where life choices are usually strictly imposed through established customs), in a world of increasing personal choice it becomes the crucial means by which individuals negotiate and make sense of the world around them. As such, lifestyle choices become an important component of self-identity, a crucial site of individual freedom that reflects a world in which identity itself is now a matter of continual renewal rather than compulsory inheritance. As Giddens points out, this means that seemingly small and everyday decisions become encoded with both 'political' and 'moral' meaning and significance (1991: 81):

Lifestyles are routinised practices, the routines incorporated into habits of dress, eating, modes of acting and favoured milieux for encountering others; but the routines followed are reflexively open to change in the light of the mobile nature of self-identity. Each of the small decisions a person makes every day – what to wear, what to eat, how to conduct himself at work, whom to meet with later in the evening – contributes to such routines. All such choices (as well as larger and more consequential ones) are decisions not only about how to act but who to be. The more post-traditional the settings in which an individual moves, the more lifestyle concerns the very core of self-identity, its making and remaking.

This proliferation of 'lifestyles' is certainly an underlining but important theme of *This Life*. Indeed, perhaps one of its most distinguishing features is the way that it nonchalantly represents contemporary attitudes towards serious 'life choices' such as drug-taking, drinking, sex, homosexuality, therapy and so on. One can detect examples of different lifestyles in the central characters themselves. While Warren is an openly gay man; Anna (Daniela Nardini) is an independent 'new woman'; Miles (Jack Davenport) is an arrogant 'new lad'; Egg is a sensitive 'slacker'; and Milly (Amita Dhiri) is an ambitious career woman. Other characters like Delilah (Charlotte Bicknell) (the manipulative and bulimic heroin addict), Ferdy (Ramon Tikaram) (the dishy but sexually confused bisexual) and Lenny (Tony Curran) (a working-class, gay plumber) add to this variation of contemporary lifestyles.[8] Although, as its critics point out, these 'lifestyle' categories risk being little more than crude stereotypes, the sheer breadth of the series (there were thirty-two forty-minute episodes) meant that there was a good deal of time to establish and change these characters (and the complexities of their lifestyles) as the storylines gradually developed.

In particular, *This Life* reveals how this generation of young people are dealing with a world in which proliferation of choice is now the norm, a world in which many of the social taboos of the past (such as drug-taking, casual sex and relationship instability) have become an accepted part of everyday life. It created a fictional world that viewers could intimately identify with, a version of contemporary life that reflected the wider scope of social and cultural change in Britain by concentrating on the private and the personal lives of a small group of friends and colleagues. Rather than exploring the wider social and political dimensions of life in Britain in a way exemplified by British social realist television of the 1960s and 1970s, 'soap dramas' like *This Life* reflected a world where politics itself was now concerned as much with the moral construction of self-identity as with wider social and political issues.

In *This Life*, for example, drugs are no longer an illicit symbol of the counter-culture but a reality all must accept. In fact, cannabis ('dope') is a permanent feature of the house, smoked and passed around with little or no comment. Although Anna drinks a good deal of vodka and wine (particularly Soave) and gets addicted to cocaine (she is caught snorting it in the toilets at work and is forced to attend Alcoholics/Narcotics Anonymous), the characters clearly have a relaxed attitude to most illegal substances (except perhaps heroin ['smack'], which is identified with the no-hoper Delilah). Their attitude, then, reflects a generation who accept drugs as a reality of everyday life, something that is simply there and has to be dealt with. Rather than taking a clear anti-drugs stance, *This Life* shows how readily available and accepted most drugs are. While the dangers and the consequences of drug-taking are revealed in the bad experiences of characters like Anna and Delilah, the fun and excitement of casual drug use is also shown with little or no moralising.[9]

This Life also deals with and portrays sex in a surprisingly fresh and frank manner. In the first episode Milly 'goes down' on Egg in the kitchen and later full frontal shots show them both getting out of the shower together.[10] However, like its portrayal of drugs, sex tends to be shown simply as another factor in the private lives of its characters; a factor that would have been conspicuous (considering the personal nature of the drama) by its absence. As Jenkins puts it, 'We decided straight at the beginning we were just going to do drugs, sex and swearing in passing. Have it all in there, but not dwell on it ... take sex as it comes, as often as it comes' (cited by McGregor, 1997: 96). In fact, the lack of sex is also an important element of the drama. Egg and Milly's diminishing sex life figures in the narrative, as does Miles's search for a sexual partner through a lonely-hearts column. Perhaps dismissing the stereotype that all twentysomethings are continuously having sex, it seemed intent on revealing the complexities and sexual realities of life in the modern age. This includes Miles's terrified trip to have an HIV test, Egg's impotency problem and Warren's interest in 'cottaging'.[11]

As Warren's sexual proclivities suggest, *This Life* particularly attracted controversy for the way that it explicitly portrayed and dealt with homosexuality. Perhaps this was partly learnt from the relative failure of earlier 'soap dramas' to realistically represent gay or lesbian characters, particularly *thirtysomething* which tried to weave a gay character (unsuccessfully) into its second series.[12] In contrast, *This Life* includes Warren from the very beginning (in fact, his session with the unseen therapist actually provides the all-important opening scene). As a crucial and original member of this small group of friends, he was arguably a radical breakthrough for the depiction of gay men in Britain on the small screen. Although not yet 'out of the closet' to his family back home in a provincial town in Wales (and when we meet his macho, rugby-playing brother we have some sympathy), Warren is open about his sexuality in London. Clearly not regarding it as an issue, something to be ashamed about or a radical statement, he simply seems at ease with his desires. He is bewildered when the sexually 'confused' Ferdy denies his feelings for him after a six-hour session of red-hot passion. 'So what happened to you last night?' he asks. 'Were you taken over by aliens from Planet Poof? You were so confused you had a tube of KY and a packet of mint condoms in your pocket?' Perhaps paving the way for the explicit sex scenes in *Queer as Folk* (Channel Four) (see below), *This Life* also showed homosexual couples having as much sex (as explicitly) as their heterosexual counterparts.

Ironically, what was perhaps most distinctive about the gay characters in *This Life* was their lack of any overtly 'camp' sensibility. In fact, Warren, Lenny and Ferdy are barely distinguishable from their heterosexual male counterparts in the drama; their sexuality not something signalled by their clothes or blatantly suggested by a particular way of talking or behaving. The decision to make Lenny a plumber and Ferdy a motorcycle courier was possibly an attempt to move away from such 'effeminate' stereotypes (in comparison, *thirtysomething* made their gay character an artist who lecturers in contemporary art). Indeed, the monosyllabic, withdrawn and sullen Ferdy is anything but camp, his sexy, black, motorcycle leathers something for both the gay and female gaze to enjoy simultaneously. Added to this, he lays out the homophobic Miles with one punch and writes off a BMW with a piece of scaffolding. While some critics might suggest that such portrayals helped to make these gay and bisexual characters more 'straight' (and thereby more acceptable to a primarily straight audience), the graphic sex scenes (at least, by the standards of the day) consistently reminded us of their sexual orientation. Inevitably such scenes caused outrage in the British tabloids. As a review in the *Daily Mail* put it (cited by McGregor, 1997: 126):

> I did not regularly watch *This Life*, but caught the final episode and was appalled at the drugs, booze and, worst of all, simulated sex between homosexuals ... We should complain more often and perhaps our comments would have some weight in preventing such trash being shown.

Yet, despite the complaints that the programme attracted, perhaps the most radical statement made by the drama was that these gay characters were not simply defined by their sexuality. As Tom McGregor has put it, 'Warren is possibly the first major gay character in television who isn't either mincing around outside the closet or cringing inside it' (ibid: 76). Like Milly (whose Asian origins are barely referred to), race and sexuality appear to be less important than individual character traits.[13] While Ferdy is clearly troubled by his sexuality, the housemates (with the possible exception of Miles) are not threatened or even bothered by it. Although this left the drama wide open to accusations of ignoring important social issues like racism and homophobia (Warren is actually praised for admitting he is gay during his interview with O'Donnell [David Mallinson]), it was a refreshing change to see 'minority' groups represented in contemporary television drama without necessarily having their 'minority' status become their only or central means of identification. To have Warren leave the series because he is arrested for 'cottaging' (he is unable to continue working as a solicitor with a criminal record) can be seen as stereotypical in its own right, but it also reveals a drama willing to show fully rounded gay characters in all manner of sexual and social situations not seen on television before (see *Queer as Folk* below).

While feminism is rarely discussed explicitly, the role of the modern woman is also an important issue in the drama. By far the majority of the female characters (with the possible exception of the drug-taking Delilah) have full-time jobs and careers. In fact, with Egg opting out of the law firm to pursue his dream to become a novelist, roles are reversed as Milly becomes the main breadwinner and is often accused by her partner of not spending enough time at home. While questions of gender and power are not completely ignored (one reason Milly is spending so much time at work are her deepening feelings for her manipulative male boss), we see women generally competing on an equal footing with men, and expecting the same rewards in return. Although Anna is not immediately taken on by the law firm, she is proved even more determined to succeed when she does finally get her tenancy. She provides the viewer with a confident and assertive woman who knows what she wants and seems to know how to get it. 'I've never heard you say you feel threatened by anyone', Milly tells her. 'That's because I don't', is Anna's self-assured reply.

Yet Anna is a fundamentally ambiguous character. Although assertive in her desires (professionally, emotionally and sexually), she also seems inherently insecure. Determined not to end up like her victimised mother back in Glasgow ('my father left when I was eleven; my mother went to bed with a packet of Temazepam'), she seems confused by the different standards by which women are judged today. While she wants to be regarded as sexy (a feature self-consciously enhanced by her characteristically long legs that she displays to maximum effect with the help of short skirts and high heels) and adored by men (particularly by the 'bastard' Miles with whom she has a complex on/off relationship), she also wants to remain as independent of the opposite sex as possible. While she is sexually assertive (she even considers sleeping with another woman to boost her career), she also wants to be wooed and seduced by a traditionally romantic male figure, perhaps someone like Cary Grant who she describes as 'charming, romantic, considerate' and 'handsome' (although typically adding that he also had 'a certain horse-like quality').

In this way, a character like Anna seems to represent a generation of young women who are trying to come to terms with and make sense of life after second-wave feminism. Although traditional feminism helped to bring about a radical liberation for women, it has been argued that some of its proposals were both simplistic and puritanical. In contrast, Anna exhibits what some commentators have referred to as a 'post-feminist' attitude to contemporary life, an independent and assertive woman who is not afraid to indulge in and celebrate aspects of female consumption (lipstick, revealing clothing, casual sex and so on) that second-wave feminism would have probably despised. As Charlotte Brunsdon explains, the 'post-feminist' woman (1997: 86):

> is neither trapped in femininity (pre-feminist), nor rejecting of it (feminist). She can use it. However, although this may mean apparently inhabiting a very similar terrain to the pre-feminist woman, who manipulates her appearance to get her man, the post-feminist woman also has ideas about her life and being in control which clearly come from feminism. She may manipulate her appearance, but she doesn't just do it to get a man on the old terms. She wants it all.

Anna wants it all. However, her personal unhappiness seems to suggest that 'post-feminism' is also not without its problems. While she gets drunk, takes drugs, has a great deal of casual sex and is clearly money-orientated (as she openly admits in her interview at the beginning of episode one), she seems far from emotionally content. In particular, many of the men she encounters (in and outside of work) appear to feel threatened by her 'ladette' behaviour. Although she may be labelled an 'honorary bloke' for her assertive demeanour, she is clearly not the 'marrying kind' (Miles chooses the more traditionally 'feminine' Francesca [Rachel Fielding] to wed), nor does she receive whole-hearted respect in her career where her personality (rarely her work) is frequently in question. 'She did well on a drugs case', Miles admits, but it's 'hardly surprising, she *is* a fucking drugs case.'

Anna represents a woman struggling to come to terms with the changing face of gender at the turn of the twentieth century. Although she is far from simply a passive victim of patriarchy like her defeated mother, she is filled with the complex contradictions of her age, reflecting a society whose view of women is still clearly in the process of radical transformation. While many of the battles of first-wave feminism have been won (equality of education, economic independence, sexual liberation), Anna represents a new breed of ('post-feminist') women for whom these changes have also produced chaos and confusion. No longer 'centred' either by traditional gender roles (the pre-feminist world epitomised by the likes of Cary Grant and his screen partner, Doris Day) or oppositional gender roles (puritanical second-wave feminism), they are left in a world of increasing uncertainty and ambiguity (see *Sex and the City* below). It is certainly a gender landscape more blurred and complex than the one experienced by Anna's mother's generation. 'I wish there was a place women could go for uncomplicated sex', Milly confesses at one point. 'There is', Anna sarcastically replies, 'the 1960s'.

As one might suspect, the instability of this new gender landscape is also reflected in many of the central male characters. Miles, for example, is an embodiment of the traditional male reacting to the demands and pressures inflicted by increasingly powerful and independent women like Anna. Not a sensitive New Age ('Hornby-esque') man like Egg, Miles embodies contemporary masculinity as it struggles to accept, resist and come to terms with the rise of feminism. Miles is perhaps best understood as representing a new type of male, a version of contemporary masculinity that aches to return to a world before feminism so radically changed the gender divide. With his sexist attitude to women (he is threatened by Anna's assertiveness and even votes against her tenancy), his homophobic attitude to Warren and Ferdy (he constantly makes jibes about their homosexuality), and his disloyal behaviour towards his intended wife (he has sex with Anna on the sofa while Francesca sleeps upstairs), Miles (an anagram of 'slime') personifies the sexist and insensitive 'new lad'.

But the name Miles is also an anagram of 'smile', suggesting hidden ambiguities at the heart of the 'new lad'. On more than one occasion he covers for Anna at work (with little gratitude from her), he is best friends with the more sensitive Egg (who he even tries to help, albeit ineptly, with his emotional problems), he refuses to become part of the 'old boy' network represented by his corrupt father and does (however grudgingly) publicly apologise to Ferdy for his homophobic behaviour. So, while he (like Egg), seems to revel in reclaiming traditional male pleasures (drinking, football, cars, music, pornography), this does not necessarily make him an old school, conservative misogynist. In fact, the 'new lad' is the name given to the modern male who claims to enjoy many of the masculine pleasures of the past without necessarily becoming involved in their traditional connotations. As one of the editors of British men's magazine *Loaded* has put it (cited by Southwell, 1998: 101):

> We like football, but that doesn't mean we're hooligans. We like drinking, but it doesn't
> mean that as soon as the pub shuts we turn into wife-beating misogynists. We like looking at
> pictures of fancy ladies sometimes, but that doesn't mean we want to rape them.

Miles exhibits both the arrogance and the insecurities of the so-called 'new lad'. As is reflected in *Loaded*'s focus on beauty products for men (we know Miles secretly has facials), stylish clothes (he takes great care in his sartorial elegance), male fitness/health issues (he is constantly trying to give up smoking and get fit) and ways of improving the male sexual performance (his rampant homophobia perhaps suggests some deep level of sexual anxiety), Miles reflects the personal ambiguities at the heart of the contemporary male. In this sense, a character like Miles dramatises a world in which a stable version of masculinity can no longer be conceived as something confidently handed down from father to son, but a confusing and complex set of cultural and social identities that is now more fluid and unstable than ever before. As David Gauntlett puts it (2002: 180):

> ... the playfulness of the [*Loaded* type] magazines and their (usually) cheerful, liberal attitude to most things – apart from the occasional nasty sting of homophobia – suggests that some fluidity of identities is invited. Furthermore, the humour and irony found throughout these publications doesn't hide a strong macho agenda, but conceals the nervousness of boys who might prefer life to be simpler, but are doing their best to face up to modern realities anyway.

As this suggests, *This Life* does not explicitly explore a macro-political environment, but does clearly address the sort of *personal politics* that have helped define a generation and its various 'lifestyles' (contemporary gay culture, post-feminism, new ladism and so on). Of course, this partly reflects television drama's tendency to adopt more 'soap opera'-like aesthetics, particularly in its concentration on the private lives of its characters.

This Life: where the political is always personal

However, it also explores the notion that politics is now as much part of our personal lives as something that exists simply in the public sphere, i.e. outside the home, the family and the bedroom.

It is more than simply a realisation of the feminist insight that 'the personal is political', it is the notion that the very concept of what constitutes 'the political' itself may have changed. Although the individual storylines of *This Life* are crucial (further dramatising 'personal' and 'political' dilemmas), it is central characters like Warren, Anna and Miles that really drive the drama; providing a personal insight into contemporary life from the point of view of the self. Indeed, according to Giddens, soap opera is almost unique in the way that it allows complex narratives of the subject to be constructed and experimented with. He argues that such televisual narratives provide a self-reflexive exploration of the individual that will inevitably have implications on actual situations and events (1991: 199):

> No doubt soap operas, and other forms of media entertainment too, are escapes –
> substitutes for real satisfactions unobtainable in normal social conditions. Yet perhaps more
> important is the very narrative form they offer, suggesting models for the construction of
> narratives of the self. Soap operas mix predictability and contingency by means of formulae
> which, because they are well known to the audience, are slightly disturbing but at the same
> time reassuring.

This Life may certainly be seen as constructing and interrogating narratives of the self within a contemporary and intensely self-reflexive context. Arguably, its soap opera characteristics (especially its emphasis on personal relationships) enable it to explore, investigate and critically examine 'politics' itself on a number of different narrative levels. In particular, the series appeared to critique the 'emancipatory politics' of a previous generation that could talk about equality on a macro-political scale but whose personal lives were frequently riddled with intolerance and inequality.

In contrast to their parents' generation, the twenty-year-olds in *This Life* are forced to confront the fact that lifestyle choices (such as casual sex, drug-taking, monogamy and infidelity) bring with them important and crucial responsibilities that define both the moral and 'political' nature of their lives. While its characters may dream of a more traditional and less complicated world, their self-reflexive attitude to their private lives (the 'pros' and 'cons' of therapy, for example, play an important part in the narrative as a whole)[14] reveals a generation that can no longer deny moral or 'political' responsibility for their actions. It is no surprise therefore that the 'feminised' politics of soap opera became the radical arena within which this drama explored, dramatised and even occasionally deconstructed the politics of the everyday.

Queer as Folk (Channel Four, 1999–2000)[15]

> The term 'queer' is a provocative description that appropriates an earlier, generally offensive,
> description of gay life and turns it to an advantage. To 'be queer' is to openly adopt a non-

'straight' life, while 'to queer' is to estrange or defamiliarise identities, texts and attitudes that are taken for granted and assumed to have fixed meanings.

Peter Brooker (2002: 212)

This Life's exploration of the personal politics of contemporary life was continued and developed two years later on British television in *Queer as Folk*. Made by the Red Production Company, its eight forty-minute episodes first appeared on 23 February to 13 April 1999. Based in Manchester's 'gay village' (particularly Canal Street where someone has appropriately 'scrubbed out the C' [Davies, 1999: 11] and later the 'S' [ibid: 50]), it took an unapologetic if not *celebratory* attitude to gay life and culture as a whole. Quickly amassing over four million viewers an episode, its success was soon followed a year later by *Queer as Folk II* (*Same Men – New Tricks*) in February 2000. Created and written by Russell T. Davies, directorial duties were divided between Charles McDougall (episodes 1–4), Sarah Harding (episodes 5–8) and Menhaj Huda (series II).

Sold to over thirteen countries, *Queer as Folk* created more than its fair share of controversy both in Britain and abroad. All of Australia's terrestrial channels refused to broadcast it, fearing that some scenes could be judged as child pornography. When pay TV providers Foxtel did finally screen it, a separate channel had to be created to ensure no children could accidentally watch (see McKee, 2002: 235). In America, the British version was never actually shown in its entirety although it was reported to have received standing ovations at screenings in movie theatres in Hollywood. Perhaps this may partly explain why America finally produced a remake of the original drama, first broadcast on the cable channel Showtime (whose slogan is 'No Limits') on 3 December 2000.[16] Transferring the action from Manchester to Pittsburgh, USA, many critics originally regarded it as a toned down, poor imitation of the original. Yet, the sheer length of the American series meant that it was inevitably forced to invent and develop its own characters and storylines, some critics arguing that it gradually found a convincing voice of its own. Backed by Hollywood director Joel Schumacher, at the time of writing, it is into its second series and has already broadcast forty episodes, blurring the line between 'soap drama' and 'soap opera' even further.

Both versions of *Queer as Folk* became notorious for their frequently graphic portrayal of gay life. In Britain the controversy focused on the scene of two men, one of them a fifteen-year-old schoolboy (changed to seventeen for the American version) having sex in the opening episode with a man nearly twice his age. This sequence was particularly sensitive in Britain as its first broadcast coincided with the Labour government's plan to lower the homosexual age of consent to sixteen. Not surprisingly then, *Queer as Folk* received more complaints in Britain than any other television drama broadcast in the same year (see Gerrard, 1999). One gay viewer even argued that scenes such as these could fuel homophobic fears about the seduction of vulnerable young boys by older predatory men (see Channel Four, 2000). Others accused the drama of reinforcing stereotypes of all gay men as 'pill-popping, sex obsessed disco bunnies', while many criticised the drama's lack of fully-rounded lesbian characters (see Collins, 2000: 7).

However, many critics came to *Queer as Folk*'s defence, insisting that it was a radical breakthrough for the portrayal of gay men (Davies makes no secret of the fact that it was the *men* and not the women he was really interested in depicting). Alistair Pegg, the editor of the *Pink Paper* (cited by Gibson, 1999), argued that:

> The show is probably the best representation we have seen of ordinary gay lives on television so far. It is not representative and it is not a public information film about being gay, it's about three gay men who happen to be real, interesting characters.

Mark Watson, communications director for the campaign group Stonewall agreed, arguing that '[w]e should never treat it as anything more than a television drama. If it is good, people will watch it, regardless of their sexuality, if it is rubbish, nobody will watch it, including gays and lesbians' (cited Gibson, 1999). Its writer Russell T. Davies has continually defended his screenplay in similar terms, arguing that the show was never meant to represent the *whole* of the gay community (Davies, 1999: 6):

> at first, I did feel this incredible pressure to be representative, to include every single angle of gay life. Lesbians, older gay men, monogamous gay couples, AIDS. And it's just too big, trying to represent an entire world – that's never going to create good drama. God, it would have been so bland and worthy. And besides, no straight drama has that kind of remit. In the end, I realised I had to focus – to find good characters, good stories, and to hell with representation.

Queer as Folk represents a radical departure for the treatment of homosexuality on the small screen. Early portrayals of gay and lesbian life on television, like American documentaries *The Rejected* (KQED-TV, 1960) and *CBS Reports: The Homosexuals* (CBS, 1967), tended to shroud the subject in medical and scientific discourse or else treat it as an unfortunate 'disease' that was best restrained. In 1973, for example, in an episode of *Marcus Welby, M.D.* (ABC, 1969–76) called 'The Other Martin Loring', a closeted gay man talks to the doctor about the effect of his homosexuality on his family. Both Welby's advice and the resolution of the episode is to simply repress his desires for the good of all concerned (see Buxton, 1997: 1478). Television at this time certainly seemed to rely on and perpetuate crude stereotypes of gay and lesbian life, preying on people's fear and ignorance about homosexuality as a whole. As Steven Capsuto puts it (2000: 5):

> TV script writers of the early 1970s finally settled down on two main genres of 'gay script': the 'coming out' script, in which a show's regulars learn to tolerate a gay guest character, and the 'queer monster' script, in which the sexual-minority guest role are killers or child molesters. From fall 1973 to summer 1975, lesbian and gay characters seldom appeared as doctors, detectives, or other problem solvers. Instead, viewers tuned into shows like the *Police Woman* episode 'Flowers of Evil' which portrayed a trio of murderous lesbians who ran around killing old women.

Although attitudes to homosexuality slowly changed during the 1970s, gay people were still generally depicted on television as either social oddities, objects of ridicule or dangerous outsiders. But, perhaps most commonly, gay characters were presented as harmless figures of fun, famously immortalised in Britain by John Inman's exaggerated portrayal of the mincing, limp-wristed menswear assistant Mr Humphries in the BBC sitcom *Are You Being Served?* (BBC, 1972–84). Such portrayals have often been viewed as an attempt to contain the apparent 'threat' of homosexuality through ridicule and mockery.[17] At best, gay characters were simply secondary, isolated or single episode figures that would momentarily introduce a gay presence or issue, but usually as a means of containing or articulating a homosexual 'threat'.

Even when a breakthrough TV movie like *That Certain Summer* (ABC, 1972) (the first American network drama to depict a stable, same gender couple and the first gay-themed show to win an Emmy®) attempted to tackle the serious subject of a gay father 'coming out' to his son, some critics argued that it was still inherently apologetic in tone. The father was particularly criticised by gay groups for saying to his son that, 'If I had a choice, it's not something I'd pick for myself' (see Capsuto, 2000: 81–5).[18] In this way, homosexuality was presented as something that its 'sufferers' should feel inherently ashamed about, a 'disease' or 'condition' to be endured rather than accepted and enjoyed.

Not surprisingly, physical desire between gays or lesbians was rarely dramatised on television. Although by the 1980s homosexual characters were making regular appearances in primetime dramas like *Dynasty* (ABC, 1981–9), *Soap* (ABC, 1977–93) and *Melrose Place* (Fox TV, 1992–8), they were almost always portrayed as strangely 'asexual'. In 1998 a scene of two lesbian characters dancing together in the American series *Heartbeat* (ABC, 1988–9) was reportedly 'banned' by ABC (see Capsuto, 2000: 329), while a kiss between two women in the American sitcom *Roseanne* (ABC, 1988–97) and the British soap opera *Brookside* (Channel Four, 1982–2003) managed to create enormous controversy. Although the award-winning British television drama *Oranges Are Not the Only Fruit* (BBC, 1992) went considerably further in its depiction of lesbian sex, some critics still accused it of sanitising the lovemaking scenes. The 'two girls' tentative exploration of each other's bodies', wrote Steve Clarke in *The Sunday Times*, 'was almost Disneyesque in its innocent wonderment' (cited by Hinds, 1992: 165).

Even when gay or lesbian characters did transgress this 'asexual' guideline it was usually as a means of expressing subversive or dangerous tendencies. In fact, sexualised gay or lesbian characters often took the role of psychotic murderers or serial killers. This seemed to be particularly emphasised in the 1980s, with the growing awareness of AIDS, with TV drama relying on and helping to perpetuate social ignorance and prejudice about the subject. The American series *Midnight Caller* (NBC, 1988), for example, controversially created an evil predatory bisexual man who was knowingly and viciously spreading the virus to heterosexual women, thereby presenting his sexuality in an inherently dangerous (if not murderous) light. In contrast, American TV dramas such as *An Early Frost* (NBC, 1985) and *In the Gloaming* (HBO, 1997) depicted 'saintly' homosexual men whose sexual life had been prematurely terminated by their HIV status. As a result, the sick son's return to the 'safety' of the heterosexual home meant that his previous sex life was conveniently positioned in the past, where it could be contained and glossed over both for the family and the imagined heterosexual audience.[19] In this way, 'good gays' and 'bad gays' could be categorised only and according to their sexual desires. As Capsuto puts it (2000: 7):

> The 'bad gays' were easy to spot: they were the ones with a sex drive. 'Good gays' were almost asexual. Except for a few recurring roles, they usually did not date anyone of their own sex, form a relationship, or seem to even know other gay people. Gay villains, on the other hand, were seen leering at people of the same sex, could have long-term relationships, and were physically affectionate with their partners on screen.

As a result, gays and lesbians were nearly always portrayed as a *problem* (both for the individual and society); something to be worked through, suffered, or at best, tolerated. As this suggests, the treatment of homosexuality on television has primarily been defined from a *heterosexual* rather than a *homosexual* perspective, one that tends (by definition) to conceive it as something 'Other' (and implicitly threatening) to the heterosexual 'norm'. Hence there has been a predominance of television shows that deal with the subject as something 'strange' and 'foreign', that is always in the process of becoming (or not becoming) approved by heterosexual society. According to Alina Bernstein (2002: 295),

> gay and lesbian media representations are not representing, in most cases, a gay/lesbian perspective – they are constructed from a heterosexual point of view and aimed at a heterosexual audience. One consequence is that, in many cases, media texts deal with storylines of tolerance and/or acceptance.

What helped make *Queer as Folk* so unusual then, was the way that it placed homosexuality at the very centre of the action, arguably presenting the whole drama from a primarily homosexual perspective. As a 'soap drama' (despite only running for eight episodes many critics referred to it as Britain's 'first gay soap') it was able to explore the everyday intimate and personal details of life for its three central gay characters in remarkable depth. In this 'soap drama' then, it is the heterosexuals who are the 'support characters' while the homosexuals are consistently defining, determining and implicitly controlling its narrative point of view. In this way, it immediately signified a crucial break from the past. These are not gay men living on the fringes of society, tortured and driven to despair by their social alienation, but men unapologetically enjoying and openly celebrating who they are. As the camera follows Vince (Craig Kelly) and Phil (Peter O'Brien) as they stride down Canal Street in the opening minutes of the first series, their confident, affirmative and dominant point of view is reflected by the long line of gay men and male couples happily displaying and indulging in affection all around them. As James Keller has put it (2002: 1):

> The characters in *Queer as Folk* exhibit little of the shame and self-loathing that is staple in the mainstream depictions of gays and lesbians, nor do they make an effort to apologize for

their behaviour to the uninitiated and the unsympathetic. The show is a strident affirmation
of the personal choices of a collection of young adults.

This general affirmation of homosexuality is also reflected in the very look and style of
the drama as a whole. The bright primary colours and vibrant dance music (a successful
soundtrack was immediately released of popular hits from the series) that came to typify the drama seemed to inherently celebrate (rather than apologise for) its characters'
lifestyle. From the bight, blurred, orange city lights of the opening credits accompanied
by the infectiously bouncy music of Murry Gold's catchy theme tune, *Queer as Folk*
dramatised the refusal of gay and lesbian people to be closeted or 'toned down' by rigid
heterosexual norms. This is immediately signalled by the appearance of characters
addressing the camera in the opening few minutes of the drama, their bright clothes and
the intense coloured backdrops revealing a confident, assured and defiant attitude.
Compare this opening, for example, with the beginning of the AIDS-centred movie
Philadelphia (Demme, 1993), the world-weary tones provided by Bruce Springsteen's
melodic but sombre theme in direct contrast to the flamboyant energy that came to
encapsulate *Queer as Folk*. This self-conscious (and perhaps even self-reflexive) spectacle
is clearly meant to offer a striking contrast to the way the subject of homosexuality may
have been represented on television in the past. As Lez Cooke explains (2003: 188), its

> postmodern televisual style [was] far removed from the social realism of other issue-based
> series – rapid cutting between scenes, a vibrant and colourful *mise en scène*, lively
> camerawork and a pounding soundtrack – *Queer as Folk* was indeed a celebration not only
> of Manchester's gay scene but of its more radical and confrontational elements.

According to *Queer as Folk*'s executive producer Nicola Shindler, such a vibrant and brilliant aesthetic was blatantly borrowed from the colourful, high production values of
American television drama such as *Ally McBeal* (Fox, 1997–2001) and *L.A. Law* (NBC,
1986–94) (and no doubt *Sex and the City* [HBO, 1998–2004] [see below]). In particular, the decision to shoot everything with very long lenses meant that everyone in the
foreground was made to look incredibly sharp while the background remained soft and
somewhat 'beautiful', a crucial if not defining part of its overall look and feel (see Channel Four/Red Production Company, 2000). The drama seemed to deliberately revel in
its high-octane and self-conscious depiction of contemporary gay life. As a result, it
immediately constructed an aesthetic sensibility that attempted to encapsulate the sheer
energy and excitement of the contemporary gay scene rather than dwelling on its 'issues'
and 'problems'.

   Perhaps this can be seen as a crucial part of the drama's own 'camp' aesthetic; a
colourful, accelerated and flamboyant sensibility that refused to betray its own playful
sense of the world. *Queer as Folk* broke away from the rather sombre, respectable and
sober portrayal of gay men in television and films from the past, particularly the attempt
to make many of them overtly 'straight'. As David Gauntlett points out, the Tom Hanks
character in *Philadelphia* is 'seen as part of a loving family, adores opera, is always polite

and pleasant, and never shocks anyone with physical displays of affection for his male partner' (2002: 87). Although a television drama like *This Life* had clearly gone much further in its physical portrayal of gay desire than a film like *Philadelphia*, the gay and bisexual men it portrayed were often peculiarly 'straight'. While this could be seen as a break from television's 'camp' stereotypes of the past, it could also be interpreted as a ploy not to offend or alienate its heterosexual audience more than necessary (see above).

In contrast, the visual style of *Queer as Folk* immediately confronts the viewer with an unashamedly 'camp' aesthetic, refusing to 'straighten up' its men or its visual style to accommodate or pander to a heterosexual audience. In this sense, *Queer as Folk* refuses to 'decamp' itself and attempts to reclaim 'campness' for the homosexual community. In doing so, it resembles the project of gay critics like Richard Dyer and Jack Babuscio who attempted to claim 'camp' back from earlier critics like Susan Sontag (1969) who, they argued, had 'desexualised' it. As Dyer puts it (1977: 11):

> It is just about the only style, language and culture that is distinctively and unambiguously gay male. In a world drenched in straightness all the images and the words of society express and confirm the rightness of heterosexuality. Camp is the one thing that expresses and confirms being a gay man.

In particular, *Queer as Folk* clearly helped to reinvent the means by which same-sex desire could be represented on the small screen. Compared even with the groundbreaking gay images that characterised *This Life*, it pushed the boundaries even further beyond what had previously been seen on television. As early as the first episode we see two naked men in bed and in the shower together. They famously indulge in wet, sweaty, sticky and passionate French-kissing, later moving on to oral sex, anal intercourse and even 'rimming'.[20] Although British law prevents the public transmission of an erect penis, these scenes were unashamedly graphic and erotic in the way in which they simulated the sexual act, going much further than any British television drama had dared to go in the past. Although Stuart's (Aidan Gillen) anal penetration of Nathan (Charlie Hunnam) is not seen in close-up, there is little doubt as to the nature of the act that is taking place, with Nathan's legs thrown over Stuart's shoulders in, what the script describes as, 'a classic fucking position' (Davies, 1999: 29).

Yet, this sexualisation of gay desire is not reserved purely for the promiscuous and manipulative Stuart or the naive but selfish Nathan. Indeed, despite Vince being a typically 'good gay' (at least, in comparison with some of his selfish, arrogant and destructive friends), his relationship with the dishy Cameron (Peter O'Brien) is far from de-sexualised. When, for example, they first sleep with each other at the end of episode five the passion is as strong, furious and spontaneous as anything Stuart indulges in. As their clothing is frantically removed and deep French kisses exchanged, it becomes apparent that Vince can be very passionate indeed. 'Good shag?' Alexander (Antony Cotton) later asks him. 'Magnificent shag' (ibid: 148) is Vince's emphatic reply. This is an important moment, as it explicitly goes against the assumption that only 'bad gays' can have passionate sex lives; that 'good gays' can be sexualised and still retain their 'good guy' status; that homosexual desire is not somehow implicitly linked with evil, corrupt or even murderous behaviour.

However, it was not just in the explicit sex scenes that *Queer as Folk* re-articulated the portrayal of gay men on the small screen. Conceived from a primarily homosexual perspective, much of the drama revolves around the objectification of the male body as a site of erotic spectacle (no wonder then, it became so popular with heterosexual women).[21] In doing so, the serial clearly *re*-presented the way that homosexuality had been 'de-normalised' by heterosexual televisual norms in the past. By explicitly constructing the story from the point of view of its gay characters, *Queer as Folk* arguably constructed homosexuality as the sexual 'norm'; the dominating gaze through which the drama as a whole could be viewed.

For example, episode two of the first series begins with a two-minute-and-forty-second montage of quickly edited images of men looking at men – explicitly positioning the television viewer to identify with the homosexual gaze. The scene begins with Nathan swaggering down a corridor at school to the sound of the French pop group Air's 'Sexy Boy', his predatory and sexually wanton stares searching out and finding male objects of desire to gaze upon. However, when his focus appears to rest on the rear of a fellow schoolboy, the camera moves to reveal that it is now actually the gaze of Vince who is also illicitly staring at men while at work. As Vince disappears from view behind a supermarket shelf, Stuart appears to come out the other side, although we are now at the PR office where he works. Like Nathan and Vince, Stuart is also casting predatory glances around him, his wanton gaze coming to a halt when his eyes finally fall upon a new male client. And so the sequence continues, travelling backwards and forwards between these three different yet surprisingly similar scenarios.

In this way, all three men are united by their gaze, a series of looks that establishes their sexual identity and the unified object of their desire. Indeed, the script describes them at the beginning of this scene as 'members of a secret society' (Davies, 1999: 37), a covert alliance whose watching eyes single them out as viewing the world from a particular (sexualised) point of view. This clearly undermines the traditional notion of the 'male gaze', for although man is still the 'maker of meaning', here he is also the *'bearer of the look'* (see Mulvey, 1992: 27). For critics like Steven Durkman, such a subversion of the 'male gaze' may best be described as a 'gay gaze', a way of looking that produces 'a new position of interpretation, desire, meaning and subjectivity' (1995: 82). This 'gay gaze' unsettles the very apparatus upon which looking has tended to be constructed in conventional heterosexual discourse, producing another level of meaning that inherently undermines traditional notions of who should be looked at and by whom. As a result, the viewer is asked to view the world from a radically different point of view, one that disturbs and re-constructs the very means by which television has traditionally viewed and portrayed homosexuality in the past.

Indeed, even the programme's title seemed to explicitly refuse to let heterosexual norms dictate homosexual identity (its similarity to 'Queer as *Fuck*' suggests unrepentant celebration), helping to turn an originally abusive term into a joyful and triumphant declaration of personal choice. This is dramatically revealed at the end of the first episode

Queer as Folk: celebrating gay culture

when children spray the word '*QUEERS*' in red paint on the side of Stuart's black Jeep. Stuart insists, however, that they still drive Nathan to school in the morning, the term of abuse emblazoned along the side of the vehicle. Of course, when they inevitably attract attention from the school kids who surround them, Stuart is there to counteract any ridicule. 'I'll give you a fuck, you tight little virgin', he quickly replies to one sarcastic schoolboy, 'you won't be laughing then' (Davies, 1999: 34–5). Thus the defaced Jeep becomes a potent symbol of gay pride and defiance, representing these gay characters' refusal to hide, repress or compromise their real (sexual) identities.

So while the derogatory term 'queer' has tended to be used by heterosexual culture to contain and control homosexuality, here the word is re-employed so that it becomes a positive, celebratory and potent weapon. Such a linguistic reversal reveals the artificiality of the way in which heterosexual culture defines what is 'normal' (straight) and what is 'abnormal' (queer), perhaps even undermining those very categories in the process. In fact, the amount of married and supposedly 'straight' men that a character like Stuart sleeps with does suggest that such (heterosexual) categorisations are now (and perhaps were always) inherently fluid and problematic. 'Jesus Christ' Stuart exclaims when a dull, middle-aged, married client approaches him for sex, 'is there no one straight left in the world?' (ibid: 125). In this way, the drama forces us to investigate the boundaries between 'straight' and 'queer' culture, asking us to examine the apparently rigid categorisations that heterosexual society (partly though television and the media) constructs. In doing so, it clearly shares a great deal in common with recent 'queer theory'. As theorist Annamarie Jagose suggests (1996: 1):

> Once the term 'queer' was, at best, slang for homosexual, at worst, a term of homophobic abuse. In recent years 'queer' has come to be used differently, sometimes as an umbrella term for a coalition of culturally marginal self-identifications and at other times to describe a nascent theoretical model which has developed out of more traditional lesbian or gay studies. What is clear ... is that queer is very much a category in the process of formation. It is not simply that queer has yet to solidify and take on a more consistent profile, but rather that its definitional indeterminacy, its elasticity, is one of its constituent characteristics.

However, despite these breakthroughs in its depiction of gay life, *Queer as Folk* was criticised for being too celebratory, failing to address many of the 'problems' and 'issues' facing gays and lesbians in contemporary society. In particular, the British version seemed to have no safe-sex message, promiscuity and drug-taking seemed to be the norm and underage sex was apparently encouraged if not tolerated. Because of this, it was regarded as an essentially 'empty' exploration into gay culture, a bright, colourful and exciting dramatic concoction that was ultimately light on any real serious debate or socio-political discussion. 'The series was the Millennium Dome of homosexuality', Michael Collins wrote in the *Observer*. 'It was received as though it represented the epitome of all that was native and modern to a culture and a community. And, like the Dome, it looked spectacular, had lots of rides, yet was thin on content' (2000: 7).[22]

Yet, regardless of its vibrant style and its general tone of celebration and affirmation, *Queer as Folk* did still deal with some complex social and personal issues, such as gay prejudice and homophobia. At one point in the British series, for example, Alexander's (Antony Cotton) parents callously ignore him when they accidentally come across him in the street. 'I said hello!' he shouts at them as they continue to walk by without any acknowledgement. 'Oy, I said hello! Look at me', he continues, '*I said hello!*' (Davies, 1999: 154). In *Queer as Folk II*, Stuart is even forced to tell his parents he is gay by a blackmailing eight-year-old nephew who demands cash after discovering his website 'Big Cock City' on his uncle's computer. But it is probably Nathan's story that offers the most detailed account of the difficulties of 'coming out' in contemporary Britain. Bullied at school, he suffers cruel and blatant prejudice from both students and teachers alike. Although his well-meaning mother (Caroline O'Neill) tries to understand, his father (Paul Copley) turns to violence in desperation. In episode six he repeatedly rams the back of Stuart's Jeep with his own car, furiously attacking both his son and his apparent 'corrupter' in a fit of blind rage. Meanwhile, the American version has Justin (Randy Harrison) hospitalised after a particularly vicious homophobic attack.

But it is the way in which these social problems are presented and challenged which suggests a subtle difference in the treatment of 'gay issues' generally by the drama as a whole. In particular, these gay characters repeatedly stand up for themselves, refusing to let homophobia have the final moral victory over them or their friends. As a result, the 'camp' aesthetic of the drama is allowed to infiltrate even its most 'serious' issues and concerns. When, for example, one of his school bullies later turns up in a gay bar in Canal Street, Nathan uses the karaoke microphone to tell everyone about his 'queer bashing' (refraining only to inform them about the time the boy let Nathan masturbate him in the changing rooms). But perhaps the most dramatic statement against gay prejudice comes from Stuart. When he visits a car showroom with the lesbian Romey (Esther Hall) and their baby (conceived through artificial insemination – 'Most expensive wank I've ever had' [Davies, 1999: 25]), he is mistaken by a salesman for a happily married, heterosexual man. Warning him off the Sport Jeep because it is popular with 'gay guys', the salesman tells him that, at least, 'they die young, so we get the resale value' (ibid: 198). As the salesman returns to his desk, Stuart starts the engine of the new car and drives the Jeep straight through the plate glass window that separates them.

Despite the explicit and controversial lack of reference to condoms (although Brian does offer a clear message of safe sex in the US version [see Keller, 2002: 2]), *Queer as Folk* also addresses some of the inherent dangers concerning gay casual sex.[23] At the end of episode three, for example, Phil (Jason Merrells) meets a man while hailing a taxi and quickly invites him home. Within minutes he is accepting drugs from the stranger and falling into a 'hypoxic fit' (ibid: 86) on the kitchen floor. As his guest realises the seriousness of Phil's condition he quickly takes his jacket and runs, only coming back momentarily to steal the cash from Phil's wallet. Such a scene then, might be seen as a moral condemnation of gay promiscuity. Indeed, Phil's mother articulates such fears at his funeral, asking Vince if her son would have found 'himself at thirty-five taking heroin with a casual *fuck* if he was *straight*?' (emphasis in the original, Davies, 1999: 102).

As this reveals then, *Queer as Folk* deals with some explicitly 'serious' gay issues, but does so in such a manner that they are never allowed to completely determine its overall narrative structure or aesthetic style. While Phil's death is an inherent warning about the dangers of (gay) casual sex, it is only one example of gay desire depicted in the drama as a whole, a reality of gay life that clearly does not make the act itself either morally corrupt or corrupting. In fact, Phil's deadly encounter is interspersed with a number of other sexual scenarios from the same evening which self-consciously refuse to allow only one version of homosexual desire to remain dominant. While Phil is casually accepting drugs from a stranger, Stuart embarks on an erotic threesome, Dane (Adam Zane) and Alexander have a farcical (and decidedly unerotic) encounter with a morbid, snake-loving undertaker, and Vince has an unsuccessful rendezvous with a man who claims to have Brazilian beach parasites living in his anus! By intercutting and contrasting these four different sexual encounters, the viewer is allowed to simultaneously witness a vast array of gay casual scenarios; ranging from the pornographic, the funny, the dangerous and the outright ridiculous. Rather than focusing on one particular example of gay desire and making it representative of the whole, different aspects of gay life are subsequently portrayed and revealed.

As a result, homosexual desire is not itself deemed inherently 'evil', but casual gay sex is represented as erotic, dangerous, frequently bizarre and often strangely unsatisfying. Phil's overdose certainly gives a tragic twist to the evening's proceedings, but it is never allowed to completely dominate the narrative to such an extent that it might suggest that homosexuality itself inevitably leads to illness or even death. Instead, by intercutting various casual encounters, the drama explores the inherent and inevitable dangers that casual sex can bring without turning homosexuality itself into an 'evil' or inevitably 'murderous' act. The drama does away with the implicit premise of earlier gay or lesbian television drama which tended to treat homosexuality as something determined by one overriding characteristic. Instead, various aspects of gay life are represented so that the sheer plurality and complexity of homosexuality (and, all sexuality) is dramatically revealed.

There are many criticisms that can be levelled at *Queer as Folk*. Its depiction of a world of urban, young, affluent, beautiful and liberated gay men may have little to say to those gay men (and, of course, lesbians) who are older, poorer, less trendy, live outside the cities or who do not have access to a contemporary gay scene as vibrant or as open as Manchester's or Pittsburgh's. The very glossy and slick style of its *mise en scène* may even alienate viewers who feel it presents gay and lesbian life as one endless and flamboyant party (or even orgy) with few social or individual consequences to pay for such hedonistic (particularly sexual) indulgence. It could be argued that the drama fails to adequately reflect the more humdrum social reality of many gay and lesbians in Western societies at the end of the twentieth century. Indeed, despite Russell T. Davies' claims that the series was not meant to be a dramatic 'representation' of gay issues, its portrayal of homosexuality is itself inevitably part of a wider ideological, political and historical struggle.

Yet, the crucial difference between this and earlier gay-or lesbian-orientated TV drama, is that the narrative itself refuses to depict homosexuality as something inherently 'abnormal', 'serious' or inevitably 'problematic'. Partly articulated through its flamboyantly 'camp' sensibility, the characters in *Queer as Folk* have little problem in displaying their desires, openly enjoying their sexuality without any apparent shame, guilt or introspective turmoil. Its extensive use of primary colours, vibrant music, explicit (same-gender) sex scenes etc. constructs a world no longer defined simply in relation to heterosexuality, but a blatantly unapologetic narrative landscape, defined only, or mainly, by its own set of complex rules and social (sexual) relations.

As a result, *Queer as Folk* can be remembered as one of the first 'post-AIDS' television dramas, a depiction of contemporary gay life that deliberately refused to simply *dwell* on the 'problems' of being gay. Indeed, perhaps the great strength of this 'soap drama' is that viewers get to know these characters in intimate detail, so rather than simply seeing them as 'gay characters' (and therefore emblematic of certain 'gay issues') their sexuality eventually becomes only a small (although crucial) part of their complex psychological make-up. The real subject of the drama is not homophobia or the dangers of casual gay sex, but friendship and the eternal and universal dilemma of unrequited love. At its heart, the narrative revolves around a love triangle between three men that goes far beyond contemporary 'gay issues' and perhaps even sexual orientation itself. But this does not make it any less 'serious' or 'socially aware' than earlier gay dramas. In fact, by refusing to make being gay an issue in 'itself', it makes the most radical statement of all. As Joel Schumacher has put it, 'It was the most political thing I have ever seen … because it wasn't political at all' (cited by Channel Four/Red Production Company, 2000).

Sex and the City (HBO, 1998–2004)

> Wearing lipstick is no longer wicked, and notions of identity have moved away from a rational/moral axis and are much more profoundly informed by ideas of performance, style and desire.
>
> Charlotte Brunsdon, 'Post-feminism and Shopping Films' (1997: 85)

In 1995, the American television producer Darren Star (best known for creating *Melrose Place* [Fox, 1992–9] and *Beverly Hills 90210* [Fox, 1990–2000]) was in the process of making a new TV show called *Central Park West* (CBS, 1995–6) in New York.[24] While living there he became a fan of a column in the *New York Observer* called 'Sex and the City' written by journalist and 'Manhattan girl-about-town' Candace Bushnell.[25] Legend has it that the idea of adapting her column for television was first conceived after Bushnell interviewed Star about his new show. According to Star, what really appealed to him about the project 'was the idea of a single woman in her thirties writing about relationships and using that column as a tool of self-discovery about her own life, sometimes even unbeknownst to herself' (cited by Sohn, 2002: 14). In particular, he hoped that this 'comedy of manners' would centre on the intimate life of its female characters, pushing the boundaries of how women's personal preoccupations had been depicted on television before. As Amy Sohn has put it (ibid):

> Having cut his teeth on drama, Star wanted to try his hand at a comedy, a comedy about sex from a female point of view, which was a totally uncharted arena on TV. He had some early discussions with ABC, but felt that the network couldn't fulfil what he had in mind. 'They weren't even sure they could call it *Sex and the City*', he recalls. In addition, he didn't like the way networks tended to handle adult sexuality: in a wink-wink, nudge-nudge style, euphemistic and adolescent. Instead he wanted to create a true adult comedy in which the sex could be handled in an upfront and honest way.

Initially this new 'adult comedy' was conceived as an anthology series centred on Bushnell's central character Carrie Bradshaw (her fictional alter ego who also writes a column
called 'Sex and the City').[26] The idea was that each episode would revolve around her
but would include a separate storyline and different characters each week. However,
when the column was later turned into a best-selling book (also called *Sex and the City*,
published in 1996) it was decided to focus all the stories around Carrie and three of her
closest friends. This allowed a close-knit female group to provide the continuous narrative framework around which the series would gradually develop and evolve. It was
decided that these friends would be Charlotte York (an art dealer and good old-fashioned romantic traditionalist), Miranda Hobbes (a cynical and pragmatic,
Harvard-educated lawyer) and Samantha Jones (a sex-obsessed, fortysomething PR
executive who owns her own company).[27] It was through these varied and contrasting
personalities and perspectives that *Sex and the City* tried to reveal the intimate complexities of life for the contemporary single, urban woman.

After a pilot show in 1997 (directed by Susan Seidelmann, who directed *Desperately
Seeking Susan* [1985]) the first series of *Sex and the City* was aired in America on HBO
[Home Box Office]) in 1998.[28] An almost instant hit; it eventually attracted viewers from
around the world such as Asia, Australia, New Zealand, Europe and Canada, winning
numerous awards (including four Emmys®, three Golden Globes, and a Screen Actors
Guild award) in the process.[29] As testament to its huge influence '*Sex and the City* Tours'
were soon available in New York where clubs and eateries such as *Il Cantinori*, *Bunga-
low 8* and *Tao* saw huge surges in their clientele after being featured in the series. Indeed,
the accompanying book *Sex and the City: Kiss and Tell* (2002) includes its own '*Sex and*

Sex and the City: an unashamedly female-centred universe

the City Map' of New York, locating all forty-one real places visited by its female characters (see ibid: 146–7 and Ackass and McCabe, 2004: 226–7). In keeping with its
reputation as a show-piece for fashion, it also frequently promoted or helped influence
the next big fashion item (Burberry coats, the Birkin Bag, Ray-Ban Aviator sunglasses,
Manolo Blahnik shoes and so on) with surprising consistency.[30] Compared with the work
of Edith Wharton, Evelyn Waugh and F. Scott Fitzgerald, the series captured the
contemporary *Zeitgeist* like no other television show, producing a huge fan base and a
surprising amount of social comment and cultural discussion.[31]

It was, of course, no surprise that the cable channel HBO became the show's final
home. Not only was it more at ease with its adult subject matter, but it also understood
the style of production that its makers were after. Above all, Star was reluctant to turn
Sex and the City into a traditional situation comedy. He consequently insisted that it would
do away with the conventional ingredients of the genre, dispensing with a live audience,
canned laughter, a fixed set and the traditional four cameras. In contrast, its more 'filmic'
style of production suited its narrative sensibility, never allowing the comedy or 'slapstick'
elements of the show to completely eclipse its dramatic aspirations. As Star suggests, the
'filmic' quality of the drama reflected a desire to blur the boundaries between the big and
small screen, perhaps indicative of his wish that the programme would be taken 'seriously'
rather than simply conceived as a 'TV comedy'. 'I wanted people to be able to watch the
show and not feel like they were suddenly watching television', he has explained. 'I wanted
it to bridge the gap between a television series and a movie' (cited by ibid).

Certainly the style and form of *Sex and the City* signalled exactly how far television
drama had come from the early dynamics of the single play. In particular, its cumulative
narrative structure (rather than completely self-contained episodes as is traditional in
situation comedy) allowed both characterisation and plot development to become as
detailed and as complex as any serial or miniseries. By the end of series five, the characters and events in *Sex and the City* were as recognisable and familiar as those from any
long-running soap opera, its gradual evolution and narrative development producing its
own carefully structured, sequential trajectory. However, like situation comedy, the series
never lost sight of its intimately contained world, which (as in most successful sitcoms)
primarily revolved around one small 'family' (see Hartley, 2001: 66–7). As a result, *Sex
and the City* cleverly combined elements of soap opera with the series, serial and situation comedy to produce a form of 'soap drama' that allowed different narrative levels
to take place simultaneously. As with shows like *Cold Feet*, *Friends* (NBC, 1994–) and
Ally McBeal, *Sex and the City* pushed the boundaries of what could and could not be
defined as television drama, allowing traditionally 'comedic' genres to become infused
with more 'serious' narrative content. A term such as 'dramedy' perhaps best describes
such a form, acknowledging the impact of both narrative traditions and generic forms
in equal measure (see Nelson, 2001: 45).[32]

It was possibly this hybridity of narrative genres that enabled *Sex and the City* to tackle
surprisingly controversial issues, the comedic elements of the drama (particularly
renowned for its smart one-liners and pithy commentaries) sometimes 'sugaring' difficult or taboo subjects. Indeed, it soon acquired a reputation for discussing and

portraying 'female-centred' issues with sometimes surprising honesty and frankness. Topics such as marriage, commitment, divorce, pregnancy, miscarriages, compatibility, fidelity and (of course) shopping were discussed alongside conversations about female masturbation, the joy of vibrators, oral/anal sex, threesomes, lesbianism, sexual perversion, 'funky spunk' and female ejaculation. From the very first episode ('Can Women Have Sex Like Men?'), these subjects became the central issues around which the drama revolved as its four principal characters ceaselessly looked (usually with very little luck) for Mr Right. The show took the contemporary relationship between men and women as the backdrop around which notions of love, romance and sex could be dramatised and discussed within an explicitly modern setting. In particular, its narrative seemed preoccupied with dramatising a world where traditional romantic sensibilities were gradually disappearing. As Carrie's (Sarah Jessica Parker) narration appears to suggest at the start of episode one:

> The glittering lights of Manhattan that served as backdrops for Edith Wharton's bodice-heaving trysts are still glowing – but the stage is empty. No one has breakfast at Tiffany's and no one has affairs to remember – instead we have breakfast at 7am and affairs we try to forget as quickly as possible. How did we get into this mess?

With this central dilemma in mind, each episode of *Sex and the City* is structured in a similar way, the most common narrative pattern revolving around Carrie as she researches her next newspaper column, each of her friends providing a personal perspective on particular topics and debates. These have included questions such as: 'Is there a secret Cold War between marrieds and singles?', 'Are threesomes the new sexual frontier?', How often is normal?', 'Are relationships the religion of the nineties?', 'Can you change a man?', 'How do you know if you're good in bed?' and so on. At the end of each episode Carrie usually arrives at a loose moral conclusion, a frequently perceptive but open-ended insight into contemporary sexual mores that is consistently framed from a primarily female perspective. In this way, the show explores both the joys and the tribulations of female liberation, revealing the modern woman as surprisingly erotic, funny, bright, independent and assertive.

As Star intended and its title suggests, *Sex and the City* was particularly interested in female desire. In particular, it sparked debate for its provocative portrayal of the modern woman as sexually experienced and assertive, a new, liberated woman who is not afraid to go out and get what she feels is her legitimate birthright. The way these four central female characters talk openly about sex reflected both the language and the topics of *Cosmopolitan*'s problem page, but put them firmly on to the small screen. Protocols of lovemaking (such as whether to swallow or not, whether to use sex toys, whether to involve a third person or the laws about kissing after giving oral sex) are discussed with considerable ease alongside discussions about which shoes to buy or where to eat. By the standards of the traditional situation comedy the sex scenes were also highly provocative, pushing sexual representation further than most comedy or TV drama (with the possible exception of *Queer as Folk* [see above]) had dared to in the past. The programme shows women experimenting with sex, openly discussing it and above all enjoying them-selves physically. As Madeleine Bunting puts it, the four female characters (2001)

> discuss every kind of sex – masturbation, dildos, telephone sex and blowjobs – comparing
> experiences, offering advice and encouragement. Nothing is out of bounds, sex is an
> adventure playground which doesn't necessarily have much to do with love … The sex stuff
> works because it turns on its head the age-old female sexual victimhood. The whole rationale
> of *Sex and the City* is that these women want pleasure, know how to get it and are
> determined to do so. And the kick is in the assumption that the women are always great in
> bed, the men more variable.

Samantha (Kim Cattrall) is the most sexually aggressive of the four central characters. In the course of the first four series she sleeps with thirty-eight men, two women, uses a strap-on, takes Viagra and Ecstasy, experiments with multiple partners, celibacy and all manner of sex toys.[33] 'I'm tri-sexual', she tells her friends, 'I'll try anything sexual'. Only rarely does she have to resort to masturbation to satisfy her sexual needs, but this is another taboo she is only too willing to break. 'I'll admit I've had to polish myself off once or twice', she explains, 'but when I *RSVP* to a party, I make it my business to come'. Of course, Samantha is a classic role reversal, a woman taking the attitude to sex that men have taken for centuries, treating her partners as sex objects and caring little for emotional commitment. 'There isn't enough wall space in NYC to hang all of my exes', she explains. 'And let me tell you, a lot of them were hung.'[34] Yet Samantha also reveals the sexually liberated woman, a female for whom equality means living and loving as men do. 'A guy could just as easily dump you', she tells her friends, 'if you fuck him on the first date as he can if you wait until the tenth.'

Although the more traditional Charlotte (Kristin Davis) tries to resist this sexual assertiveness ('A vibrator does not call you on your birthday', she tells her friends. 'A vibrator doesn't send you flowers. And you cannot take a vibrator home to meet your mother'), *Sex and the City* reveals a world where women now want and demand as much (sexual) freedom as men, and are determined to put men to the test in the process. No wonder so many of the male characters look anxious; these women display the kind of confidence and liberated attitude to sex that only a generation before would have had them labelled as cheap, stupid and even (certainly in the case of Samantha) mentally unstable. However, this is a world where men no longer hold all the powerful cards either in or out of the bedroom. As Miranda (Cynthia Nixon) puts it, 'In fifty years men are going to be obsolete, anyway. Already you can't talk to them. You don't need 'em to have kids with. You don't even need them to have sex any more.'

Despite this focus on female sexuality and desire, *Sex and the City* has been criticised for its portrayal of women generally. Like its 'post-feminist' contemporaries (in particu-lar, *Bridget Jones's Diary* [Maguire, 2001] and *Ally McBeal*), many critics argued that its female representations were ultimately weak and reactionary. According to its critics, the show simply revealed a world where feminism and liberation had brought the modern woman nothing but confusion, misery and desperation. As funny, outrageous and 'postmodern' as a show like *Sex and the City* seemed, they argued that it ultimately constructed inherently old-fashioned female stereotypes that, despite their open sexuality, still centred their lives around finding the right man to settle down with. According to the critic Stacey D'Erasmo, the show not only suggests that feminism is over but that it also failed. For Erasmo, viewers will sit back and exclaim, '[L]ook how unhappy the "liberated" woman is! Men don't want to marry her' (cited by Ackass and McCabe, 2004: 9). As the ever pragmatic and cynical Miranda complains, 'How did it happen that four such smart women have nothing to talk about but boyfriends? It's like seventh grade with bank accounts.' Indeed, despite its frank portrayal of female desire, most of the women in the show (with the possible exception of Samantha) still continually hanker for Mr Right, each episode centred around that endless and exhausting search for romantic love. As Carrie herself puts it, 'I couldn't help but wonder: inside every confident, driven, single woman, is there a delicate, fragile princess just waiting to be saved?'

Other commentators have criticised *Sex and the City* for constructing a dangerously misleading and idealised view of life for the contemporary urban woman. According to Jonathan Bignell, the affluence of its four central characters (they all have large, comfortable apartments in Manhattan, constantly wear expensive designer clothes and are rarely seen at work) renders invisible the 'questions of economic status, work and social power for women' (2004a: 217). For Bignell, the central characters' 'fascination with clothes, shoes, hair and personal style is a focus on relatively trivial aspects of women's lives, in contrast to questions of gender equality and the difficulty that real women face in employment and opportunity' (ibid). This is reinforced by its comedic impulse that forces its viewers (notably from the high-spending 18–35 age group) to identify with its characters' problems rather than encouraging them to critically engage with the issues it might arise.[35] In conclusion, Bignell argues that *Sex and the City* perpetuates (ibid: 220; also see Bignell, 2004b: 161–76)

> discourses about women's self-absorption, the focus on heterosexual sex as the barometer
> of personal and social success, and the normalisation of commodity fetishism as the
> environment in which women exist 'by nature'. For more than thirty years feminist critics
> have been reacting against these kinds of representation, and aiming to liberate women from
> their oppressive restrictions on what being female and feminine mean.

It is true that *Sex and the City* deliberately sets itself up as an ostentatiously glamorous show that reproduces a world of beauty, wealth and cosmopolitan decadence. Not only does it seem obsessed with affluence and consumption, its explicitly colourful, glossy and expensive (Star's self-consciously 'filmic') *mise en scène* appears to take great delight in displaying and indulging in material wealth and glamour. Such a narrative world flies in the face of the early feminist movement, which traditionally tended to deride or downgrade female consumption. Consumerism in all its forms but particularly that which tended to promote a particular view of 'femininity' (such as make-up, fashion, beauty products, women's magazines and so on) were generally regarded as the enemy of 1970s' feminism. These forms of consumption were perceived as instruments of patriarchy that

helped keep women oppressed by primarily defining them through their physical attractiveness to men (see Brunsdon, 1997: 86–7).

This way of thinking is clearly at odds with a programme like *Sex and the City* which
openly celebrates female consumption. Its obsession with shopping, clothes, fashion,
make-up, designer labels and its focus on the romantic possibility of heterosexual love
seem to explicitly contradict the traditional feminist quest for female independence, particularly the rejection of women as commodified sex objects designed to satisfy the male
gaze. Like their early prototype, Madonna, these are unashamedly 'material girls' who
appear to derive great joy (albeit in an ironic or self-consciously flamboyant manner)
from indulging and revelling in traditionally 'feminine' pleasures.

This self-conscious and ironic use of style and performance reveals the men in the
series to be profoundly unstylish and one-dimensional – a gender that seems simply
unable (or at best unwilling) to face up to the changing face of modern women. Indeed,
if the four central characters are obsessed with finding the right man, is it not because
the men they consistently meet are unable to satisfy their 'post-feminist' desires on any
level at all? As Janet McCabe and Kim Ackass point out, few male characters are even
named by the women and are addressed by titles such as Mr Big, Mr Pussy, Groovy Guy,
Mr Marvellous or Artist Guy (Ackass and McCabe, 2004: 7). Freaks, liars, 'toxic bach-
elors' (commitment phobics), married, repressed, porn-obsessed, 'modelisers' (they will
date only female models) and narcissistic, men are consistently portrayed as shallow,
immature and emotionally inadequate for these four surprisingly strong, intelligent, stylish and financially solvent women. In particular, the men seem to have missed the fact
that modern women have changed and are still obsessed with traditional representations
of femininity that these women refuse to live up to.[36]

Rather than suggesting a return to traditional patriarchal relationships, then, *Sex and
the City* could perhaps reveal and portray a generation of women who have actually
become more discerning, choosy and fastidious about what they want out of life and men.
The show arguably depicts a world where women are now granted the sort of choice and
opportunity that their mother's generation could only dream about. Rather than marry
the first man that asks or gets them pregnant, these women are given greater choice than
ever before to select their life partners with considerable care, skill and endless (particularly female) discussion. As such, Carrie and her friends obsess about men partly because
they can't find any that match their increasingly high standards. Seen in this light, the
endless search for a good, honest and *desirable* man becomes not so much a longing to
return to romantic tradition as a seething critique of the contemporary male, particularly
of those men who are threatened by this new breed of strong and independent women.
This tendency is immediately established in the opening of the first episode:

(All in direct address to the camera):

PETER MASON (ADVERTISING EXECUTIVE – TOXIC BACHELOR):   The problem is expectation.
　　　　　　　　　Older women just won't settle for what is available.

MIRANDA: By the time you reach your mid-thirties you think, why should I settle? You
　　　　　　know?

CHARLOTTE: It's like the older we get, the more we keep self-selecting to a smaller and smaller group.

CAPOTE DUNCAN (PUBLISHING EXECUTIVE – TOXIC BACHELOR):   What women really want is Alec Baldwin.

PETER: There's not one woman in New York City who hasn't turned down ten wonderful guys because they were too short, too fat or too poor.

MIRANDA: I have been out with some of those guys, the short, fat and poor ones. And it makes absolutely no difference. They're still as self-centred and unappreciative as the good-looking ones.

PETER: Why don't some of these women just marry a fat guy? Why don't they just marry a big fat tub of lard?[37]

Even when the traditional and hopelessly romantic Charlotte gets married, it turns out that her husband Trey (Kyle MacLachlan) is unable to satisfy her sexually (he seems to prefer the pictures of naked women in *Juggs*, his porn magazine). While her mother's generation may have put up with this unhappy situation, Charlotte refuses to do so and relies on her woman-centred world for emotional love, advice and support. 'Look at me', she tells her sexually repressed husband, 'This is me. I'm not Madonna, and I'm not a whore, I'm your wife … and I'm sexual, and I love you.' Similarly, when Carrie refuses to marry the seemingly perfect Aidan Shaw (John Corbett), she does so not because he won't make a good husband and father (in fact, we later see him playing the role of an ideal parent) but because she does not love him. This perhaps reveals women's new-found determination not to settle even for a 'good' and 'decent' man when he is not 'the one'.[38] While Carrie's Mr Big (Chris Noth) may be 'the one', he seems to be emotionally inadequate and unable to commit to her, revealing a world where endless choice does not always bring total fulfilment. However, this does not suggest that female choice is inherently bad, only that endless choice can sometimes produce as many problems as it solves. As Carrie laments, 'In a city of infinite options, sometimes there's no better feeling than knowing you have only one'.

Consequently, *Sex and the City*'s obsession with finding Mr Right could suggest a world in which women everywhere (and not just successful, middle-class New Yorkers) are starting to demand more out of their lives. If these thirtysomething women are delaying settling down, getting married and having babies, it is not simply because they now have careers, economic status and social independence, it is because they inevitably desire and demand more than any generation of women before them. These are not simply passive and attractive women waiting patiently for dashing Prince Charming to arrive and sweep them off their feet, but a group of smart, funny and highly critical women who insist that the men in their lives finally face up to the fact that women have changed. Rather than return to 'traditional' modes of courtship, the show re-interprets courtship for a contemporary audience. As Joanna di Mattia puts it (2004:18):

Sex and the City renders a landscape where the rules of heterosexual relations are in a state of flux – with women no longer content to adopt traditional models of femininity, and men unsure what is expected of them in both public and private roles. Faced with a newly independent, sexually liberated woman, hegemonic masculinity repositions itself as an unstable identity in need of revision. As a result, the formula for the ideal romantic hero has become imprecise.

The changing role of women in society is also reflected in the world of conspicuous consumption that the programme indulges in. Indeed, as these successful women now have highly paid careers, would it not be odd if they didn't take great care and delight in spending their hard-earned money? Clothes, shoes and cosmetics may appear 'trivial' to (male) critics like Bignell, but for these four women they represent a world where female desire is now no longer repressed, ridiculed or downgraded (see Bruzzi and Church Gibson, 2004: 115–29). Refusing to be (or, at least delaying the time when they are) tied to the demands of children and domestic drudgery ('The only thing I've ever successfully made in the kitchen is a mess,' Carrie confesses. 'And several small fires'), these four women have almost complete freedom to choose exactly what to do with their lives, their free time, their bodies and their (yes, quite considerable) income. That means refusing to settle for cheap and unfashionable shoes and refusing to tolerate insensitive, sexually inadequate and emotionally immature men. While this may construct an unrealistic world for viewers who are not so economically (or socially) independent, it also creates a narrative space in which notions of female freedom can be articulated, dramatised and discussed.

Clearly this 'narrative space' has strong elements of fantasy within it. The version of New York constructed by *Sex and the City* owes more to the bourgeois, middle-class comedies of Woody Allen (see Grochowski, 2004: 149–60) than the gritty realism of Martin Scorsese, Spike Lee or even David Chase (see *The Sopranos* above).[39] Its makers self-consciously constructed a highly stylised and fashionable world that is built (perhaps like its real generic predecessors such as *The Mary Tyler Moore Show* [CBS, 1970–7] and *Rhoda* [CBS, 1974–8]) on a combination of real and idealised representations. The self-reflexive direct address to camera that typified the first series suggests as much, as does Carrie's narrative voice-over which helps to frame and conceptualise much of the series from an essentially ironic and profoundly personal perspective. As Helen Richards' revealing account of Carrie as a 'postmodern' *flâneuse* points out (2003: 148):

> Whilst *Sex and the City* is concerned with all four women's sexual adventures, the programme concentrates mainly on the character of Carrie. She is the show's observer and commentator, typified in her career as a newspaper columnist. . . . The occurrences that happen within the programme are told from her point of view, which is emphasized by the use of her voice-over narration. Carrie is not an omniscient narrator, but she is the viewer's guide to life in the city.

It could be argued that *Sex and the City* actually uses notions of fantasy, subjectivity and consumption in order to re-examine contemporary conceptions of femininity.[40] In this 'semi-fantasy' world, female desire knows no bounds, it is let free to self-reflexively test its own limitations, to subvert traditional (masculine) social boundaries and to provide a ceaseless indulgence in the very topics, longings and materials that have been denied to women for so long. Seen in this light, female consumption is not just an escapist element of *Sex and the City* but possibly a crucial factor in its ideological potential. As white, affluent and educated women, its four central characters clearly possess more personal and economic freedom than most. Yet it could be argued that it is this very freedom that provides the real subject of the narrative. The show is not about the 'real' struggle of women to attain economic power and equality with men, but about what women will do when a good deal of that struggle has been won.

The feminist critic Naomi Wolf (2003) argues that *Sex and the City* finally addresses the question posed in Virginia Woolf's groundbreaking feminist essay, 'A Room of One's Own' (1929), that is, what will women do when they have five hundred pound a year and their own place to live? In addressing this central question, *Sex and the City* constructs a partly fictional landscape where women's endless consumption (whether it be materially, socially or even sexually) consistently refuses to limit itself to traditional social ('feminine') norms. The intense desire for sexual fulfilment, the ceaseless enjoyment of consumerism and even the 'luxury' to keep looking for a decent man (like the proverbial 'needle in a haystack'), construct a female-centred universe where women refuse to settle for anything less than complete satisfaction. As a result, *Sex and the City* creates a fictional universe where women's desires have few limits and where women's concerns are finally allowed to dominate, consume and dictate the action. In this way, the series allows itself the possibility to create a world that explicitly goes against masculine power and desire, and produces a radical form of narrative that re-interprets life from a wholly 'feminine' perspective. As Wolf puts it (ibid):

> *Sex and the City* ... resonates because it is the first cultural document to treat women's concerns on an epic scale. I hear you laughing – but it is true. In what other novel or series do women's concerns mark and guide the dates, the events, the turns of the action? In *The Iliad*, war and battles set the pace. In *The Odyssey*, feats of seamanship determine the action. In a woman's epic, sex and intimacy, fashion and matrimony are the landmarks on the horizon. Yet even great women writers were not as narcissistically women-centred as the writers of *Sex and the City*. One show featured the portentous sentence: 'The next day Samantha and I went to the Valley for Fendi bags. We had found fake Fendi paradise.' You can go on laughing, but this sentence is as important, in its own way, as Virginia Woolf's iconic take on female friendship: 'Chloë liked Olivia'. For women do secretly mark time and goals and accomplishments by fashion, bodies, children, sex, relationships. *Sex and the City* has the audacity to treat women's internal concerns as if they were actually important.

Not surprisingly then, *Sex and the City* has strong similarities with *Queer as Folk*, portraying female culture for a contemporary audience in the way that *Queer as Folk* portrayed gay culture. As *Queer as Folk* attempted to reflect its flamboyantly 'camp' aesthetic through the style of the drama itself (see above), so the very look and consumerist obsessions of *Sex and the City* seem to self-consciously *celebrate* the so-called 'trivial' aspects of women's lives. However, rather than ignoring feminist concerns, this re-examination of contemporary female culture actually asks important questions about the nature and possibility of feminism today. In particular, issues of consumerism, the romantic (essentially heterosexual) notion of love and the strength and endurance of female friendship become the means by which feminism is dramatically re-interpreted and re-examined for a new generation. Like Anna in *This Life* (see above), these four women want to be independent, liberated and successful but also 'feminine', fashionable and intensely desirable to men. While some (old school) critics may see these desires as inherently contradictory, *Sex and the City* reflects the 'post-feminist' belief that consumerism, feminism and romantic idealism should no longer be seen as mutually exclusive.

Ironically, it is *Sex and the City*'s obsession with traditional female pleasures (sex, love and shopping) that finally forces the programme to re-evaluate feminism itself in the contemporary era. By indulging in such high levels of fantasy and consumption it could be argued that it is deliberately and self-consciously reacting against the traditional limitations of 1970s' feminism. Arguably, the show represents a generation of ('third-wave') women for whom traditional feminism is now identified as rather sombre, weary, tired and reactionary. In contrast, the explicit consumption of its four main female characters becomes a direct response against old school feminism's puritanical tendencies and a celebration of contemporary feminism as playful, fluid and shamelessly flamboyant. As Astrid Henry puts it (2004: 70):

> Growing up with the gains of the women's movement has given this generation a decidedly different perspective on their life choices and, consequently, on the feminism they choose to advocate. For many, the first stage in defining a feminism to call their own is to critique those aspects of second-wave feminism that they find limiting and dogmatic.

It is in this context that *Sex and the City* is perhaps best understood. Above all, the series re-examines female expectations in a world where 1970s' feminism is no longer adequate to sustain or articulate contemporary female desire. Indeed, rather than female expectations being reduced to a 'pre-feminist' state through its obsession with fantasy and consumption, the show actually reveals a world where female expectations are increasingly higher than ever before. Yes, this is a semi-fantasy world (part of its appeal is its aspirational sense of fashion and lifestyle) but it is a fantasy world that also deals with issues, concerns and anxieties that a large majority of women appear to identify with.

In this way, *Sex and the City* actively confronts the contemporary construction of the self, using elements of fantasy, fashion and consumption to both dramatise and explore the means by which identity is now articulated and interpreted in the contemporary world. As John Hartley suggests, the old 'authentic' notions of identity are being increasingly undermined by a world in which identity is now open to the cultural accumulation and examination of individual lifestyles (Hartley, 1999: 178–9):

> While cultural identity has classically been conceived as proceeding from natural or territorial authenticity, being determined in other words by heritage and territorial location, more recent identities arise from the private, domestic world of individual lifestyle, choice and preference; identity based on sexual orientation and preference, for instance, and subcultural identities on youth, taste or fanship of various kinds.

Sex and the City addresses this process of 'DIY citizenship' (ibid.), exploring the means by which identity is now formed and developed within a world of seemingly endless lifestyles and personal choice. In particular, it prioritises the emotional life of its four central characters, employing sexuality and eroticism as a force through which their devotion to 'life politics' (to love, sex, relationships, friendship and community) can be examined, dramatised and thoroughly interrogated. These women are not 'evil' commodity fetishists engaged only on ruthless and aimless consumption. Instead, they are women dedicated to their emotions, to their 'inner lives', to their desires, to their pleasures and to each other. Rather than exemplifying the increasing commodification of modern life, a show like *Sex and the City* ironically reveals a growing interest in Giddens' conception of 'lifestyle' and the need to re-examine all manner of desires in a world where desire itself (in whatever form) is now a potent 'political' issue. While style and fashion are clearly important themes in the show, so is the desire for women to initiate, enjoy and experiment with sex; to find a deep and emotionally worthwhile relationship with a man; to work on and nurture the importance of female friendship and to keep believing in (despite every reason to be cynical) the romantic conception of true love. As unpalatable as some of this may seem to 'traditional' feminists, these are contemporary concerns that *Sex and the City* addresses and explores for a new generation of men and women alike.

Sex and the City reveals many of the most important narrative aspects and aesthetic characteristics of 'soap drama'. Although soap drama tends to unashamedly prioritise the 'personal' over the 'political', it does so frequently in order to examine and interrogate issues surrounding the personal nature of politics in an age where even the notion of what is 'political' is increasingly uncertain. It does so, I would argue, not simply in order to 'downplay' the political nature of the social world but often to heighten and explore the frequently complex relationships between the 'social' and the 'private', between the 'personal' and the 'political'. To many critics concerned with 'emancipatory politics', serial (even 'soap-like') television drama such as *This Life*, *Queer as Folk* and *Sex and the City* must look surprisingly apolitical. However, what these shows possibly are is a dramatic re-examination of 'politics' itself, a contemporary dialogue about 'choice' that reveals the part we all play in the political nature of ourselves and inevitably the world around us.

NOTES

1. Many critics have now condemned the war narrative in *The Deer Hunter* as a rather biased (if not racist) view of American involvement in Vietnam.

2. Part of the success of *The Big Chill* depended on its cast that included (before many of them had hit the big time): Glenn Close, William Hurt, Kevin Kline, Jeff Goldblum and Tom Berenger.

3. During the 1980s this preoccupation with narratives surrounding small communities and friends seemed particularly pronounced with a plethora of 'teen' films like *The Breakfast Club* (Hughes, 1985) and *St Elmo's Fire* (Schumacher, 1987), exploring the personal dynamics of a small group of young friends. While such storylines were not exactly novel to

the movies, in these newer films there seemed to be a more self-conscious and self-reflexive interest in how friendship and small communities are formed and maintained despite (and perhaps even because of) the pressures and fragmentation of modern life. As with the later *Boyz N the Hood* (Singleton, 1991), they seemed to take social dislocation as the narrative drive that would enable them to examine what friendship and community actually means in a frequently hostile and socially fragmented world.

4. *This Life* was made by Garnett's World Production Company. After trying his luck in America during the 1980s, Garnett returned to Britain in the 1990s and set up the independent company which, as Cooke points out, was intent on 'making drama series, recognising that this was where the potential for innovative drama resided following the decline of the single play and the marginalisation of the progressive drama serial' (2003: 180).

5. As Tony Garnett told Lez Cooke, *This Life* was eleven minutes of screen time a day. In comparison *The Cops* (an earlier Garnett production) was between seven and eight minutes a day (2003: 181).

6. This meant that the style of *This Life* (particularly its shaky camerawork) appeared to mimic the semi-documentary style of American dramas like *Hill Street Blues* and *NYPD Blue*. However, Garnett told Cooke that he was not simply aping those earlier dramas but trying to create an aesthetic of his own that centred on close-ups and the human face (see 2003: 183).

7. According to Cooke, the narrative tempo of *This Life* was also very fast compared to other contemporary TV dramas. Compared with *Coronation Street* and *Casualty* whose average shot length was over six seconds, *This Life*'s ASL was only 4.6 seconds (see Cooke, 2003: 181).

8. These characters also appeared to neatly represent different aspects of a fragmented British society. While Warren was Welsh, Anna and Lenny were Scottish, Miles and Egg were English (although from inherently different sides of the tracks), Milly was Asian and Ferdy of mixed race.

9. 'Last time I had stuff this good', Anna says at one point, 'I had a dream about Michael Portillo. It was good actually.'

10. The complex sleeping patterns of its characters are neatly summed up by McGregor as such (1997: 100):

> 'Who's Slept With Who?
> *Miles*: Delilah, Anna and Francesca.
> *Anna*: Miles, Jo and Jerry.
> *Milly*: Egg and O'Donnell.
> *Ferdy*: Mia, Warren, Lenny, an unnamed man and a one-night (female) stand.
> *Jo*: Anna and Kira.
> *Kelly*: Nat.
> *Warren*: Figures unavailable at time of going to press.'

11. Having sex with strangers in public lavatories.

12. Because the character was not a member of the original seven friends upon which *thirtysomething* was based, its writers apparently found it difficult to fully integrate him into

the show. This may not have been helped by a drop of $1.5 million in advertising revenue when the sponsors of the programme discovered that one episode involved two gay men in bed with each other (see Capsuto, 2000: 24–5).

13. According to Kramer, 'We all agreed . . . that the radical approach to material like this was not to sensationalize it . . . I remember Marshall saying "Let's go into Russell's bedroom, just like we go into Hope and Michael's" ' (cited by ibid).

14. As Giddens puts it, '[t]herapy seeks to create a confident and prosperous individual without a sense of higher moralities; it dispenses with the great riddles of life in exchange for a modest and durable sense of well-being' (1991: 179). While Warren is a 'believer' in therapy, Anna constantly offers an opposing point of view. 'Why is it?', Warren tells Anna, 'the people who are most hostile towards therapy are – coincidentally – also the ones with most to gain?'

15. Parts of this section first appeared as 'Queer as Folk' in Creeber (ed.) (2004c), Fifty Key Television Programmes.

16. It was reported that its controversial subject matter meant that those owners of brands such as Polo, Prada and Versace refused to be associated with the series. However, it quickly became one of Showtime's highest-rated programmes of all time.

17. However, other critics have argued that, despite their exaggerated features, such camp figures were still nonetheless important in bringing more visibility to homosexuality as a whole. For example, although initially a target of gay protest in the USA, Inman (a former Austin Reed window-dresser) eventually became a homosexual icon.

18. Perhaps less apologetic in tone was The Naked Civil Servant (ITV, 1975), a groundbreaking British drama that explicitly dealt with a gay man's flamboyant struggle to live without prejudice, harassment and humiliation. Based on the biography of extravagant and effeminate homosexual Quentin Crisp (played by John Hurt), it was particularly praised for its refusal to present its leading gay protagonist as 'suffering' from homosexuality.

19. Interestingly, although An Early Frost did extremely well in the ratings, it actually lost money for NBC due to the advertisers being afraid to have their commercials shown during its broadcast.

20. The stimulation of the anus with the tongue.

21. Perhaps not surprisingly, it was widely reported that the audience for the first series of Queer as Folk was made up of over fifty per cent women (see Collins, 2000: 7).

22. 'The Millennium Dome' in London's East End was a national humiliation and public relations disaster for the British Labour government. Meant to celebrate the year 2000, for many critics its disastrous ticket sales never made up for the millions of pounds of taxpayers' money spent on it.

23. Although the issue of safe sex is never foregrounded by the drama, condoms are clearly visible in various sequences.

24. Central Park West, set in a New York publishing house, failed to ever really find an audience. Although it premiered in the autumn of 1995 it was cancelled a year later.

25. Bushnell initially wrote about the New York party-going scene for the magazine Beat before writing freelance for Self, Mademoiselle and other magazines.

26. Sarah Jessica Parker went on to play Carrie but also became executive producer on the show (see Sohn, 2002: 22–3).

27. Charlotte's surname was Ross in the book but was changed to York for the TV show.

28. The show regularly attracts a large audience for a cable network programme, with 10.6 million when shown on HBO. Seidelman went on to direct a number of episodes, as did the director of *Gas Food Lodging* (1992), Allison Anders.

29. *Sex and the City* won the Emmy® for Outstanding Comedy Series in 2001, while 2002 saw it pick up two Golden Globes for Best Television Musical/Comedy and Best Performance by an Actress in a Television Series/Musical (Sarah Jessica Parker), the Screen Actors Guild award for Outstanding Performance by an Ensemble in a Comedy Series, as well as another three Emmys® for Casting, Costuming and Outstanding Directing for a Comedy Series. And in 2003 Kim Cattrall won the Golden Globe Award for Best Supporting Actress in a Series, Miniseries or TV Musical.

30. Its star Sarah Jessica Parker has even become a fashion icon, with magazines such as *Harpers & Queen* and *People Magazine* devoting covers to her and the clothes she wears.

31. 'Fans of the show can even visit the HBO and Bravo websites to take part in the interactive quizzes to see which of the series' four female characters they are most like' (Richards, 2003: 147).

32. While 'comedy drama' might better describe a programme like *Cold Feet*, dramedy perhaps better conveys *Sex and the City*'s debt to situation comedy. Each episode lasting only thirty minutes, programmes like *Sex and the City* and *Ally McBeal* are different from those programmes which simply employ comedy in a more traditional form of television drama.

33. Particular vibrators that appeared on the show (most memorably the 'Rabbit' and the 'Hitachi Magic Wand') sold out soon after they were featured.

34. However, ironically when Samantha does finally fall in love she is devastated to find that her man is cheating on her.

35. According to Bignell, there is a 'connection between the commodification represented narratively in the programme and the commodity status of the programme itself' (2004a: 219). He notes, for example, that HBO is owned by the media conglomerate Time Warner that also publishes many women's magazines which trade in similar images of women and femininity (see ibid: 210–20).

36. 'I know how to please a man', Miranda confesses. 'You just give away most of your power.'

37. It is worth nothing that this dialogue has the men either furiously working out in the gym or rock climbing on an artificial slope while the women are seen sitting calmly at work or eating lunch. The point being that the men seem more concerned about their bodily appearance than the women who, by comparison, appear confident and relaxed.

38. As Sarah Jessica Parker (cited by Sohn, 2002: 22) puts it,

> People make sweeping judgements of the show and say it's about four women looking for sex, and it's just not. Someone who only cared about sex would not have told her boyfriend she has had an affair. She would have said 'I can get away with it'. But it haunted her, and that says a lot about who she is.

39. However, New York City is a crucial part of the narrative of *Sex and the City* as a whole. As Helen Richards points out, 'at least three or four scenes per episode are shot on location on

actual New York streets and not sets, unlike other New York-set sitcoms such as *Friends* and *Seinfeld* which use constructed sets to recreate the city's streets' (2003: 148).

40. Interestingly, a great deal of recent gender studies has re-examined the radical potential of fantasy and consumption as a whole. For example, Jackie Stacey (1994) examined the complex relationship between British female audiences and Hollywood cinema during the 1940s and 1950s. She found that 'glamorous' Hollywood films allowed British women to negotiate, play around with and actually *extend* their own national (arguably limited) versions of femininity. 'Paradoxically', she argued,

> whilst commodity consumption for female spectators in the mid- to late 1950s' Britain concerns producing oneself as a desirable object, it also offers an escape from what is perceived as the drudgery of domesticity and motherhood which increasingly comes to define femininity at this time (223).

In other words, despite their obsession with glamour and consumption, she found that Hollywood images actually enabled British women to re-examine their own culturally limited roles and aspirations.

CONCLUSION[1]

That's the promise and the contract we have with our subscribers. Films by sophisticated
film-makers, of the sort they can't get in a movie theatre.

Colin Callender, head of HBO films (cited by Wolf, 2004: 11)

The British journalist David Aaronovitch recently argued that the influence, quality and
relevance of television was rapidly in decline. In particular, he suggested that the arrival
of satellite and cable television was slowly eradicating the shared national experience
that the old three-channel system (at least in Britain) had once gloriously produced. In
contrast, the present multichannel system was now creating mindless and diverse
entertainment, watched by an ever-decreasing audience. According to Aaronovitch
(2000: 1):

> An increasingly fragmented market is served by an increasingly risk-adverse industry. The
> consequence of this is likely to be the reduction of the part that television plays in our
> national conversation ... And you can't help wondering, what with all the other diversions
> and possibilities open to the citizens of the millennium, whether we are not seeing the dying
> era of what Clive James called the crystal bucket. The age of television is over.

This lament for the death of television is nothing new, neither is the claim that the end
of the terrestrial monopoly has led to an increasing fragmentation of (British) society.
Aaronovitch's views represent a whole generation of critics who assume that the changes
taking place in television equal the destruction of the medium itself. Brought up on a
diet of traditional broadcasting methods, these critics tend to despise many of the
changes that define the new broadcasting age. They look back longingly to a time when
the whole nation was seemingly bound together by a limited number of choices, bathed
in the warm glow of what Raymond Williams once referred to as a 'common culture'
(1971).[2] Not surprisingly, Aaronovitch chooses the BBC's 1970 adaptation of Jean Paul
Sartre's *Roads to Freedom* to highlight this unique period, a play that he remembers
(through personal experience) transcending the class system of British society. For him,
this drama stands as a symbol of an age when the whole nation could be brought together
by the healing power of high art on the small screen.[3]

However, what I hope this book has attempted to point out is that such appraisals of
both the past and the present are dangerously deluded, that each age has its triumphs,
its mediocrity and its trash. As Aaronovitch himself admits, his own 'golden age' also
included *Miss World* (BBC/ITV, 1951–88) and the *The Black and White Minstrel Show*

(BBC, 1958–78), programmes that today are quite rightly regarded with distaste and contempt for their sexist and racist representations. In particular, what I refuse to accept is that somehow the very nature of television today makes it impossible for intelligent, challenging and innovative drama to still be made, distributed and consumed.

Indeed, despite the claims of commentators like Aaronovitch, the new broadcasting age (particularly the spread of cable and satellite channels) has clearly not meant the end of television. Ironically, the number of cable and satellite channels may have actually enhanced the power and potential of television drama in the contemporary age. One need look no further than the American cable channel Home Box Office (HBO) to see how the emerging forms of broadcasting may actually provide a fertile environment for new drama. In fact, this mini television 'studio' has built a growing reputation for producing high-quality television drama and comedy such as *The Sopranos* (HBO, 1998–), *Band of Brothers* (2000), *Sex and the City* (1998–2004) and *Angels in America* (2003). In particular, HBO reveals the ability of new television companies to transgress the traditional demands of either the 'public' or 'commercial' sector. As HBO is financed purely by subscription this means that it can bypass the wishes and demands of advertisers who have historically tended to put explicitly conservative pressure on television channels for fear of upsetting their potential customers (see Patterson, 2003: 9–10).

The success of HBO also has had a positive effect on other American television channels with ABC, CBS, NBC and Fox all attempting to reinvigorate their own programmes in the light of the channel's success. While not all cable channels live up to the standards set by HBO, its success reveals a market for adult 'quality' and comedy drama that other channels are eager to emulate. According to Matt Wells, 'Once there was a time when British acquisition scouts had little to choose from at the annual LA screenings; now, the difficulty is which show to spot before it becomes a hit and shoots up in price' (2003: 7). As the creator of the controversial police drama *The Shield* (Fox, 2002–), Shaun Ryan puts it (cited by ibid: 6):

> It's the golden age of drama right now on American TV. The film industry has become so taken with the global market and simplifying things to sell around the world, that TV has filled a niche that film occupied in the 70s and 80s. It used to be that film people wouldn't work in TV. Now look around: Aaron Sorkin, creator of *The West Wing*, came out of the film world, Bruckheimer on *CSI* [*Crime Scene Investigation*] and Alan Ball of *Six Feet Under* came out of that world, too. TV as a medium has benefited from that.

Despite the success of contemporary television drama, critics like Wilsher will no doubt point to its 'soap operaisation' in recent years, in which, as he puts it, 'personal life is privileged at the expense of questions of "power" and "politics" (1997: 11). However, I hope to have shown how contemporary TV drama is no less challenging and sophisticated that it has ever been. In fact, it could be argued that the serialisation of television drama has actually helped the genre to come of age, to address issues and concerns in a more complex, ambiguous and pluralistic manner that ever before. Who could imagine a television drama like *The Sopranos* or *Sex and the City* being made in the 1960s? Not

only in terms of content, but also thematically, structurally and formally these programmes talk about, examine and reflect the period in which they were made. Each new
age requires new ways of portraying the world, of engaging with social and political
themes and revealing its complexity. Surprisingly, television drama still manages to do
this and the success of HBO reveals the desire for audiences to tune into its sometimes
controversial and unsettling portrayals of the here and now.

With hindsight, every age has its 'golden' moments and this age is no exception.
Indeed, as Shaun Ryan points out, contemporary television drama could currently be in
a new 'golden age', one that inevitably pushes the boundaries and conventions by which
an earlier age was conceived and represented. No doubt, in twenty years' time, commentators will also be predicting 'the end of television' and looking back longingly to a
time when the television schedules were filled with 'classics' like *Buffy the Vampire Slayer*
(WB, 1997–), *The X-Files* (Fox, 1993–2002) and *The West Wing* (NBC, 1999–). While
television may no longer 'cement' the nation in quite the same way as it once did (unit-
ing a country primarily through the scarcity of channels available), it still plays a crucial
role in the means by which we begin to understand ourselves and the world around us.
In fact, many critics would argue that television has actually matured in the last ten or
twenty years to become a more sophisticated and complex medium in its own right. As
Robert J. Thompson puts it (1996: 12):

> The fact is that most of the programmes during the golden age of the 1950s weren't very
> good. Although the same holds true of more recent times, the medium has significantly
> matured in the last decade and a half. Much of the best television ever to appear in this
> country [America] was made after 1980. Some of the programmes from this period were,
> and are, truly outstanding.

In fact, it could be argued that a multichannel system of broadcasting is actually able to
better represent the multicultural society that defines so much of contemporary life, and
now (albeit it gradually) is informing more and more of its dramatic and artistic life (see
Creeber, 2004b: 27–39). Television is not a static and intransigent medium, but an ever-
growing, evolving and expanding industry that continually attempts to reflect, respond
to and engage with the world around it. Each age is faced with its problems, its chal-
lenges and its possibilities. In my own small way then, I hope to have shown how this
current age (despite and maybe because of the problems it faces) still manages to rise
to the challenge of making television drama that dramatises, reflects and at times even
deconstructs, the period in which it is made. Since the arrival of *Roots* in 1977 there have
been millions upon millions of hours of television drama, not all of which will be remembered and some of which may be remembered for all the wrong reasons. However, I
hope this book will remind us in years to come of some of its most interesting and
remarkable moments. If this is what the end of television looks like then there is little
need for concern. On the strength of this account alone, TV drama is alive and well and
rapidly maturing in a living room near you. The age of the single play may be dead but
a vibrant age of serial television drama is now upon us.

NOTES

1. Part of this section first appeared in a different form in Creeber (2004b).

2. This opinion is shared by many within the industry of a certain generation. As the British television playwright Dennis Potter once put it (Interview with Paul Madden, unpaginated programme notes for a National Film Theatre screening of the *Nigel Barton Plays*, November 1976):

   > Television seemed to me the most democratic medium. I thought that if I wanted to write both for my parents and the people I grew up with, and the people I was now moving amongst, there was only one medium capable of that, and that was television, and that's still the case. It cuts across the lines, the hierarchies inherent in, for instance, print culture.

3. Aaronovitch remembers the difficult experience of watching his own *middle-class* father meeting his girlfriend's *working-class* father. *Roads to Freedom*, he argues, provided the 'bridge over which they advanced towards each other' (2000: 1).

TELEOGRAPHY

ROOTS: THE TRIUMPH OF AN AMERICAN FAMILY (ABC, 1977)
Length: 12 hours
Number of episodes: 8
Based on the book by Alex Haley
Developed for television by William Blinn
A David L. Wolper Production
Producer: Stan Margulies
Executive Producer: David L. Wolper
Writers include: William Blinn, M. Charles Cohen, Ernest Kinoy, James Lee
Directors include: Marvin J. Chomsky, John Erman, David Greene, Gilbert Moses
Music: Gerald Fried, Quincy Jones
Cast includes:
Kunta Kinte (LeVar Burton/John Amos)
Chicken George Moore (Ben Vereen)
Fiddler (Louis Gossett Jr)
Binta (Cicely Tyson)
Kizzy (Leslie Uggams)
Captain Davies (Edward Asner)
John Reynolds (Lorne Greene)
Tom Moore (Chuck Connors)
Evan Brent (Lloyd Bridges)
Sam Bennett (Richard Roundtree)
Tom Harvey (Georg Stanford Brown)
Irene Harvey (Lynne Moody)
Ames (Vic Morrow)
Dr William Reynolds (Robert Reed)
Kadi Touray (O. J. Simpson)
Nyo Boto (Maya Angelou)
Sir Ian Russell (Ian McShane)
Available on DVD and video: *Roots: The 25th Anniversary Edition*, Warner Bros

HOLOCAUST: THE STORY OF THE FAMILY WEISS (NBC/TITUS, 1978)
Length: 7 hours 30 minutes
Number of episodes: 4
Producer: Robert Berger
Executive Producer: Herb Brodkin

Writer: Gerald Green
Director: Marvin J. Chomsky
Photography: Brian West
Music: Morton Gold
Supervising Film Editor: Stephen A. Rotter
Executive Producer: Herbert Brookin
Cast includes:
Dr Josef Weiss (Fritz Weaver)
Berta Weiss (Rosemary Harris)
Karl Weiss (James Woods)
Inga Helms/Weiss (Meryl Streep)
Rudi Weiss (Joseph Bottoms)
Anna Weiss (Blanche Baker)
Moses Weiss (Sam Wanamaker)
Erik Dorf (Michael Moriarty)
Marta Dorf (Deborah Norton)
Kurt Dorf (Robert Stephens)
Reinhard Heydrich (David Warner)
Heinrich Himmler (Ian Holm)
Adolf Eichmann (Tom Bell)
Available in America on Worldvision Home Video

HEIMAT: A CHRONICLE IN ELEVEN PARTS (WDR/SFB, 1984)

Length: 15 hours 30 minutes
Number of episodes: 11
Creator: Edgar Reitz
Director: Edgar Reitz
Screenplay: Edgar Reitz and Peter Steinbach
Costume: Regine Bätz, Reinhild Paul
Make-up: Lore Sottung
Photography: Gernot Roll
Editor: Heidi Handorf
Art Director: Franz Bauer
Music: Nicos Mamangakis
Cast includes:
Maria (Marita Breuer)
Paul (Michael Lesch/Dieter Schaad)
Pauline (Karin Kienzler/Eva Maria Bayerswalter)
Eduard (Rüediger Weigang)
Hermann (Peter Harting)
Glasisch-Karl (Kurt Wagner)
Anton (Mathias Kniesbeck)
Otto (Jörg Hube)

Lucie (Karin Rasenack)
Katharina (Gertrud Bredel)
Mathias (Willi Burger)
Anton (Rolf Roth)
Ernst (Ingo Sottung)

TWIN PEAKS (ABC, 1990–1)

Number of series: 2

Producers include: David Lynch, Mark Frost, Robert Engels, Harley Peyton, Gregg D. Fienberg

Writers include: David Lynch, Mark Frost, Robert Engels, Harley Peyton, Scott Frost

Directors include: David Lynch, Tim Hunter, Mark Frost, James Foley, Todd Holland, Duwaynne Dunham, Tina Rathone, Graeme Clifford, Lesli Linka Glatter, Caleb Deschanel

Music: Angelo Badalamenti

Cast includes:

Annie Blackburne (Heather Graham)
Deputy Andy Brennan (Harry Goaz)
Bobby Briggs (Dana Ashbrook)
Major Garland Briggs (Don Davis)
Denis(e) Bryson (David Duchovny)
Gordon Cole (David Lynch)
Special Agent Dale Cooper (Kyle MacLachlan)
Windom Earle (Kenneth Welsh)
Laura Palmer, Maddy Ferguson (Sheryl Lee)
Audrey Horne (Sherilyn Fenn)
Shelley Johnson (Mädchen Amick)
The Log Lady (Catherine Coulson)
Man from Another Place (Michael J. Anderson)
Catherine Martell (Piper Laurie)
Pete Martell (Jack Nance)
Lucy Moran (Kimmy Robertson)
Josie Packard (Joan Chen)
Leland Palmer (Ray Wise)
Sheriff Harry S. Truman (Michael Ontkean)
Available on video and DVD, Universal Pictures

RIGET (*THE KINGDOM*) (DANISH TELEVISION, 1994)

Number of series: 3

Creator: Lars von Trier

Language: Danish

Production: Zentropa Entertainments and Danmarks Radio TV in cooperation with other European production entities

Co-production: Ib Tardini
Associate Producer: Philippe Bober
Writers: Niels Vørsel and Lars von Trier
Screenplay: Tomas Gislason and Lars von Trier
Art Director: Jette Lehmann
Shooting format: 16mm (blown up to 35mm for theatrical release)
Directors include: Lars von Trier and Niels Vørsel
Photography: Eric Kress (Steadicam: Henrik Harpelund)
Original Music: Joachim Holbek
Cast includes:
Stig G. Helmer (Ernst-Hugo Järegård)
Mrs Stig Drusse (Kirsten Rolffes)
Rigmer (Ghita Nørby)
Dr Krogshøj (Søren Pilmark)
Porter Hansen (Otto Brandenburg)
Bulder (Jens Okking)
Dr Einar Mosegaard (Holger Juul Hansen)
Video/DVD available on Manga/ICA Projects, A Division of Manga Entertainment Ltd,
    An Island International Company

COLD LAZARUS (CHANNEL FOUR/BBC, 1996)
Number of episodes: 4
Production Company: Whistling Gypsy
Producers: Kenith Trodd and Rosemarie Whitman
Executive Producers: Michael Wearing and Peter Ansorge
Writer: Dennis Potter
Director: Renny Rye
Editor: Clare Douglas
Production Designer: Christopher Hobbs
Director of Photography: Remi Adefarasin
Costume Designer: Charlotte Holdich
Music: Christopher Gunning
Cast includes:
Daniel Feeld (Albert Finney)
Martina Masdon (Diane Ladd)
David Siltz (Henry Goodman)
Emma Porlock (Frances de la Tour)
Fyodor Glazunove (Ciaran Hinds)
Tony Watson (Grant Masters)
Luanda Partington (Ganiat Kasumu)
Blinda (Carmen Ejogo)
Kaya (Claudia Malkovich)
Nat (Jonathan Cake)

Nigel (Richard Karlsson)

Bill (Ian Kelly)

Celestine (Lisa Shingler)

Beth Carter (Tara Woodward)

Young Chris (Joe Roberts)

Young Daniel (Joe Roberts)

Tramp (John Forgeham)

PRIME SUSPECT (GRANADA, 1991–)

Number of series: 7

Created by Lynda La Plante

Producers include: Don Leaver, Paul Marcus, Brian Park, Lynne Horsford

Executive Producer: Sally Head

Directors include: Christopher Menaul, John Strickland, David Dury, Sarah Pia, John Madden, Philip Davis

Writers include: Lynda La Plante, Allan Cubitt, Eric Deacon, Guy Hibbert, Guy Andrews, Paul Billing

Music: Stephen Warbeck

Cast includes:

DCI Jane Tennison (Helen Mirren)

DS Bill Otley (Tom Bell)

DCI John Shefford (John Forgeham)

George Marlow (John Bowe and Tim Woodward [4])

Moyra Henson (Zoë Wanamaker)

Superintendent Thorndike (Stephen Boxer)

Dr Patrick Schofield (Stuart Wilson)

DCI Mitchell (Christopher Fulford)

DI Haskons (Richard Hawley)

Chief Superintendent Kernan (John Benfield)

Available on video/DVD, Granada and Video Collection International

CRACKER (GRANADA, 1993–6)

Number of separate stories: 10

Created by: Jimmy McGovern

Producers include: Paul Abbott, Gub Neal, Hilary Bevan Jones

Executive Producer: Gub Neal

Writers include: Jimmy McGovern, Paul Abbott, Ted Whitehead

Directors include: Michael Winterbottom, Andy Wilson, Simon Cellan Jones, Roy Battersby, Charles McDougall, Julian Jarrold., Richard Standeven, Tim Fywell

Music: Stephen Warbeck

Cast includes:

Eddie 'Fitz' Fitzgerald (Robbie Coltrane)

Judith Fitzgerald (Barbara Flynn)
DS Jane Penhaligon (Geraldine Somerville)
DCI David Bilborough (Christopher Eccleston)
DS Jimmy Beck (Lorcan Cranitch)
CI Wise (Ricky Tomlinson)
Albie Kinsella (Robert Carlyle)
Mr Cassidy (Christopher Fulford)
Kelly (Adrian Dunbar)
Mark Fitzgerald (Kieran O'Brien)
Det. Chief Harriman (Colin Tierney)
Temple (Robert Cavanah)
Skelton (Wilbert Johnson)
Available on video/DVD, Granada and Video Collection International

THE SOPRANOS (HBO, 1999–)

Number of series: 5
Created by: David Chase
Producers include: David Chase, Ilene Landress, Brad Grey, Mitchell Burgess, Robin Green, Frank Renzulli
Writers include: David Chase, Frank Renzulli, Robin Green, Mitchell Burgess, Terence Winter, Todd A. Kessler, Michael Imperioli, Lawrence Konner
Directors include: David Chase, John Patterson, Allen Coulter, Tim Van Patten, Henry J. Bronchtein, Steve Buscemi
Cast includes:
Giacomo Jr (Jackie Jr) Aprile (Jason Cerbone)
Richie Aprile (David Proval)
Salvatore (Big Pussy) Bompensiero (Vincent Pastore)
Artie Bucco (John Ventimiglia)
Ralph Cifaretto (Joe Pantoliano)
Adriana La Cerva (Drew De Meteo)
Dr Jennifer Melfi (Lorraine Bracco)
Christopher Moltisanti (Michael Imperioli)
Johnny (Johnny Sack) Sacramoni (Vincent Curatola)
Anthony (AJ) Soprano, Jr (Robert Iler)
Carmela Soprano (Edie Falco)
Carrado (Uncle Junior) Soprano (Dominic Chianese)
Janice (Parvati) Soprano (Aida Turturro)
Livia Soprano (Nancy Marchand)
Meadow Soprano (Jamie-Lynn Sigler)
Tony Soprano (James Gandolfini)
Paulie Walnuts (Tony Sirico)
Available on DVD and video, HBO Video/Bradgrey Television

THIS LIFE (BBC, 1996–7)

Number of series: 2
Created by Amy Jenkins, Tony Garnett and Michael Jackson
Executive Producer: Tony Garnett
Producer: Jane Fallon
Directors include: Audrey Cooke, Nigel Douglas, Sallie Aprahamian
Writers include: Amy Jenkins, Matthew Graham, Richard Zajdlic
Cast includes:
Miles Andrews (Jack Davenport)
Milly Nassim (Amita Dhiri)
Edgar 'Egg' Cook (Andrew Lincoln)
Anna Forbes (Daniela Nardini)
Warren Jones (Jason Hughes)
Ferdy (Ramon Tikaram)
Hooperman (Geoffrey Bateman)
Kira (Luisa Bradshaw-White)
O'Donnell (David Mallinson)
Paul (Paul Medford)
Nicki (Juliet Cowen)
Jo (Steve John Shepherd)
Graham (Cyril Nri)
Kelly (Sacha Craise)
Rachel (Natasha Little)
Available on DVD and video. A World Production for the BBC

QUEER AS FOLK (UK, CHANNEL FOUR, 1999–2000 AND US, SHOWTIME, 2000–)

(UK version)
Number of series: 2
Directors: Charles McDougall, Sarah Harding, Menhaj Huda
Writer/Co-producer: Russell T. Davies
Executive Producer: Nicola Shindler
Associate Producer: Tom Sherry
Designer: Claire Kenny
Director of Photography: Nigel Walters
Editor: Tony Cranstoun, Tony Ham
Composer: Murry Gold
Cast includes:
Stuart Jones (Aidan Gillen)
Vince Tyler (Craig Kelly)
Nathan Maloney (Charlie Hunnam)
Hazel Tyler (Denise Black)
Sonna Clarke (Carla Henry)

Alexander Perry (Antony Cotton)
Cameron Roberts (Peter O'Brien)
(US version)
Based on the British series created by Russell T. Davies
Developed for American television by Ron Cowen and Daniel Lipman
Director: Kevin Inch
Writer: Richard Kramer
Executive Producers: Tony Jonas, Ron Cowen and Daniel Lipman
Cast includes:
Brian Kinney (Gale Harold)
Michael Novotny (Hal Sparks)
Justin (Randy Harrison)
Emmett (Peter Paige)
Ted (Scott Lowell)
Debbie Novotny (Sharon Gless)
Melanie (Michelle Clunie)
Lindsay (Thea Gill)
Available on video/DVD, Channel Four and Video Collection International

SEX AND THE CITY (HBO, 1998–2004)

Number of series: 5
Based on the book by Candace Bushnell
Producer: Darren Star
Co-producer: Jane Raab
Executive Producer: Sarah Jessica Parker
Writers include: Darren Star, Michael Patrick King, Jenny Bicks, Nicole Avril, Susan
    Kolinsky, Terri Minsky, Michael King, Matthew Harrison, Cindy Chupack, Allan
    Heinberg, Jessica Bendinger
Directors include: Susan Seidelman, Alison Maclean, Nicole Holofeener, Darren Star,
    Michael Fields, Matthew Harrison, Allen Coulter, John David Coles, Victoria
    Hochberg, Pam Thomas, Allison Anders, Alan Taylor, Dan Algrant, Michael Spiller
Post-production: Antonia Ellis
Directors of photography: Michael Spiller and John Thomas
Editors: Michael Berenbaum and Wendy Stanzler
Costume: Patricia Field
Set Design: Jeremy Conway
Casting: Jennifer McNamara
Props: Sabrina Wright
Cast includes:
Carrie Bradshaw (Sarah Jessica Parker)
Charlotte York (Kristin Davis)
Miranda Hobbes (Cynthia Nixon)
Samantha Jones (Kim Cattrall)

Trey MacDougal (Kyle MacLachlan)
Steve Brady (David Eigenberg)
Stanford Blatch (Willie Garson)
Aidan Shaw (John Corbett)
Mr Big (Chris Noth)
Available on video and DVD, Warner Vision International

BIBLIOGRAPHY

Aaronovitch, David (2000), 'The Great Telly Turn-Off', *Independent on Sunday*, 'Culture', 10 September.

Abercrombie, Nicholas (1996), *Television and Society*, Cambridge: Polity Press.

Ackass, Kim and McCabe, Janet (eds) (2004), *Reading* Sex and the City, London and New York: I. B. Tauris.

Allen, Robert C. (1995), *to be continued . . .: Soap Operas around the World*, London and New York: Routledge.

Allen, Robert C. (ed.) (1992), *Channels of Discourse, Reassembled: Television and Contemporary Criticism*, London and New York: Routledge.

Anderson, Benedict (1991), *Imagined Communities: Reflections on the Origins and Spread of Nationalism*, London: Verso.

Andrew, Geoff (1998), *Stranger than Paradise: Maverick Film-makers in Recent American Cinema*, London: Prion.

Ang, Ien (1985), *Watching Dallas: Soap Opera and the Melodramatic Imagination*, London and New York: Methuen.

Avisa, Ilan (1988), *Screening the Holocaust: Cinema's Images of the Unimaginable*, Bloomington and Indianapolis: Indiana University Press.

Baehr, Helen and Dyer, Gillian (1987), *Boxed In: Women and Television*, New York and London: Pandora Press.

Baldick, Chris (1990), *The Concise Oxford Dictionary of Literary Terms*, Oxford: Oxford University Press.

Baudrillard, Jean (1984), *The Evil Demon of Images*, Sydney: Power Institute.

Bellour, Raymond (1979), 'Psychosis, Neurosis, Perversion', *Camera Obscura*, nos 3/4: 105–32.

Bennett, Tony, Boyd-Bowman, Susan, Mercer, Colin and Woollacott, Janet (eds) (1981), *Popular Television and Film*, London: BFI with the Open University Press.

Bernstein, Alina (2002), 'Gender and the Media: The Representation of Men, Masculinity(ies), Gays and Lesbians', in Chris Newbold, Oliver Boyd-Barret and Hilde Van Den Bulck (eds), *The Media Book*, London and New York: Arnold.

Bier, Jean-Paul (1980), 'The Holocaust and West Germany: Strategies of Oblivion 1947–1979', *New German Critique*, 19 (Winter): 9–29.

Bignell, Jonathan (2004a), 'Gender Representations: *Sex and the City*', in Jonathan Bignell (ed.), *Television Studies: An Introduction*, London and New York: Routledge.

Bignell, Jonathan (2004b), 'Sex, Confession and Witness', in Kim Ackass and Janet McCabe (eds), *Reading* Sex and the City.

Blimes, Alex (2000), '*The Sopranos* Hit London', *GQ Magazine*, July.

Bondebjerg, Ib (1992), 'Intertextuality and Metafiction: Genre and Narration in the Television

Fiction of Dennis Potter', in M. Skormand and K. C. Schroder (eds), *Media Cultures: Reappraising Transnational Media*, London: Routledge: 161–79.

Botting, Fred and Wilson, Scott (2001), *The Tarantinian Ethics*, London, Thousand Oaks, CA. and New Delhi: Sage.

Bradshaw, Peter (2000), 'The Lars Dance', *Guardian*, Arts, 23 May.

Bragg, Melvyn (1996), *The South Bank Show: Jimmy McGovern*, ITV.

Brooker, Peter (2002), 'Queer Theory', in Peter Brooker, *A Glossary of Cultural Theory* (2nd edn), London and New York: Arnold.

Brookes, Rod (2001), 'Sport', in Glen Creeber (ed.), *The Television Genre Book*.

Brookes, Rod (2004), '24', in Glen Creeber (ed.), *Fifty Key Television Programmes*.

Brown, Rob (2001), 'I Never Saw *Queer as Folk* as a Gay Drama' (interview with producer Nicola Shindler), *Guardian*, 9 April 2001.

Brunsdon, Charlotte (1997), 'Post-feminism and Shopping Films', in Charlotte Brunsdon, *Screen Tastes: Soap Opera to Satellite Dishes*, London and New York: Routledge.

Brunsdon, Charlotte (1997), *Screen Tastes: Soap Opera to Satellite Dishes*, London and New York: Routledge.

Brunsdon, Charlotte (1998), 'Structure of Anxiety: Recent British Television Crime Fiction', *Screen*, vol. 39, no. 3, Autumn.

Bruzzi, Stella and Church-Gibson, Pamela (2004), 'Fashion is the Fifth Character: Fashion, Costume and Character in *Sex and the City*', in Kim Ackass and Janet McCabe (eds) (2004), *Reading* Sex and the City.

Bunting, Madeleine (2001), 'Loadsasex and Shopping: A Woman's Lot', *Guardian*, 9 February.

Burton, Graeme (2000), *Talking Television: An Introduction to the Study of Television*, London and New York: Arnold.

Buxton, Rodney A. (1997), *'An Early Frost'* and 'Sexual Orientation and Television', in Horace Newcomb (ed.), *Encyclopaedia of Television*, Chicago, IL and London: Fitzroy Dearborn Publishing.

Caldwell, John Thornton (1994), *Televisuality: Style, Crisis, and Authority in American Television*, New Brunswick, NJ: Rutgers University Press.

Cameron, Ian (ed.), (1994), *The Movie Book of Film Noir*, London: Studio Vista.

Canby, Vincent (2000), 'From the Humble Mini-Series comes the Magnificent Megamovie', in Stephen Holden (ed.), The New York Times *on* The Sopranos, New York: ibooks.

Capsuto, Steven (2000), *Alternate Channels: The Uncensored Story of Gay and Lesbian Images on Television: 1930s to the Present*, New York: Ballantine Books.

Carpenter, Humphrey (1998), *Dennis Potter: The Authorized Biography*, London: Faber & Faber.

Carter, Bill (2000), 'He Engineered a Mob Hit, and Now It's Time to Pay up', in Stephen Holden (ed.), The New York Times *on* The Sopranos, New York: ibooks.

Caughie, John (2000), *Television Drama: Realism, Modernism and British Culture*, London and New York: Oxford University Press.

Channel Four/Red Production Company (2000), *Queer as Folk 2: Same Men, New Tricks*, DVD extras featuring documentary, *What the Folk?*.

Channel Four (2002), *Sex on TV* (a documentary in three parts presented by David Aranovitch), episode three, 31 May.

Chapman, Rowena (1988), 'The Great Pretender: Variations on the New Man Theme', in Rowena Chapman and Jonathan Rutherford (eds), *Male Order: Unwrapping Masculinity*, London: Lawrence & Wishart.

Chase, David (2001), *The Sopranos Scriptbook*, London: Macmillan.

Childs, Peter (2000), *Modernism* (New Critical Idiom), London and New York: Routledge.

Clarke, Alan (1986), ' "This Is Not the Boy Scouts": Television Police Series and Definitions of Law and Order', from Tony Bennett *et al.* (eds), *Popular Culture and Social Relations*, Milton Keynes: Open University.

Clover, Carol J. (1999), 'Her Body, Himself: Gender in the Slasher Film', in Sue Thornham (ed.), *Feminist Film Theory: A Reader*.

Collins, Jim (1992), 'Postmodernism and Television', in Robert C. Allen (ed.), *Channels of Discourse, Reassembled*.

Collins, Michael (2000), 'Sing If You're Glad to Be Gay (and Cute)', *The Observer: Television*, 30 January: 6–7.

Connery, Donald, S. (1967), *The Scandinavians*, London: Eyre & Spottiswoode.

Cook, John (1998), *Dennis Potter: A Life on Screen*, Manchester and New York: Manchester University Press.

Cook, Pam and Bernink, Mieke (eds) (1999), *The Cinema Book* (2nd edn), London: BFI.

Cooke, Lez (2003), *British Television Drama: A History*, London: BFI.

Coolidge, Archibald C. (1967), *Charles Dickens as Serial Novelist*, Ames: Iowa State University Press.

Cowie, Peter (1997), *The Godfather Book*, London and Boston, MA: Faber & Faber.

Creeber, Glen (1996), 'Banality with a Beat: Dennis Potter and the Paradox of Popular Music', *Media, Culture & Society*, vol. 18, no. 3, July: 501–8.

Creeber, Glen (1998), *Dennis Potter: Between Two Worlds, A Critical Reassessment*, London and New York: Macmillan.

Creeber, Glen (1998b), ' "Reality or Nothing?": Dennis Potter's *Cold Lazarus*', in Mike Wayne (ed.), *Dissident Voices: The Politics of Television and Social Change*, London, Sterling, VA: Pluto Press: 12–22.

Creeber, Glen (2000), ' "Adapted for Television": Dennis Potter's Last Interview', in Martin Crowley (ed.), *Dying Words: The Last Moments of Writers and Philosophers*, Amsterdam and Atlanta, GA: Rodopi.

Creeber, Glen (2001a), 'Taking Our Personal Lives Seriously: Intimacy, Continuity and Memory in the Television Serial', *Media, Culture & Society*, vol. 23, no. 4: 439–55.

Creeber, Glen (2001b), 'Cigarettes and Alcohol: Investigating Gender, Genre and Gratification in *Prime Suspect*', *Television and New Media*, vol. 2, no. 2, May.

Creeber, Glen (ed.) (2001c) (associate editors: John Tulloch and Toby Miller), *The Television Genre Book*, London: BFI.

Creeber, Glen (2001d), 'The Mini-Series', in Glen Creeber (ed.), *The Television Genre Book*.

Creeber, Glen (2002a), 'Old Sleuth or New Man?: Investigations into Rape, Murder and Masculinity in *Cracker* (1993–1996)', *Continuum: Journal of Media and Cultural Studies*, vol. 16, no. 2, July.

Creeber, Glen (2002b), 'Surveying *The Kingdom*: Explorations of Medicine, Memory and Modernity in Lars von Trier's *The Kingdom*', *European Journal of Cultural Studies*, vol. 5, no. 4, November.

Creeber, Glen (2002c), ' "TV Ruined the Movies": Television, Tarantino and the Intimate World of *The Sopranos*', in David Lavery (ed.), *This Thing of Ours: Investigating* The Sopranos.

Creeber, Glen (ed.) (2004), *Fifty Key Television Programmes*, London: Arnold.

Creeber, Glen (2004a), '*Heimat*', in Glen Creeber (ed.), *Fifty Key Television Programmes*.

Creeber, Glen (2004b), 'Hideously White: British Television, Glocalisation and National Identity', *Television and New Media*, vol. 5, no. 1, February.

Creeber, Glen (2004c), '*Queer as Folk*', in Glen Creeber (ed.), *Fifty Key Television Programmes*.

Creeber, Glen (2004d), '*Prime Suspect*', in Glen Creeber (ed.), *Fifty Key Television Programmes*.

Culler, Jonathan (1975), *Structuralist Poetics: Structuralism, Linguistics and the Study of Literature*, London: Routledge.

Danaher, Geoff, Schirato, Tony and Webb, Jen (2000), *Understanding Foucault*, London, Thousand Oaks, CA and New Delhi: Sage.

Davies, Russell T. (1999), Queer as Folk: *The Scripts*, Basingstoke and Oxford: Channel Four Books/Macmillan.

Day-Lewis, Sean (1998), *Talk of Drama: Views of the Television Dramatist Now and Then*, Luton: University of Luton Press.

di Mattia, Joanna (2004), ' "What's the Harm in Believing?": Mr Big, Mr Perfect, and the Romantic Quest for *Sex and the City*'s Mr Right', in Kim Ackass and Janet McCabe (eds), *Reading* Sex and the City.

Dolan, Marc (1995), 'The Peaks and Valleys of Serial Creativity: What Happened to/on Twin Peaks?', in David Lavery (ed.), *Full of Secrets: Critical Approaches to Twin Peaks*.

Donatelli, Cindy and Alward, Sharon (2002), ' "I Dread You"?: Married to the Mob in *The Godfather*, *Goodfellas* and *The Sopranos*', in David Lavery (ed.), *This Thing of Ours: Investigating* The Sopranos.

Doneson, Judith, E. (2002), *The Holocaust in American Film* (2nd edn), Philadelphia, PA: Jewish Publication Society.

Durkman, Steven (1995), 'The Gay Gaze, or Why I Want My MTV', in Paul Burston and Colin Richardson (eds), *A Queer Romance: Lesbians, Gay Men and Popular Culture*, London and New York: Routledge.

Dyer, Richard (1977), 'It's Being So Camp as Keeps Us Going', *Body Politic*, 10: 11–13.

Eaton, Mary (1995), 'A Fair Cop? Viewing the Effects of the Canteen Culture in *Prime Suspect* and *Between the Lines*', in David Kidd-Hewitt and Richard Osborne (eds), *Crime and the Media: The Postmodern Spectacle*, London and East Haven, CT: Pluto Press.

Eaton, Michael (1999), 'A Review of *Great Expectations*', *Sight and Sound*, vol. 9, no. 6, June: 29.

Ellis, John (1982), *Visible Fictions: Cinema, Television, Video*, London and New York: Routledge.

Elsaesser, Thomas (1996), 'Subject Positions, Speaking Positions: From *Holocaust*, *Our Hitler*, and *Heimat* to *Shoah* and *Schindler's List*', in Vivian Sobchack (ed.), *The Persistence of History: Cinema, Television and the Modern Event*, London and New York: Routledge.

Epstein, Jacob (1994), 'A Dissent on *Schindler's List*', *New York Review of Books*, vol. 41, no. 8, 21 April: 65.

Ettedgui, Peter (1998), *Cinematography: Screencraft*, Switzerland: RotoVision Book.

Feuer, Jane (1992), 'Genre Study and Television', in Robert C. Allen (ed.), *Channels of Discourse, Reassembled*.

Feuer, Jane, Kerr, Paul and Vahimagi, Tise (eds), (1984), *MTM – 'Quality Television'*, London: BFI.

Feuer, Jane (1995), *Seeing through the Eighties: Television and Reaganism*, London: BFI.

Fishbein, Leslie (1983), '*Roots*: Docudrama and the Interpretation of History', in John E. O'Connor (ed.), *American History/American Television: Interpreting the Video Past*, New York: Frederick Ungar Publishing Co.

Fiske, John (1992), *Television Culture*, London and New York: Routledge.

Foucault, Michel (1991), 'Nietzsche, Genealogy, History', in Paul Rabinow (ed.), *The Foucault Reader: An Introduction to Foucault's Thought*, London, New York, Victoria, Ontario and Auckland: Penguin.

Freud, Sigmund (1958), *The Standard Edition of the Complete Psychological Works of Sigmund Freud*, tr. and ed. Strachey, James *et al.*, London: The Hogarth Press.

Fukuyama, Francis (1992), *The End of History and the Last Man*, London: Penguin.

Fuller, Graham (ed.) (1993), *Potter on Potter*, London: Faber & Faber.

Gabbard, Glen O. (2002), *The Psychology of* The Sopranos: *Love, Death, Desire and Betrayal in America's Favorite Gangster Family*, New York: Basic Books.

Gardner, Carl and Wyver, John (1983), 'The Single Play: From Reithian Reverence to Censorship and Cost-Accounting', *Screen*, vol. 24, nos. 4–5: 114–29.

Gascoyne, David (1970), *A Short Survey of Surrealism*, London: Frank Cass & Co Ltd.

Gauntlett, David (2002), *Media, Gender and Identity*, London and New York: Routledge.

Geraghty, Christine (1981), 'The Continuous Serial – A Definition', in Richard Dyer, Christine Geraghty, Marion Jordan, Terry Lovell, Richard Paterson and John Stewart (eds), *Television Monograph: Coronation Street*, London: BFI.

Gerrard, Nicci (1999), 'Overexposure', *Guardian*, 18 July.

Gibson, Janine (1999), 'Channel Four Glad to Pioneer the First Gay Drama on British TV', *Guardian*, 24 February.

Giddens, Anthony (1991), *Modernity and Self-Identity: Self and Society in the Late Modern Age*, London and New York: Routledge.

Giddens, Anthony (1999), 'The 1999 Reith Lectures: New World Without End', *Observer*, 11 April: 31.

Giddings, Robert and Sheen, Erica (2000), *The Classic Novel: From Page to Screen*, Manchester and New York: Manchester University Press.

Gilbert, Sandra M. and Gubar, Susan (1979), *The Madwoman in the Attic: The Woman Writer and the Nineteenth-Century Literary Imagination*, New Haven, CT and London: Yale University Press.

Gledhill, Christine (1994, orig pub. 1978), '*Klute* 1: A Contemporary Film Noir and Feminist Criticism', in E. Ann Kaplan (ed.), *Women in Film Noir*, London: BFI.

Goldhagen, Daniel Jonah (1996), *Hitler's Willing Executioners: Ordinary Germans and the Holocaust*, London: Little, Brown & Company.

Granada Television (2000), *This Is Personal: The Hunt for the Yorkshire Ripper*, January–February.

Grant, Barry Keith (1986), *Film Genre Reader*, Austin: University of Texas Press.

Grochowski, Tom (2004), 'Neurotic in New York: the Woody Allen Touches in *Sex and the City*', in Kim Ackass and Janet McCabe (eds), *Reading* Sex and the City.

Hallam, Julia with Marshment, Margaret (2000), *Realism and Popular Cinema*, Manchester and New York: Manchester University Press.

Hartley, John (1999), *The Uses of Television*, London and New York: Routledge.

Hartley, John (2001), 'Situation Comedy', in Glen Creeber (ed.), *The Television Genre Book*.

Haskell, Molly (1978), 'A Failure to Connect', *New York Times*, 11, no. 20, 15 May: 79.

Hattenstone, Simon (1999), 'Danish Blue', *Guardian*, Friday Review, 22 January.

Hayward, Anthony and Rennert, Amy (eds) (1996), *The* Prime Suspect *Book*, London: Carlton Books.

Hayward, Susan (1996), *Key Concepts in Cinema Studies*, London and New York: Routledge.

Heide, Margaret J. (1996), 'Gender and Generation: The Case of *thirtysomething*', in John Corner and Sylvia Harvey (eds), *Television Times: A Reader*, London and New York: Arnold.

Henry, Astrid (2004), 'Orgasms and Empowerment: *Sex and the City* and Third-Wave Feminism', in Kim Ackass and Janet McCabe (eds), *Reading* Sex and the City.

Herf, Jeffrey (1980), 'The 'Holocaust' Reception in West Germany: Right, Centre and Left', *New German Critique*, 19 (Winter): 30–52.

Higson, Andrew (1986), ' "Britain's Outstanding Contribution to the Film": The Documentary– Realist Tradition', in Charles Barr (ed.), *All Our Yesterdays: 90 Years of British Film*, London: BFI.

Hinds, Hilary (1992), '*Oranges Are Not the Only Fruit*: Reaching Audiences Other Lesbian Texts Cannot Reach', in Sally Munt (ed.), *New Lesbian Criticism: Literary and Cultural Readings*, New York: Columbia University Press.

Hobsbawm, Eric (1994), *Age of Extremes: The Short Twentieth Century 1914–1991*, London: Michael Joseph.

Hodge, B. and Tripp, D. (1986), *Children and Television: A Semiotic Approach*, Cambridge: Polity Press.

Hohne, Heinz (1979), 'Schwarzer Freitag für die Historiker: Holocaust: Fiktion oder Wirklichkeit?', *Spiegel*, 29 January: 22.

Holden, Stephen (ed.) (2000), The New York Times *on* The Sopranos, New York: ibooks.

Holland, Patricia (1997), *The Television Handbook*, London and New York: Routledge.

Holquist, Michael (1990), *Dialogism: Bakhtin and His World*, London and New York: Routledge.

Horowitz, Sara R. (1997), ' "But Is It Good for the Jews?": Spielberg's Schindler and the Aesthetics of Atrocity', in Yosefa Loshitzky (ed.), *Spielberg's Holocaust: Critical Perspectives on Schindler's List*, Bloomington and Indianapolis: Indiana University Press: 119–152.

Hughes, David (2001), *The Complete Lynch*, London: Virgin.

Hurd, Geoffrey (1981), 'The Television Presentation of the Police', in Tony Bennett *et al.* (eds), *Popular Television and Film*, London: BFI with the Open University Press.

Jacobs, Jason (2000), *The Intimate Screen: Early British Television Drama*, Oxford: Oxford University Press.

Jacobs, Jason (2003), *Body Trauma TV: The New Hospital Dramas*, London: BFI.

Jagose, Annamarie (1996), *Queer Theory: An Introduction*, New York: New York University Press.

James, Caryn (2000), 'Addicted to a Mob Family Potion', in Stephen Holden (ed.), The New York Times *on* The Sopranos.

Jameson, Fredric (1991), *Postmodernism, or the Cultural Logic of Late Capitalism*, London and New York: Verso.

Jenkins, Amy (last accessed August, 2003), <This Life-TVHeaven.com>.

Jenkins, Keith (1991), *Re-Thinking History*, London and New York: Routledge.

Jordan, Marion (1981), 'Realism and Convention', in Richard Dyer *et al.* (eds), *Coronation Street*, London: BFI.

Kaes, Anton (1989), *From Hitler to Heimat: The Return of History as Film*, Cambridge, MA and London: Harvard University Press.

Kalinak, Kathryn (1995), ' "Disturbing the Guests with this Racket": Music and *Twin Peaks*', in David Lavery (ed.), *Full of Secrets: Critical Approaches to* Twin Peaks.

Kelly, Richard (2000), *The Name of This Book Is Dogme 95*, London: Faber & Faber.

Kozloff, Sarah (1992), 'Theory and Television', in Robert C. Allen (ed.), *Channels of Discourse, Reassembled*.

Krutnik, Frank (1991), *In a Lonely Street: Film Noir, Genre, Masculinity*, London: Routledge.

Kuenzli, Rudolph E. (ed.) (1987), *Dada and Surrealist Film*, New York: Willis Locker & Owen.

Kuhn, Annette (1993 orig. pub. 1982), *Women's Pictures: Cinema and Feminism*, London and New York: Verso.

Lanzmann, Claude (1979/80), 'From the Holocaust to *Holocaust*', *Telos*, no. 42, Winter: 3: 137–143.

Lauzen, Martha (2001), 'Don't Forget the Brutalized Women behind *The Sopranos*', *Los Angeles Times*, 16 April.

Lavery, David (ed.) (1995), *Full of Secrets: Critical Approaches to* Twin Peaks, Detroit, IL: Wayne State University Press.

Lavery, David (ed.) (2002), *This Thing of Ours: Investigating* The Sopranos, New York: Columbia University Press.

Lavery, David (2004), '*The Sopranos*', in Glen Creeber (ed.) *Fifty Key Television Programmes*, London: Arnold.

Lewis, Jon E. and Stempel, Penny (1999), *The Ultimate TV Guide*, London: Orion.

Liebman, Stuart (1987), '*Un Chien andalou*: The Talking Cure', in Rudolph E. Kuenzli (ed.), *Dada and Surrealist Film*.

Loshitzky, Yosefa (1997) (ed.), *Spielberg's Holocaust: Critical Perspectives on* Schindler's List, Bloomington: Indiana University Press.

MacInnes, John (1998), *The End of Masculinity: The Confusion of Sexual Genesis and Sexual Difference in Modern Society*, Buckingham and Philadelphia, PA: Open University Press.

MacIntyre, Ben (2001), 'Godfathers Who Wish to Play the Starring Role', *Times*, 28 April.

Macmurraugh-Kavanagh, Madeleine, K. (1997), 'The BBC and the Birth of *The Wednesday Play*, 1962–66: Institutional Containment versus "Agitational Contemporaneity" ', *Historical Journal of Film and Television*, vol. 17, no. 3, August.

Mandel, Ernest (1984), *Delightful Murder: A Social History of the Crime Story*, Minneapolis, MN: University of Minnesota Press.

Martin, Robert Bernard (1985), *With Friends Possessed: A Life of Edward Fitzgerald*, London: Faber & Faber.

McFarlane, Brian (1996), *Novel to Film: An Introduction to the Theory of Adaptation*, Oxford: Clarendon Press.

McGregor, Tom (1997), This Life: *The Companion Guide*, London: Penguin/BBC Books.

McKee, Alan (2002), 'Interview with Russell T. Davies', *Continuum: Journal of Media and Cultural Studies*, vol. 16, no. 2, July: 235–44.

McQuire, Scott (1998), *Visions of Modernity: Representation, Memory, Time and Space in the Age of the Camera*, London, Thousand Oaks, CA and New Delhi: Sage.

Millington, Bob (1997), 'The Sweeney', in Horace Newcomb (ed.), *Encyclopaedia of Television*, Chicago, IL and London: Fitzroy Dearborn.

Morin, Edgar (1960), *The Stars*, New York: Grove Press.

Mort, Frank (1996), *Cultures of Consumption: Masculinities and Social Space in Late Twentieth-Century Britain*, London and New York: Routledge.

Moseley, Rachel (2001), 'The Teen Series', in Glen Creeber (ed.), *The Television Genre Book*.

Mulvey, Laura (1992), 'Visual Pleasure and Narrative Cinema', in *Screen* (editorial collective), *The Sexual Subject: A Screen Reader in Sexuality*, London and New York: Routledge. Originally published in *Screen*, vol. 16, no. 3, 1975: 16–18.

Neale, Steve (2000), *Genre and Hollywood*, London and New York: Routledge.

Neale, Steve (2001), 'Studying Genre', in Glen Creeber (ed.), *The Television Genre Book*.

Nelson, Robin (1997), *TV Drama in Transition: Forms, Values and Cultural Change*, London and New York: Macmillan.

Nelson, Robin (2001), '*Ally McBeal*', in Glen Creeber (ed.), *The Television Genre Book*.

Nelson, Robin (2004), '*Hill Street Blues*', in Glen Creeber (ed.), *Fifty Key Television Programmes*.

Newcomb, Horace (1974), *TV: The Most Popular Art*, New York: Anchor Books.

Newcomb, Horace (1984), 'On the Dialogic Aspects of Mass Communication', *Critical Studies in Mass Communication*, vol. 1, no. 1, March.

Nochimson, Martha (1995), 'Desire under the Douglas Firs: Entering the Body of Reality in *Twin Peaks*', in David Lavery (ed.), *Full of Secrets: Critical Approaches to* Twin Peaks.

Papke, David Ray (1996), 'Myth & Meaning: Francis Ford Coppola and Popular Response to *The Godfather* Trilogy', in John Denvir (ed.), *Legal Reelism: Movies as Legal Texts*, Urbana and Chicago: University of Illinois Press.

Patterson, John (2003), 'Knocking the Dead' (on HBO), *Guardian, The Guide*, 16–22 August.

Pattie, David (2002), 'Mobbed up: *The Sopranos* and the Modern Gangster Film', in David Lavery, *This Thing of Ours: Investigating* The Sopranos.

Place, J. A. and Peterson, L. S. (1996), 'Some Motifs in Film Noir', in Alain Silver and James Ursini (eds), *Film Noir Reader*, New York: Limelight. Originally published in *Film Comment*, vol. 10, no. 1, Jan/Feb 1974.

Postman, Neil (1985), *Amusing Ourselves to Death: Public Discourse in the Age of Show Business*, London: Methuen.

Potter, Dennis (1984), *Waiting for the Boat: On Television*, London: Faber & Faber.

Potter, Dennis (1986), *The Singing Detective*, London and Boston, MA: Faber & Faber.

Potter, Dennis (1994), *Seeing the Blossom: Two Interviews and a Lecture*, London and Boston, MA: Faber & Faber.

Potter, Dennis (1996), Karaoke *and* Cold Lazarus, London: Faber & Faber.

Prince, Stephen (1998), *Savage Cinema: Sam Peckinpah and the Rise of Ultraviolent Movies*, London: The Athlone Press.

Rabinbach, Anson G. and Zipes, Jack (1980), 'Lessons of the Holocaust', *New German Critique*, 19 (Winter): 3–7.

Radio, Nick (2003), 'Where Now for the Single Play?', *Journal of RTS* (Royal Television Society), April.

Reeves, Jimmie L., Brent, Elizabeth, Campbell, Richard, Eagle, Herb, Jenkins, Jennifer, Rogers, Marc C., Saaf, Lisa and Zuberi, Nabeel (1995), 'Postmodernism and Television: Speaking of *Twin Peaks*', in David Lavery (ed.), *Full of Secrets: Critical Approaches to* Twin Peaks.

Rich, Frank (1994), 'Extras in the Shadows', *New York Times*, 2 January, sect. 4.

Richards, Helen (2003), '*Sex and the City*: A Visible *Flâneuse* for the Postmodern Era?', in *Continuum: Journal of Media and Cultural Studies*, vol. 17, no. 2.

Ricks, C. (ed.) (1969), *The Poems of Tennyson*, London: Longman.

Ridgman, Jeremy (2000), 'Patriarchal Politics: *Our Friends in the North* and the Crisis of Masculinity', in Bruce Carson and Margaret Llewellyn-Jones (eds), *Frames and Fictions on Television: The Politics of Identity within Drama*, Exeter and Portland, OR: Intellect.

Roberts, Yvonne (1991), 'Tough Lady with the Blue Lamp', *Observer*, 14 April.

Rodley, Chris (ed.) (1997), *Lynch on Lynch*, London: Faber & Faber.

Root, Jane (1986), *Open the Box: About Television*, Littlehampton and Ontario: Comedia Pub. Group.

Ross, Karen (1996), *Black and White Media: Black Images in Popular Film and Television*, Cambridge: Polity Press.

Rucker, Allen (2000), The Sopranos: *A Family History*, London: Channel Four Books/Macmillan.

Rying, Bent (1967), *Danish in the South and North, Vol. 2, Denmark: History*, Copenhagen: Royal Danish Ministry of Foreign Affairs.

Scott, Rebecca (ed.) (1996), *Tennyson: Longman Critical Readers*, London and New York: Longman.

Shandler, Jeffrey (1997), 'Schindler's Discourse: America Discusses the Holocaust and its Mediation, from NBC's Miniseries to Spielberg's Film', in Loshitzky, Yosefa (ed.), *Spielberg's Holocaust: Critical Perspectives on* Schindler's List, Bloomington: Indiana University Press.

Shattuc, Jane M. (1997), *The Talking Cure: TV Talk Shows and Women*, London and New York: Routledge.

Smith, Anthony (1995), *Television: An International History*, Oxford and New York: Oxford University Press.

Sohn, Amy (2002), Sex and the City: *Kiss and Tell*, London: Macmillan.

Sontag, Susan (1969), 'Notes on Camp', in Susan Sontag (ed.), *Against Interpretation*, New York: Dell Publishing Company.

Southwell, Tim (1998), *Getting Away with It: The Inside Story of* Loaded, London: Ebury Press.

Stacey, Jackie (1994), *Star Gazing: Hollywood and Female Spectatorship*, London and New York: Routledge.

Staiger, Janet (1999), 'Taboos and Totems: Cultural Meanings of *The Silence of the Lambs*', in Sue Thornham (ed.), *Feminist Film Theory: A Reader*.

Stark, Steve D. (1997), *Glued to the Set: The 60 Television Shows and Events that Made Us Who We Are Today*, New York, London, Toronto, Sydney and Singapore: The Free Press.

Stein, Howard, F. (1977), 'In Search of *Roots*: An Epic of Origins and Destiny', *Journal of Popular Culture*, 11: 11–17.

Stevenson, Diane (1995), 'Family Romance, Family Violence, and the Fantastic in *Twin Peaks*', in David Lavery (ed.), *Full of Secrets: Critical Approaches to* Twin Peaks.

Stevenson, Jack (2002), *Lars von Trier*, London: BFI.

Storr, Anthony (1975), *Jung*, Glasgow: Fontana/Collins.

Tarantino, Quentin (1991), *Reservoir Dogs* (features interview with Tarantino on the making of the movie), Dog Eat Dog Productions, Universal Pictures, UK.

Tasker, Yvonne (1998), *Working Girls: Gender and Sexuality in Popular Cinema*, London and New York: Routledge.

Thompson, Robert J. (1996), *From* Hill Street Blues *to* ER*: Television's Second Golden Age*, New York: Syracuse University Press.

Thornham, Sue (ed.) (1999), *Feminist Film Theory: A Reader*, Edinburgh: Edinburgh University Press.

Tucker, Lauren R. and Shah, Hemant (1992), 'Race and the Transformation of Culture: The Making of the Television Miniseries *Roots*', *Critical Studies in Mass Communication*, vol. 9: 325–36.

Turner, Graeme (2001), 'Genre, Hybridity and Mutations', in Glen Creeber (ed.), *The Television Genre Book*.

Waldberg, Patrick (1978), *Surrealism*, London: Thames & Hudson.

Wasko, Janet (1994), *Hollywood in the Information Age: Beyond the Silver Screen*, Cambridge and Oxford: Polity Press.

Wells, Matt (2003), 'Where the Writer Is King', *Guardian*, *Media*, 27 January.

Weymouth, Anthony and Lamizet, Bernard (1996), *Market and Myths: Forces of Change in the Media of Western Europe*, London: Longman.

Wheen, Francis (1985), *Television: A History*, London: Century Publishing.

Whelehan, Imelda (2000), *OverLoaded: Popular Culture and the Future of Feminism*, London: Women's Press.

Wiesel, Elie, (1978), 'Trivialising the Holocaust: Semi-Fact and Semi-Fiction', *New York Times*, 16 April

Williams, Kevin (1998), *Give Me a Murder a Day: A History of Mass Communication in Britain*, London, New York, Sydney and Auckland: Arnold.

Williams, Linda (1981), *Figures of Desire: A Theory and Analysis of Surrealist Film*, Berkeley, CA and Oxford: University of California Press.

Williams, Raymond (1971), *Culture and Society, 1780–1950*, London: Penguin Books.

Williams, Raymond (1974), *Television Technology and Cultural Form*, London: Routledge.

Williams, Raymond (1975), *Television Technology and Cultural Form*, London: Routledge.

Willis, Ellen (2002), 'Our Mobsters, Ourselves', in David Lavery (ed.), *This Thing of Ours: Investigating* The Sopranos. Originally published in *The Nation*, 2 April 2001.

Wilsher, J. C. (1997), 'TV Series Drama: A Contradiction in Terms?', *The Author*, Spring: 11–12.

Winship, Janice (1987), *Inside Women's Magazines*, London: Pandora.

Wolf, Matt (2004), 'Winged Victory', *Sunday Times*, culture section, 25 January.

Wolf, Naomi (2003), 'Sex and the Sisters', *Sunday Times*, News Review, 20 July.

Yeates, Helen (2000), 'Sleuthing the Body', in Clare O'Farrell, Daphne Meadmore, Erica McWilliam and Colin Symes (eds), *Taught Bodies*, New York, Washington and Oxford: Peter Lang

Zielinski, Siegfried (1979), 'History as Entertainment and Provocation: The TV Series "Holocaust"', *New German Critique*, 19 (Winter): 81–96.

INDEX

Page numbers in *italics* denote illustrations

LIST OF ILLUSTRATIONS

Whilst considerable effort has been made to correctly identify the copyright holders, this has not been possible in all cases. We apologise for any apparent negligence and any omissions or corrections brought to our attention will be remedied in any future editions.

The Sopranos, Brad Grey Television/HBO/Chase Films; *The Singing Detective*, BBC/ABC; *Hill Street Blues*, MTM/NBC; *Our Friends in the North*, BBC; *Rich Man, Poor Man*, Universal Television; *Days of Hope*, BBC; *Roots*, David L. Wolper Productions/Warner Bros; *Holocaust*, Titus Productions; *Heimat*, ERF/SFB/WDR; *Twin Peaks*, Lynch/Frost Productions/Spelling Entertainment/Twin Peaks Productions, Inc.; *Riget*, Zentropa Entertainments ApS; *Cold Lazarus*, Channel Four/BBC; *The Sweeney*, Euston Films; *Prime Suspect*, Granada Television; *Cracker*, Granada Television; *thirtysomething*, MGM Television; *This Life*, BBC; *Queer as Folk*, Red Productions; *Sex and the City*, HBO.